The Logic of Surprise
in International Conflict

The Logic of Surprise in International Conflict

Alex Roberto Hybel
University of Southern California

Lexington Books
D.C. Heath and Company/Lexington, Massachusetts/Toronto

Library of Congress Cataloging in Publication Data

Hybel, Alex Roberto.
The logic of surprise in international conflict.

Bibliography: p.
Includes index.
1. Preemptive attack (Military science).   2. Surprise.   3. Military history, Modern—20th
century.   4. World politics—20th century.   I. Title.
U163.H93   1986   355.4'3   85–45924
ISBN 0–669–12371–4 (alk. paper)

Published simultaneously in Canada
Printed in the United States of America
International Standard Book Number: 0–669–12371–4
Library of Congress Catalog Card Number: 85–045924

The paper used in this publication meets the minimum requirements of American National
Standard for Information Sciences—Permanence of Paper for Printed Library Materials, ANSI
Z39.48–1984. ∞™

The last numbers on the right below indicate the number and date of printing.

10 9 8 7 6 5 4 3 2

95 94 93 92 91 90 89 88 87

To my mother
Margarita Lonsbury

Contents

Tables   ix

Acknowledgments   xi

1. **A Framework to Analyze Surprise   1**

   Two Schools of Thought   3
   A Framework for Analyzing Strategies of Surprise   9
   The Process-Tracing Procedure and the Method of Analytical Induction   18
   Notes   21

2. **Why International Actors Attempt to Achieve Surprise   25**

   Japan's Decision to Resort to Surprise   28
   Egypt–Syria's Decision to Resort to Surprise   36
   Germany's Decision to Resort to Surprise   40
   The Decision by the Soviet Union to Resort to Surprise   46
   Conclusion   51
   Notes   59

3. **Surprise with Respect to Target and Time: Pearl Harbor, 1941, and Yom Kippur, 1973   65**

   Japan's Target Strategy of Surprise   65
   Egypt–Syria's Time Strategy of Surprise   75
   Target and Time Strategies of Surprise   83
   Notes   85

4. **Why Were the Americans and Israelis Surprised in 1941 and 1973, Respectively?   89**

   Surprise at Pearl Harbor   89
   Surprise on Yom Kippur, October 1973   95
   Conclusion   100
   Notes   101

5. **Surprise with Respect to Intention: Barbarossa, 1941, and the Cuban Missile Crisis, 1963   105**

   Germany's Intention Strategy of Surprise, 1941   105
   Moscow's Intention Strategy of Surprise, 1962   115

Intention Strategy of Surprise   123
Notes   126

6. **Why Were the Soviets but not the Americans Surprised in 1941 and 1962, Respectively?   131**

   Why Was Stalin Surprised by Hitler's Actions in 1941?   131
   How the Americans Averted Being Surprised by the Soviets in 1962   136
   Conclusion   147
   Notes   148

7. **The Logic of Surprise and Surprise Avoidance   151**

   Why Would an International Actor Want to Achieve Surprise?   151
   Three Strategies of Surprise   156
   Conclusion   166
   Notes   167

Bibliography   169

Index   175

About the Author   180

Tables

7–1. Factors that Motivate or Discourage International Actors to Opt for Surprise, by Case   154

7–2. Dimensions of Surprise Sought, by Case   161

7–3. Dimensions of Surprise, Objectives of Deception Sought, and Means Used to Mislead Victims, by Case   162

7–4. Conditions and Actions that Aided or Prevented the Achievement of Surprise, by Case and Strategy   163

Acknowledgments

The environment in which a person writes and completes his first major project can have a significant impact on his work. Moreover, it can influence an analyst's disposition to engage in new research. In this respect, I have been very lucky.

To begin with, I seem to have been at the right place at the right time. One of the most difficult tasks faced by any analyst is coming up with an original question about an important subject. Here I was greatly aided by Eliahu Zeira's misfortune. In 1973, during the Yom Kippur War, Major General Zeira was Israel's director of military intelligence. His misfortune was predicting that Egypt and Syria would not attack Israel in October 1973. My fortune was meeting him at a seminar on decision making at Stanford University. Aware of his background, I sought to understand what had led him to conclude that Israel would not be attacked in October 1973. His answers were illuminating. They led me to conclude that our approach to the study of surprise had been biased by our determination to seek answers in the actions of the victims, without ever fully addressing the question of whether such actions might have been purposely prejudiced by the aggressors.

The person who has helped me the most along every step of the analysis has been Alexander L. George. The number of times that he and I met to discuss deception and surprise, and the number of drafts that he read, defy the highest expectation that any person could have. Moreover, Professor George relentlessly questioned my thoughts and arguments, always in a constructive way, hoping to add clarity to the final product. I will always be grateful to him.

Further, I would like to thank Stephen Krasner, Robert North, Richard Ned Lebow, and John Oneal. Their insightful comments convinced me to make some major changes in the presentation and structure of my original overall argument. I am also greatly indebted to the University of Southern California, and especially to the director of the School of International Relations, Michael Fry, for providing the funding necessary to complete the manuscript; and to Rosanne De Benedetti, Julie Gang, Kathy Matthes, and Mary A. Baitinger for their assistance in putting together the final draft.

There is a second environment that can also have a major effect on an individual's attitude toward research—that which is provided by his family. There are three members of my family who deserve special recognition: my mother, my mother-in-law, and my wife.

Life does not always flow in the direction that we hope. Disappointments leap at us time and time again, often when we least expect them. How well we cope with these setbacks is largely dependent on our general outlook toward life. One of the many things that I owe my mother, Margarita Lonsbury, is the belief that regardless of how often we stumble, we must bounce back, aware that life, with all its pitfalls, still has a magical tone. Her love and constant support have made me aware of the value of hope and importance of setting goals.

Rarely are mothers-in-law thanked for anything. The common perception is that we must accept them as a necessary evil. Barbara Peurifoy, my mother-in-law, could never fit such a callous description. Her attitude and involvement with my work have always been positive. In fact, it was she who volunteered to type and edit early drafts of this manuscript.

Last, I wish to acknowledge my wife's contribution. Hers cannot be measured in terms of what wives are usually thanked for, such as keeping the children quiet, typing, editing, or putting together the bibliography. Her contribution has been of a less tangible, but more important nature. She has taught me that love has a real meaning and that its fulfillment surpasses any other achievement. This knowledge and the sharing of my life with her has made the completion of this manuscript worthwhile.

1

A Framework to Analyze Surprise

It is pardonable to be defeated, but never to be surprised.
—Frederick the Great

Surprise is not exclusively a modern-day phenomenon. In some respects, the relationship between states has been the history of actors attempting, on the one hand, to exploit the advantages generated by the achievement of surprise and, on the other hand, to avert becoming the victims of surprise. As a subject of systematic analysis, however, it never truly caught the interest of scholars until 1962, following Roberta Wohlstetter's insightful study of the events and decisions preceding the Japanese attack on Pearl Harbor.[1] Since then, students of international affairs have sought to unlock the countless doors that obstruct the formulation of a theory of surprise.[2] Much of the enigma surrounding surprise, however, persists. As a distinguished analyst commented, "If the validity of a theory lies in its predictive potential, then the theory of surprise has failed time and time again."[3]

Three analytical tendencies have slowed attempts to formulate a theory of surprise with strong diagnostic powers. Initially, analysts tended to center their studies on the actions and perceptions of the victims.[4] Rarely was there an attempt to dissect systematically whether the actions of the aggressors might have been designed to prejudice the perceptions and actions of their victims. A new bias was introduced when scholars finally acknowledged that in order to understand surprise one would also have to account for the actions of the aggressor prior to the surprise. The new tendency was to assume that surprise can be viewed from one perspective—the aggressor's attempt to achieve surprise with respect to his intention.[5] This assumption is too narrow, for it overlooks the fact that surprise is multidimensional, which means that it is possible for an international actor to be surprised even when he knows about his adversary's intention. Lately, it has been recognized that surprise is multidimensional. The problem with the new tendency is that no attempt has been made to find out whether would-be surprisers select the different dimensions of surprise randomly or whether their choices are conditioned by certain factors.[6]

The primary objective of this study is the formulation of a more refined and differentiated theory of surprise. The achievement of this objective requires that three tasks be carried out. First, it is important to establish why international actors opt for surprise. Although this question has been addressed on numerous occasions by other analysts, it is worthwhile to take another look at some of the arguments that have been forwarded in order to assess whether they are relevant to the cases considered in this study. The next step will be to explain what leads those international actors who decide to resort to surprise to choose one strategy of surprise over another. This question, which has yet to be addressed systematically by other students of surprise, represents the core of this study. By developing an understanding of the conditions that dictate the choice of a strategy of surprise, we should be able to expand our comprehension of why certain international actors succeed in achieving surprise while others fail, and how potential victims succeed in averting surprise.

To establish fully the extent to which the actions of a would-be surpriser contribute to the achievement of surprise, it will be necessary to compare them systematically with the internal impediments that may have hindered the victim's ability to estimate accurately his adversary's intention. This task will be the most difficult to execute effectively. Initially, to breach many of the problems one is likely to confront while carrying out this type of comparison, it will be assumed that the intelligence processing of each potential victim is totally unhindered by internal impediments. With this assumption in mind, we will ask in each of the case studies whether it is reasonable to contend that, in view of the strategy of surprise designed by the aggressor and the type of information available to the potential victim, the victim should have been able to avert surprise. If the conclusion reached is negative, then it is clear that it would be of little theoretical value to find out whether the intelligence processing of the potential victim was hindered by internal impediments. On the other hand, if a positive conclusion is reached—that is, if it is concluded that the strategy of surprise adopted by the would-be surpriser and the information available to the victim were such that the latter should have been able to avert surprise—then it would be justifiable to contend that, if the potential victim were surprised, he was surprised because of internal impediments that hindered his intelligence processing. At this juncture, an attempt will be made to establish which internal impediments prevented the victim from correctly interpreting the actions of the aggressor.

To limit the number of exogenous factors that needs to be controlled, this study will concentrate solely on events in which (1) both the aggressor and the target were sovereign states; (2) the aggressor tried to surprise the victim; (3) the intended victim showed—before the surprise—a real interest in areas that subsequently became the target of the aggressor's action; and (4) the surprise was attempted during a period in which the two parties were not at war with one another.

Two Schools of Thought

The study of surprise has been influenced by two schools of thought. The first, which can be referred to as the *victim's school,* has one central goal: to uncover the factors that constrain a victim's attempt to avert surprise. Members of the second school, which can be referred to as the *surpriser's school,* have sought to explain the means an actor is likely to use to deceive an adversary in order to surprise him.

Students of the first school of thought, those who argue that much of the blame for failing to avert surprise can generally be placed on the victim, can be categorized according to the level of analysis they use to advance their explanations. The literature on the failure of intelligence has focused on three levels: (1) the individual decision makers, (2) the organizational factors, and (3) the political decision-making channels.[7]

Analysts who focus on the individual decision maker see him as the victim of his own distorted perceptions. They evaluate (1) the impact of specific images of the other and of the self on the decision maker's information processing, (2) the filtering effects of the perceptions on information processing, or (3) the limitations of human cognition in general. Those who evaluate the impact of specific images of the other and of the self on the decision maker's information processing maintain that the individual's cognitive structures shape the beliefs he has of external reality and limit any objective examination of the appropriateness of the images. However, they disagree in their assessments of the component elements underlying this basic cause of intelligence failure. Lloyd Etheredge contends that the perceptual blindness of policy makers is a consequence of the personalities of those who succeed in political life. Wasserman argues that intelligence failures result from the official theory of intelligence and from the relationship of intelligence to policy. DeWeerd maintains that, in order to assess intelligence effectively, it is necessary to separate signals from noise and then be efficient in the coordination and assessment of intelligence signals. The successful execution of these steps is often hampered by what DeWeerd calls the "climate of opinion" that prevails among policy makers.[8]

Those who evaluate the impact of specific images of the other and of the self suggest that the calculations of foreign intentions are often carried out in a relatively objective manner by intelligence analysts, but are rejected by biased decision makers. In contrast, those who look at the filtering effects of perceptions on information processing observe that perceptual biases are pervasive among both groups. Avi Shlaim, in a study of Israeli decision making just prior to the Egyptian–Syrian attack of 1973, argues that the monopolistic structure of Israeli intelligence permitted the heads of military intelligence to put forth a concept of Arab intentions that was accepted without challenge by Golda Meir and her cabinet.[9]

The general theme that the perceptions of decision makers and intelligence specialists distort the realities of the international environment has been developed in greater detail by Wohlstetter, George and Smoke, and Handel. According to Wohlstetter, Americans failed to perceive a clear pattern of Japanese intentions prior to Pearl Harbor because the conditions of their human perceptions limited their ability to perceive signals as warnings. George and Smoke proposed that the recognition of intentions requires hypotheses and models about the adversary's approach to political conflict and his behavioral style, respectively. But the ability to formulate the proper hypotheses and create models that accurately reflect the opponent's behavioral style, they add, depends largely on whether the perceiver's cognitive and perceptive factors are unbiased.[10]

Handel's conceptual framework consists of two parts. In the first part, he deals with the way in which three types of noise barriers affect the flow of information to analysts and policy makers. His contention is that when information passes through noise barriers it is distorted, weakened, or attenuated. In the second part of the framework, Handel describes the causes that can lead to erroneous estimations of enemy intentions. There are six:[11]

1. One's own intentions influence the perceptions of enemy intentions.

2. Misunderstanding of the opponent's character and of his willingness to take risks prevents the analyst from accurately picturing how the opponent approaches the balance between capabilities and intentions.

3. Ignorance about what the enemy knows about oneself makes it easier to misunderstand his willingness to take risks.

4. The assessment of enemy intentions, when based on the assessment of his capabilities, will be inaccurate if the enemy has hidden the true state of his capabilities or provided erroneous information.

5. There is a tendency to underestimate or overestimate the opponents capabilities.

6. Cry-wolf syndrome.

The last theme of the perceptual group steps beyond the emphasis on perceptual filters and examines the overall process of reasoning involved in all decision making. According to Steinbruner, cognitive tendencies determine how information is considered and analyzed. The tendency, he notes, is (1) to control uncertainty via mechanisms that screen out information established beliefs are not programmed to accept, (2) to process a few relevant incoming variables, and (3) to make decisions by a set of established rules.[12] Thus, policy makers who believe that an opponent state is unwilling to risk war but who are confronted with reports that the state is preparing its military forces can make such information consistent by denying the reliability of the source of information or by asserting that the preparations are for defensive purposes.[13]

In the organizational model of intelligence failure—that is, the model at the second level of analysis—the unit of analysis is the policy agency, and the perspective can be psychological, sociological, or structural.[14] Those adhering to the psychological perspective maintain that cognitive and psychological processes can influence not only the information processed by individuals, but also information flows and decision making by organizations. According to Steinbruner, three models of organizational thinking can be derived from these processes.[15]

The first—grooved thinking—refers to the tendency to look systematically at a small number of variables and apply consistent decision criteria to them. This sort of process provides stability by handling the burdens of uncertainty, political pressure, heavy work loads, and potential controversy over the outcomes.

The second model of organizational thinking—uncommitted thinking—occurs at the top decision-making level, where it is impossible to give routine responses because the decision makers must contend with a broader set of issues posed to them by agencies that compete and contend with each other. Thus, because decision makers confront uncertainty, each one oscillates in his thinking among competing belief patterns in order to protect and reinforce his own belief.

Finally, the third model of organizational thinking is what Steinbruner refers to as "theoretical thinking." Theoretical thinking has to do with the elaborate and stable belief pattern that the decision makers develop over time. It enables the decision makers to develop a long-range framework that can be used to discard inconsistent information. Because the development of such a framework requires time and a supportive environment, it is found in organizations that support the interaction between small, close groups.

Writers focusing on the organizational aspects of intelligence failure, who have a largely sociological perspective, contend that the social relations and forces between individuals in the organization influence the manner in which the estimation of intentions proceeds. In a series of articles, Abraham Ben-Zvi argues that one of the main reasons that states are surprised is that decision makers tend to give priority to the strategic assumptions of possibilities over the tactical assumptions of actualities and to assume that their enemy will adhere to the same line of reasoning. Greater importance is given to strategic assumptions than to tactical ones because the former reflect the image of the enemy held by the top policy makers.[16]

Those who approach intelligence failure from an organizational structural perspective maintain that the characteristics of individuals or social relationships are less important than the rules that describe organizational relationships. According to Harold Wilensky, intelligence failures are rooted in the manner in which organizations are structured. The hierarchy, specialization, and centralization of an organization are the major sources of distortion and blockage of intelligence. Another structuralist, Graham Allison, maintains that because organizational outputs shape the situation and the choices open to leaders, intelligence failures can be seen largely as a result of the programmed character of organizational activity and the limitations created by pre-established organizational routines.[17]

Finally, at the third level of analysis is the bureaucratic political model, in which the central unit of analysis is the set of individuals who act as representatives of different organizations during action on a particular decision. Governmental decisions, as viewed by Morton Halperin, are the results of bargaining between actors who have different interests and powers. The consensus-building process depends on how much power each actor can exert during the discussion of issues. The rules that govern the bureaucracy determine influence paths and power resources, constrict the range of decisions, and sanction or prohibit various actions.[18]

Bureaucratic politics influence the estimation of intentions in several ways. First, the bureaucratic actor will be confronted with varying outlooks from different subordinates attempting to push competing estimates of enemy intentions. Under such circumstances, the bureaucratic actor will tend to withhold acceptance of any one estimate while he attempts to build some form of consensus behind a policy solution. This means that the policy solution may not be based on the most accurate estimation of intentions, but on the estimation of intentions of those who possess the greatest power resources. Second, because competition permits only limited attention to any one issue, the estimation of intentions may be relegated to a secondary role. Third, the competition for time and attention often forces the subordinates to be more confident about their estimations than is warranted by their analyses. And finally, as Halperin notes, bureaucratic players are known for transmitting only that information that serves their purposes.[19]

Having summarized what members of the victim's school of thought perceive to be the central problem faced by those whose job it is to evaluate intentions and make decisions, we can now measure their success. Our task demands the answering of two questions: (1) What have we learned about surprise? (2) How successful have these scholars been in proposing theories of surprise?

With respect to the first question, we are now more cognizant of the types of internal impediments that targeted countries must overcome in order to interpret correctly the intentions of their opponents and, thus, to avert surprise. These impediments, we have learned, are the by-products of the cognitions of individuals and organizations, of the way in which organizations are structured, and of the rules that dictate the relationships between the different organizations involved in the making of decisions.

However, to contend that we are more knowledgeable about the internal impediments that targeted countries must overcome during their decision-making processes is not the same thing as saying that we have a clear understanding of the relative relevance of such impediments under specific circumstances. In fact, nobody has yet been able to consolidate all of these factors, or even those that are presumed to be the most relevant, into some form of theoretical framework capable of predicting or forecasting surprise.[20]

In addition, there is the problem of determining whether the potential victim of a surprise act will be able to avert the surprise if and when he can overcome all the constraints that hinder his gathering of intelligence, its analysis, and his choice of alternative. The unspoken and unwritten assumption among members of the victim's school of thought is that if a potential victim succeeds with such tasks he will improve significantly his chances of averting surprise. Although at first glance this seems to be a reasonable assumption, the fact of the matter is that a victim who is free of psychological and organizational dynamics is not in a better position to avert surprise than one who is not, if he does not know what to do with his freedom. What many of these scholars have failed to recognize, or at least to take into account, is that even if all known obstacles are removed, the potential victim will still be unable either to gather the correct information if he does not have the correct theory of his adversary's behavioral style, or to select the best alternative if he does not know which one would be the most effective and under what conditions. In other words, the absence of impediments does not guarantee the presence of wisdom.

Of those who have centered their analyses on the actions of the surprisers, only Barton Whaley has attempted to create a general theory of stratagem.[21] Taking Liddell Hart's concept of alternative objectives as his central theme, Whaley maintains that the main task of a stratagem is to make the victim select a false or unfavorable alternative. Such a choice, he claims, can be brought about via a two-step operation. The first step is to introduce ambiguity into the situation with which the victim must cope. If the victim already feels uncertain about the situation—that is, if he is unsure about his opponent's intentions or the direction of his operation—then the deceiver needs only to find out how uncertain his victim feels. If, on the other hand, the victim has accurate knowledge of his opponent's objectives or the direction of his operation, then it is the deceiver's task to provide him with an alternative interpretation. In either case, the second step is to encourage the victim to formulate alternative solutions to his predicament.[22]

In the introduction to his theory of stratagem, Whaley argues that the problem with Liddell Hart's theory of "indirect approach" is that it does not explain the precise manner in which the planning deception fits with the principle of surprise.[23] It seems reasonable, therefore, to look at Whaley's own theory in light of this criticism—that is, by asking whether he is successful in filling the gap left by Liddell Hart. To fulfill such a task, we must investigate how well Whaley addresses two questions. The first question deals with whether significant differences exist in the ways in which different actors use deception to surprise their victims. The second question deals with whether significant differences exist in the ways in which different targets are surprised. At first glance these two questions seem to overlap, but as we shall see shortly they do not fully do so.

To test his theory, Whaley compares a total of 115 cases. His main concerns are to determine (1) how often deception was used by the aggressor to surprise his victim, (2) the types of deception used, (3) whether deception was coordinated and, if so, at what administrative level, and (4) whether the intended victim was surprised and, if so, in what ways.

Prior to carrying out the comparative analysis, Whaley, in defining surprise, argues that "strategic surprise is distinguished from tactical surprise by the degree to which the action of the aggressor affects the victim's mobilization, deployment, or grand strategy." But then he acknowledges that the strategic-tactical dimension should also include grand tactics and grand strategies. What this means, in effect, is that Whaley is quite aware of the possibility that the means employed to deceive a target in order to surprise him strategically may differ from those means employed to surprise him tactically. Yet, he argues that there are no strong or consistent distinctions among grand strategy, strategy, and grand tactics in the application to them of the theory of stratagem.[24] From Whaley's perspective, this means two things. On the one hand, surprise is generally preceded by deception. And, on the other hand, only a small repertory of stratagems is needed to ensure surprise. In other words, regardless of the type of surprise, be it grand tactical, strategical, or grand strategical, surprisers tend to rely on the same means of deception.

Whaley has not fully addressed our first question. To formulate a comprehensive theory of stratagem, the analyst must also deal with the variety of constraints the deceivers have to overcome in order to draw their victims away from the correct solutions. These conditions are likely to determine how surprisers must arrange their means in order to be able to draw their victims away from the correct solutions. Thus, although Whaley could be correct in pointing out that surprisers tend to rely on the same means of deception, what we do not know is how they determine which means to choose in any given situation, and the extent to which their objectives affect their decisions. In other words, Whaley's generalization may be very elegant, but it is of little help to the policy makers interested in detecting different forms of deception.

Because surprise is multidimensional, it is very difficult to draw specific guidelines about how to spot deception.[25] The task, however, can become more manageable if three things are kept in mind. The first, as Whaley points out, is that the number of stratagems used to achieve surprise is quite small. Second, it is possible that only some means of deception will help achieve specific types of surprises. And, finally, it may be that only some means of deception can be used concurrently without risking unexpected and unwanted responses from the victim. When these three factors are taken into consideration, one can argue that it may be possible to construct a typological theory of surprise that identifies a finite number of patterns linking types of surprises intended with types of means employed. Accordingly, it is relevant to investigate how the choice of means used for deception is conditioned by the objectives of the aggressor and by the types of constraints the means must overcome to fulfill the designated objectives. Employing this analytical method may make it feasible to go beyond Whaley's generalization that surprise is preceded by deception.

With respect to the second question—that is, whether there are any significant distinctions with regard to how targets are surprised by the actions of aggressors—Whaley barely addresses it. He acknowledges that there are various dimensions in which intended victims can be surprised. Such a broad conclusion, however, does not tell much about what aspects of the aggressor's stratagem were effective and what dimensions of surprise they produced. If the analyst were able to address and answer this question, he then would have a clearer vision of (1) how surprisers attempt to tailor their actions to the expectations of their respective targets, (2) how the targets react to such actions, and (3) whether the surprisers should be credited for achieving surprise, or the victims blamed for failing to avoid it.

A Framework for Analyzing Strategies of Surprise

A strategy of surprise is the result of conscious, carefully calculated decisions by national foreign-policy elites made prior to the outbreak of overt hostilities. At its most basic level, a strategy of surprise entails the deliberate cultivation of misunderstanding by one part on the party of another. In order to understand the extent to which the actions of a would-be surpriser may have prejudiced the perceptions and reactions of his intended victim, international relations must be conceived of as a continuous and interdependent flow of decisions by national foreign-policy elites and subsequent actions by the corresponding states.[26] Moreover, in trying to understand the actions of a would-be surpriser and the subsequent reactions of his intended victim, the analyst must place himself in the positions of both parties and ask: (1) What alternatives could each party have chosen? (2) Were the alternatives chosen by each party justified, from a rational perspective, in view of the circumstances?[27]

According to contemporary dogma, theories of rational choice do not intend to describe actual behavior in individuals or social institutions, but instead are designed to prescribe optimal behavior. Efforts to understand actual choice behavior have led students of decision making to conclude that rationality is bounded.[28]

Theories that treat decision making as a process of maximizing expected utility and those that treat rationality as being bounded, however, are not necessarily incompatible. As Snyder and Diesing point out, both theories can be combined by taking one as basic and the other as supplementary.[29] Decision making is, by definition, a process of finding the alternative that promises to achieve the most of various desired goods. From this perspective, the notion of maximizing is basic. However, because it is humanly impossible to consider all the relevant alternatives and evaluate all the possible consequences that could follow from the implementation of each alternative, human decisions will repeatedly fall short of the ideal. Maximization, therefore, represents "the ideal limit that a good decision approaches as it becomes careful and exact, while the bounded rationality procedures are more nearly descriptive of actual decisions."[30]

In this study, both views of rationality are combined. On the one hand, it is assumed that each national foreign-policy elite will want to adopt the alternative that promises to achieve the most of various desired goals. On the other hand, it is realized that maximization, being an ideal, is unattainable. Therefore, the problem to be addressed is not whether any one decision was "rational" or not, but the extent to which the decision in question differs from the rational mode.

A bounded rational theory of surprise can best be framed from an overall systemic perspective. This contention may seem misplaced in view of the belief held by many that theories of international politics are not reducible to theories of foreign policy.[31] Such a belief is unfounded. It is based on the incorrect assumption that the study of foreign policy is limited solely to the analysis of foreign-policy processes. Foreign policy, however, also entails the examination of policy outputs.[32] In the following statement, the fact that it is feasible to derive theories of foreign policy via a systematic perspective was inadvertently acknowledged by one of the scholars who claimed that such a task is impossible:

> Each state arrives at policies and decides upon actions according to its own internal process, but its decisions are shaped by the very presence of other states as well as interactions with them.[33]

The international actions of each national foreign-policy elite are shaped by three components: (1) the structure of the international system, (2) the patterns of relations among states within the system, and (3) the interactions between states within the system. Some definitions are in order before proceeding with the analysis. The terms *structure, relations,* and *interactions* denote distinctly different phenomena.[34]

In this study, the term *structure* will be used only to account for the distribution of military and economic powers among the would-be surpriser, his victim, and their potential and actual allies.[35] *Patterns of relations,* in turn, refers to the dynamic aspects of the system's functioning, or, as Snyder and Diesing put it:

> It denotes "how states stand in relation to each other"—e.g., their images of others as opponents, allies or neutrals; their beliefs about each other's aims and intentions; their interdependence; their conflicts of interests and common interests; their ideological differences and affinities; and any other non-behavioral elements which contribute to their attitudes, expectations and potential influence vis-a-vis each other.[36]

Snyder and Diesing also point out that the two most important elements in relations, from a politico-strategic perspective, are alignments and interdependence. By *alignment* they mean a state's intentions and expectations of another state's intentions concerning supportive or opposing behavior in future interactions.[37] The central difference between a *structure* and an *alignment* is that the former accounts for the objective distribution of military and economic powers among individual states, while the latter refers to the subjective beliefs about how such powers are aggregated and how they affect the system.

The fact that two states may be part of the same alliance or belong to opposite camps does not mean that they will necessarily be dependent on each other for the realization of their respective goals and the preservation of their respective values. In politico-strategic relations, two allies are interdependent only if they are in need of each other's help for deterrence and defense purposes against adversaries. In turn, interdependence between two adversaries can be measured by the extent to which each party can deprive the other of value it possesses or give the other values it desires.[38]

The last component that must be accounted for is *interaction. Interaction* refers to the behavioral process of states—that is, the types of actions and communications they exchange. In an interaction, however, an action can sometimes have a broader effect than that of simply generating a reaction from the intended target. On certain occasions, it may engender a new set of expectations or reaffirm existing expectations of how the initiator of the action intends to continue behaving.[39]

In short, although the characteristics of the three components are significantly distinct, there exists a close connection between them. The general nature of relations in an international system is likely to be determined by the system's power structure. In turn, prevailing relations affect interactions and are established in detail by the interactions among states.[40]

The three components can now be assembled to create a framework for the analysis of strategy of surprise. An actor who decides that his best alternnative is an act of aggression must assess carefully whether surprise would facilitate the attainment of his goals. Assuming he concludes that surprise will be necessary, he must also consider what strategy of surprise to adopt and how to implement it.

Surprise is largely dependent on how successful the would-be surpriser is in controlling his victim's perception of threat. Needless to say, other factors, such as impediments to a rational decision-making process within the victim himself, can also contribute to the occurrence of surprise. But no reasonable actor who is heavily dependent on the achievement of surprise is likely to remain inactive while merely hoping that his victim will be trapped by his own shortcomings. On the contrary, he will attempt to ensure that his victim's misperceptions are consistent with what he—the would-be surpriser—wants him to perceive.

According to Raymond Cohen, the perception of a threat is the product of a subjective appraisal of events viewed selectively by decision makers acting within a given domestic political context and playing a role in a geopolitical environment on behalf of a state. This means that an actor's receptivity to threat is affected by (1) his cognitive process, (2) his domestic political environment, and (3) the conditions and salient features of the geopolitical environment of which he is part.[41] International actors rarely possess the means to exert significant control over the domestic political environments of their adversaries. Sometimes, however, they can alter the context in which they interact with their respective adversaries in the geopolitical environment and, as a result, have an impact on their adversaries' cognitive processes.

It has been suggested that in the geopolitical environment three factors seem consistently to affect any actor's perception of threat. They are: (1) whether the distribution of capabilities in the system is balanced in his favor or against him, (2) the extent to which he is involved politically and economically in any one particular geographical area, and (3) the type of relationship he has with other actors in the system.

Regarding the first geopolitical factor, an observer's receptivity to threatening signals from an adversary is likely to be greater when the strength of the adversary is known to be superior. In other words, the observer's monitoring system becomes more sensitive when he feels vulnerable. In terms of the second factor, an actor is bound to perceive greater threats when events concern geographical areas of high priority for strategic or emotional reasons or of current and urgent relevance to him. Finally, an observer's sensitivity is likely to be greater when the relationship between him and a second party is plagued with tension and mistrust.

From the above argument it could be deduced that if a would-be surpriser can exert some control over the geopolitical environment and can manipulate his intended target's receptivity to threatening signals, his best strategy would be to control (1) his victim's sense of vulnerability, (2) the concern his victim has for the areas in which he intends to stage the surprise, and (3) the degree of tension and mistrust his victim feels toward him.

Different international actors possess different abilities to control each of these geopolitical factors. An actor who is as powerful as his intended victim will have greater difficulty in controlling the latter's sense of vulner- ability than one who is much weaker than his victim. A similar variance in ability is likely to prevail between an actor who initiates actions in areas that are of high priority to the intended victim and an actor who pursues his interests in areas that have no significant strategic value to the intended victim. Finally, an actor who has had a harmonious relationship with his victim is likely to find it less troublesome to control the latter's perception of threat than one whose relationship with his victim has been plagued with tension and mistrust.[42]

It should not be inferred that only those who possess the ability to achieve maximal control over their victim's perception of threat will resort to surprise. What is important for an international actor is whether, in view of the environmental conditions, he can still control those factors that are crucial to the execution of his particular strategy of surprise. The reason an international actor may be able to achieve surprise even when he does not have full control over every geopolitical factor is that surprise is multidi- mensional. For instance, an actor who cannot control the concern his victim has over the areas where he intends to stage the surprise will most likely refrain from trying to achieve surprise with respect to *whom* he will attack. That same actor, however, may be in a position to control his victim's sense of vulnerability and thus achieve surprise with respect to *when* he will attack.

Six dimensions of surprise can be identified. They are: intention, ration- ale, capabilities, military doctrine, target, and time.[43]

1. *Intention* refers to whether the aggressor attempts to prevent his victim from learning *what* he will do.

2. *Rationale* refers to whether the aggressor attempts to prevent his victim from learning *why* he will do what he plans to do.

3. *Capabilities* can be divided into three components:
    a. *Overall capabilities* refers to whether the aggressor attempts to pre- vent his victim from learning about the aggregate economic and military strengths of his state.
    b. *Assigned capabilities* refers to whether the aggressor attempts to pre- vent his victim from learning about the forces he plans to use in his surprise attack. The characteristics of the assigned forces that the poten-

tial victim would want to know are *size, location and movement,* and *readiness*.

c. *Types of military forces* refers primarily to whether the aggressor attempts to prevent his victim from learning about the composition of the attacking forces—that is, the kinds of forces and weapons he will use. A potential victim expecting an armored assault at the opening phase of a war might be inordinately vulnerable to an airborne or amphibious assault against points unprotected by its armor. Technological innovation is also relevant to this component. Underestimated improvements in mobility, firepower, and communications can greatly affect the potential victim's ability to respond to an attack.

4. *Military doctrine* refers to whether the aggressor attempts to prevent his victim from learning *how* the operation will be executed.

5. *Target* refers to whether the aggressor attempts to prevent his victim from learning *whom* he will attack. This dimension should be viewed at two levels. At the level of grand strategy this dimension is concerned with which state will be attacked. At the level of military strategy, it refers to the specific points within the state that will be attacked.

6. *Time* refers to whether the aggressor attempts to prevent his victim from learning *when* he will attack. The goal of an international actor attempting a surprise attack is to minimize his target's warning time (Tw). Warning time equals the difference between when the victim identifies an impending attack on a specific target (Td), and the time of the attack (Ta); thus, $Tw = Ta - Td$. At the strategic level, the goal is to ensure that Tw will be smaller than the length of time the potential victim needs to ready his forces (Tr)—through mobilization, concentration, and redeployment—in order to defeat the attack or to raise its costs unacceptably. Thus, the objective is to have Tw smaller than Tr.

The Tr the potential victim needs in order to be able to defeat the attack or raise its costs is, in part, a function of the potential victim's economic capacity and domestic political climate. In most cases, the would-be surpriser has a limited ability to influence such factors. The factor Tr, however, is also a function of a factor referred to as T_1.

In some cases, a would-be surpriser may assume that his potential victim will be able to partially infer his intention to attack and to partially deduce the likely targets of attack. Under these circumstances, one of the would-be surpriser's main tasks is to maximize the difference between the victim's estimate of the time of the attack (Te) and the actual Ta. The would-be surpriser will generally want Te to lag Ta, so that $Te - Ta$ can be called time T_1.

The potential victim's ability to defend himself is a function of his ability to estimate accurately the time of the attack. To this extent, if the would-be surpriser can increase T_1, the value of Tr will also increase. In short, the value of Tw is a function of the estimate of the victim's Tr, which in turn is a function of T_1, which can be increased by manipulating the victim's Te.

In view of the numerous dimensions of surprise would-be surprisers can select from, it would seem reasonable to assume that they would attempt to combine as many as they deemed necessary to achieve surprise and would select their strategies from a vast array of combinations of dimensions of surprise. The task of choosing a strategy, however, is not so simple as just implied. A consideration of just two of the six dimensions of surprise should clarify the problems generally confronted by would-be surprisers.

Of the six dimensions, the estimation of intentions is often perceived as being the most difficult. The problem lies in the intricacy of the analysis and the large number of factors that must be considered. George and Smoke make this point clear when they note that intelligence concerning the task of estimating an adversary's intentions rarely speaks for itself, even when it is plentiful, consistent, and relatively free of noise.[44]

According to Michael Handel, evaluating an opponent's intentions requires forming the proper image of his character and willingness to undertake risks.[45] This, in turn, demands an understanding of the assumptions or interpretations of the situation upon which that particular adversary bases his decisions.[46] Put in different words, "the analyst needs a theory or model of that adversary's behavioral style and approach to calculating political action."[47]

There are several obstacles to an analyst's attempt to estimate his adversary's intentions. One of the most common is what Klaus Knorr calls "apparently irrational behavior."[48] He contends that the behavior of people with a different cultural background often appears irrational because they tend to evaluate the outcomes of alternative courses of action in terms that differ sharply from ours. This cultural gap has led many analysts to misunderstand the risks leaders of different cultures are willing to accept.

The complexity of evaluating an actor's willingness to take risks, however, does not diminish noticeably when the two adversaries share a common culture. First, there is the problem of data. A victim does not always have the luxury of having an opponent with a history of leadership that has been observed and analyzed in great detail. Second, there is the problem of determining how the belief system of an opponent mediates his responses with regard to different situations. Part of the difficulty here lies in the fact that belief systems never surrender easily to empirical analysis or quantification.[49] But even if they did, it should be kept in mind that an actor's willingness to take risks depends not only on how he feels about taking risks but also on the type of situation in which he finds himself. Hence, an actor who has the reputation of always playing it safe may find it justifiable to break his mold if he concludes that he has no other choice. But, in order for the target to be able to decide that it is in the nature of his opponent to travel riskier paths when his options are severely narrowed, he must have a series of situations from which to measure his opponent's response variance to risk. Although the spectrum of situations required need not cover every possible development, often the actual number available is so meager that it would be inconceivable for the observer to come up with a reasonable, accurate measure of how much risk his opponent is willing to take during special occasions.

This problem is not minimized even in instances in which the analyst has a fairly good idea of his adversary's mode of calculating risk under varying circumstances. The idea behind gathering data on an actor's willingness to take risks is the assumption that his patterns will persist. However, if the observed actor is aware that he is not expected to do anything drastic about a particular development because he had not done so on previous occasions under similar circumstances, he also knows that if he breaks the pattern he will probably find his adversary unprepared and thus will be taking fewer risks than originally estimated.[50] This means that dependency on the knowledge of an opponent's risk calculation can provide an incentive for the opponent to break his pattern.

Finally, there is the problem of how to assess an opponent's mode of calculating utilities. Even the most obstinate defenders of choice models have acknowledged that an observer's chances of succeeding with this task are exceedingly limited. The predominant theory used in the past to explain decisions by individuals and organizations was *rational choice*.[51] The model takes as its starting point an individual who is able to rank the consequences of each course of action open to him. This individual, when faced with a competing set of alternatives, A, B, C, D, . . . N, can also rank them in order of preferences and determine whether his preference for A over B is greater than his preference for B over C. What this requires is the development of a cardinal utility function that preserves both the rank of each alternative and the interval distance between them.[52] Furthermore, the construction of a rational-choice model is based on the assumption that preferences are exogenous and stable over time. These assumptions, however, have long been challenged. To begin with, in the case of collective choice, it is very difficult to ascertain empirically the principal preference if the goals held by decision makers conflict in the sense that the means appropriate for the attainment of one blocks the attainment of another.[53] What is more, even in cases where the preferences of only one individual are involved, it is very difficult to determine how he ranks them.[54] Any attempt to overcome these obstacles by inferring preferences from one actor's past actions would not only be tautological[55] but, more importantly, would overlook the fact that actions often reflect the actor's strategic calculations in the first instance rather than his unadulterated, fundamental preferences.[56] Thus, one cannot help but wonder how successful an international actor can be in his attempt to assess his opponent's mode of calculating utilities in order to estimate his intentions, when such an assessment is partly based on the analysis of preferences that are generally in conflict with one another, fuzzy, and alterable.

This argument seems to indicate that, since it is so difficult to estimate an actor's intention, would-be surprisers have an enviable advantage over their victims. And yet, intended victims of surprise have not always been surprised by their adversaries' decisions to attack. This development should not astonish anyone who has an inkling of how complex it is to transform an actor's intention to attack into an actual attack. As a would-be surpriser begins to deploy his forces, he is, in fact, increasing dramatically the potential victim's chances of realizing that he is going to be attacked. In 1941, for instance, Japan did not even attempt to conceal its intention to go to war, because it would have been nearly impossible to conceal the preparations that preceded the launching of the attacks throughout Southeast Asia.

The ability of an international actor to achieve surprise with respect to his target is also severely constrained. A would-be surpriser who hopes to act as though he plans to direct his aggression against targets other than his victim must take into consideration four factors. First, he must look carefully into the type of relationship he has had with his victim. If their relationship has been hostile, any troop deployment by the would-be surpriser is likely to intensify the curiosity of his adversary. Second, the aggressor must assess whether the geographical location of his victim is such that as he openly fixes his forces against some alternative targets, he can simultaneously deploy undetected martial means against his victim. A good example of the conditions under which a would-be surpriser would be wise not to attempt to achieve surprise with respect to his target is the Yom Kippur War of 1973. The Egyptian leaders seemed to have been aware that any attempt on their part to persuade Israel that it would not be a target would have been futile for several reasons: an intense level of hostility had permeated their relationship, they shared a common border, and Egypt had no other foes nearby.

The last two factors that a would-be surpriser must take into account are the strategic value of his alternative targets and the feasibility of luring his victim into believing that he—the would-be surpriser—lacks the martial means to attack him and the other targets simultaneously. It is quite unlikely, for instance, that in 1941 Japan would have succeeded in concealing the fact that Pearl Harbor was one of its targets, had the other targets been of little strategic value and had it not tried to reinforce the existing perception among American foreign-policy makers that Japan was too weak to launch two major attacks—against Southeast Asian targets and Pearl Harbor—simultaneously.

In sum, would-be surprisers rarely can select randomly the dimensions of surprise that they will resort to in their strategies. Instead, they must carefully assess which dimensions are within their reach, as determined by the impediments they must overcome and the means they can employ to surmount them, and then select accordingly.

The Process-Tracing Procedure and the Method of Analytical Induction

This study uses historical cases and relies on what is commonly referred to as a within-case explanation to explain (1) the reasons that international actors opt for surprise, (2) the factors that lead those who decide to resort to surprise to choose one strategy over another, and (3) the extent to which the actions of the would-be surprisers contribute to the achievement of surprise. The principal mode of investigation used by this explanation is the process-tracing procedure. Via this mode, the investigator attempts to identify the intervening steps or cause-and-effect links that might exist between the dependent and independent variables in different cases.[57]

Four tasks must be carried out to execute a well-designed and well-structured comparison. Several of these tasks have already been completed. The first one consists of specifying the phenomena that are being singled out for investigation, the nature of the existing theory, and the aspects of the existing theory that will be singled out for assessment and/or refinement and elaboration. Two schools of thought have already been discussed. Moreover, ways of enhancing the theoretical content and reach of the theory proposed by the surpriser's school of thought have been advanced. However, although the phenomena singled out for investigation have been identified, it is necessary to be more specific in the conceptualization of the two basic concepts.

Surprise can be gained via a coordinated campaign of deception designed to mislead the victim's analysis. Deception, in its narrowest sense, implies ruse, trickery, guile, false information, and decoy objects or activities.[58] The Soviets, however, combine *deception*—Mashirovka—with *camouflage* and *concealment* to mean measures intended to fabricate, confuse, distort, or deny information that could be of value to a foreign intelligence service.[59] To simplify the discussion, we will use deception in the broader sense and define it as an attempt to mislead a potential victim via the manipulation, distortion, falsification, camouflage, concealment, or cover of evidence in order to induce him to react in a manner prejudicial to his interest and favorable to the originator's objectives.

Students of deception and surprise often fail to establish a clear distinction between these two terms; thus, their arguments tend to fall into circular reasoning. To avoid this pitfall, *deception* is sometimes defined in its active sense—that is, as viewed by the practitioner rather than in terms of its effect on the intended victim. Conversely, *surprise* is defined as an effect, as viewed by the victim.[60]

We do not find this distinction acceptable. We have no qualm with the contention that surprise ought to be viewed from the perspective of the victim so long as it is ascertained that surprise was intended. On the other hand, if deception is viewed solely from the perspective of the practitioner, how can one argue that the victim was surprised because he was deceived and not because of internal impediments to information processing? In other words, deception must be viewed in terms of the means employed by the practitioner and the effects they had on the intended victim. Circular reasoning will not follow so long as deception and surprise are conceptualized differently.

Surprise will be conceptualized in terms of its six dimensions. *Surprise* will refer to those instances in which the intentions of international actors, the rationales for the actions, the capabilities used in the actions, the military doctrines that dictated the use of capabilities, the targets of the actions, and/or the timing of the actions were inaccurately predicted or estimated by the targets.[61]

The second task is to formulate a standardized set of general questions to be asked in each case that reflects the theoretical focus of the study. These questions, which have already been forwarded, establish the data requirements needed for a comparative analysis of the cases.

The third task requires the identification of the conditions and variables. Since the conditions and variables are quite broad and are related to the specific questions, they will not be identified until each question is addressed in greater detail.

The final task requires the specification of the cases that will be used in the analysis and the rationale for selecting them. Four instances of surprise or intended surprise were selected:

1. The 1941 attack of Pearl Harbor by Japan.
2. The 1973 attack of Israel by Egypt and Syria.
3. The 1941 invasion of the Soviet Union by Germany.
4. The Cuban Missile Crisis of 1961.

Three factors determined the selection of these four cases. To begin with, the first three cases have already been analyzed extensively, and scholars agree that in each instance surprise was attempted. Some readers may challenge the wisdom of walking over ground that has already been explored extensively. However, what is important is not that old data are being used once again, but that new ways of looking at those data—and therefore new ways of interpreting them—are being proposed.[62] The Cuban Missile Crisis of 1962 has also been studied in great detail. But analysts have yet to look at the event from the perspective of attempted surprise.

Second, this kind of study requires the consideration of cases that were both successful and unsuccessful in achieving surprise. In at least one of the cases, the attempt was uncovered early enough to avert some forms of surprise.

The third factor is also linked to a methodological requirement. Thus far it has been suggested that the choice of a strategy of surprise is rarely random and that it is conditioned generally by the types of obstacles would-be surprisers must overcome and the means they have at their disposal to surmount them. To test the validity of this argument, the investigator ideally would conduct an in-depth analysis of a vast array of cases of surprise chosen at random.

Only one of these two conditions will be satisfied in this study. The data requirement of a process-tracing procedure is quite demanding. Such a requirement enormously limits the capabilities of the investigator to analyze in depth a large number of cases. For this reason, only four cases were chosen.

If only a small number of cases is considered, the investigator must be extremely careful to ensure that his selection of cases will not influence his results. Although this investigator was aware from the outset that a significant degree of variance existed among the cases in terms of the dimensions of surprise sought and the means of surprise used, very little was known about the particulars of each case. In other words, the four cases were selected randomly and not because they might serve as examples of different types of strategies of surprise.

Reliance on so few cases, however, can create a problem. In instances in which the universe of analysis is very small, the question of sampling from such a distribution is destined to be irrelevant if the cases constitute a population rather than just a sample. On the other hand, if the cases considered do not encompass the universe, it is important to note that the propositions that result from such study will not be of a "confirmatory mode," but of an "exploratory mode."[63] This study fits within the latter mode.

The fourth factor that had an influence on the selection of the four cases has to do with the question of why international actors opt for surprise. To address this question fully, it would be necessary to include in the empirical analysis both cases in which international actors opted for surprise and cases in which they rejected the use of surprise. It should be clear by now that the emphasis here will be on considering cases in which the aggressor evaluated the benefits of relying on surprise and decided to follow such a path.

However, in two of the cases, the victims seriously considered the possibility of a launching a pre-emptive surprise attack, but in the end chose not to do so. The two cases are the Cuban Missile Crisis of 1962 and the Yom Kippur War of 1973. The reasons that the United States in 1962 and

Israel in 1973 chose not to pre-empt with surprise attacks will be discussed extensively. To offset the possibility that the rationale for opting for a *pre-emptive surprise attack* may differ substantially from the rationale for not opting for a *regular surprise attack,* this study will analyze, briefly, two additional cases: the invasion of Guatemala in 1954, and the attempt to invade Cuba in 1961.

In sum, the basic objective of this work is the proposal of a more differentiated theory of surprise. To this end, four cases will be considered by addressing three questions:

1. Why did the international actors in question opt for surprise?
2. What led the would-be surprisers to choose one strategy of surprise over another?
3. To what extent did the actions of the would-be surprisers contribute to the achievement of surprise?

Notes

1. Wohlstetter, 1962.
2. Betts, 1978; Handel, 1976; Shlaim, 1976; Perlmutter, 1975; Whaley, 1973a; Wohlstetter, 1965; Knorr, 1964.
3. Handel, 1976, p. 9.
4. The most prominent works in this category have been by Betts, 1978; Handel, 1976; Shlaim, 1976; Perlmutter, 1975; Wohlstetter, 1965, 1962; Knorr, 1964.
5. The most prominent representative of this school has been Whaley, 1973a, 1973b. It is interesting to note that, although Whaley acknowledges that there are numerous dimensions of surprise, he centers his analysis primarily on intention. Also, Robert Jervis, in his book *The Logic of Images in International Relations,* argues that his main objective is to answer the question, "how can an actor influence beliefs about himself and lead others to make predictions about his behavior that will contribute to his reaching his goals." (Jervis, 1970, p. 3.) In view of Jervis' statement, one could assume that part of his objective is to develop a theory of deception. Jervis, however, never proposes a clear set of propositions indicating the conditions under which international actors are likely to resort to deception, nor the type of strategies they are likely to adopt to succeed with their task.
6. See Knorr and Morgan, 1983.
7. For a detailed review of the first school of thought see Stech, 1979, chapter 4. The most prominent members of this school of thought have already been identified in note 4. See also Jervis, 1976, and Lebow, 1981.
8. Etheredge, 1978, pp. 434–451; Wasserman, 1960, pp. 156–169; DeWeerd, 1962, pp. 435–452.
9. Stech, 1979, p. 65; Shlaim, 1976, pp. 348–380.
10. Wohlstetter, 1962, p. 397; George and Smoke, 1974, p. 573.

11. Handel, 1976, pp. 11–28.
12. Steinbruner, 1974.
13. Stech, 1979, p. 104.
14. Ibid., p. 104.
15. Steinbruner, 1974, pp. 127, 130, and 135.
16. Ben-Zvi, 1976, pp. 381–395.
17. Wilensky, 1976; Allison, 1971.
18. Stech, 1979, p. 144; Halperin, 1974.
19. Allison, 1971, p. 175; Stech, 1979, p. 146; Halperin, 1974, p. 145.

20. One of the possible exceptions is Richard N. Lebow, who in his book *Between Peace and War* (1981) identifies some of the conditions under which certain individual pathologies are likely to contribute to the intensification of crises. See especially chapters 5 and 6.

21. We have excluded from the present discussion the argument forwarded by Knorr and Morgan in their book *Strategic Military Surprise* (1983) for the simple reason that they are primarily interested in finding out the conditions under which an actor may find it attractive to resort to surprise and the conditions that constitute an opportunity for strategic surprise. These concerns are very important and will be addressed fully later on.

22. Whaley, 1973b, p. 139.

23. Ibid., p. 128.

24. Ibid., pp. 154, 245–247.

25. According to Whaley, it is a nearly impossible task to draw guidelines to help spot deception. See Whaley, 1973b, p. 225.

26. See Snyder, Bruck, and Sapin, 1962, pp. 62 and 65. In his book, *The Logic of Images in International Relations,* Robert Jervis makes an important contribution by making the distinction between words and actions more definite by the categories of "signal" and "index." Signals are statements or actions overtly directed toward shaping the adversary's image of the sender. Hence they carry no inherent credibility and so do not generally affect any given situation unless they can be verified through the use of indices. Indices are statements or actions that, not being intended for the eyes of the adversary, carry inherent credibility and provide evidence that can either confirm or disconfirm the image projected by the actor. Examples of indices are (1) personal characteristics of leaders, (2) domestic events, (3) statements not intended for the eyes of the adversary, and (4) capability indices, or those whose change can alter the balance of power among the actors. Although indices are more reliable than signals as evidence of an actor's image, Jervis notes that they, too, can be manipulated and, due to their greater credibility, such manipulation is more likely and more influential. Moreover, even if a given index is not manipulated, it is still possible to misunderstand its linkage with the actor's behavior. (Jervis, 1970, chapters 2 and 3.)

27. As Morgenthau put it, "It is the testing of the rational hypothesis against the actual facts and their consequences that gives meaning to the facts of international politics and makes a theory of politics possible." See Morgenthau, 1966, p. 5.

28. Simon, 1957.

29. Snyder and Diesing, 1977, p. 345.

30. Ibid., p. 345. Even Alexander L. George, a major critic of rational theory, cannot escape from acknowledging that rational choice is a desirable ideal that ought to be used as a standard to evaluate the quality of decisions. See George, 1980, p. 10.

31. Waltz, 1979, p. 121.

32. It ought to be acknowledged, however, that the emphasis placed so far by students of foreign policy has been on policy processes rather than policy outputs. See Cohen and Harris, 1975, p. 383.

33. Waltz, 1975, p. 71.

34. Snyder and Diesing, 1977, p. 472.

35. For an insightful analysis of how military and economic powers are connected, see Gilpin, 1981, pp. 20–43.

36. Snyder and Diesing, 1977, p. 472. Snyder and Diesing appreciably broaden "pattern of relations" beyond the Waltzian systemic-structural concept by including state and decision-making attributes.

37. Ibid., p. 473.

38. Ibid., p. 473.

39. Ibid., p. 475.

40. Ibid., p. 475.

41. Cohen, 1979.

42. Ibid., pp. 104, 191.

43. George and Smoke, 1974, p. 582.

44. George and Smoke, 1974, p. 582. See also Jervis, 1970, pp. 3–17.

45. Handel, 1976, p. 23.

46. Wasserman, 1960, pp. 166–167.

47. George and Smoke, 1974, p. 582.

48. Knorr, 1964, p. 459.

49. Converse, 1964, p. 206.

50. This proposition is very similar to Handel's Paradox 2: "The greater the risk, the less likely it seems, and the less risky it actually becomes. Thus, the greater the risk, the smaller it becomes." See Handel, 1976, p. 16. Jervis overlooks this possibility when he notes that: "A country that has never been willing to run high risks cannot suddenly make others believe it will undertake audacious actions unless its demands are met." See Jervis, 1970, p. 14.

51. Palumbo, 1975, p. 320.

52. Ibid., p. 323.

53. Ibid., p. 334.

54. March, 1977.

55. Riker makes this point very clear in his analysis of preferences inferred from voting in the United States House of Representatives. Riker, 1952, pp. 349–366.

56. Palumbo, 1975, p. 469.

57. For an excellent discussion and example of how this method can be employed, see George and Smoke, 1974. See also Lebow, 1981. Mefford, 1984, has written an excellent article in which he transplants the strategy for building theory

via structured, focused comparison into the study of how decision makers compare cases. Finally, our method resembles the one adopted by Jervis in his book, *The Logic of Images in International Relations*. He proceeds from the assumption that rational actors try to project desired images. He then traces, deductively, the consequences of the assumption by asking questions regarding the interaction that will follow between two or more actors. See Jervis, 1970, p. 15.

58. Central Intelligence Agency, February 1981, p. 1.

59. Ibid., p. 2.

60. Whaley, 1973b, p. 156.

61. This definition is more precise than Whaley's, which states that surprise is an instance in which a sudden military action by an antagonist has not been predicted, much less anticipated, by its intended victim. See Whaley, 1973b, p. 154. Our definition conforms with George's recommendation that surprise be broken into its major dimensions. See George, 1979, p. 14.

62. Some readers will be tempted to criticize our heavy reliance on secondary sources. This criticism is misplaced for two reasons. First, the main emphasis of this study is not empirical, but theoretical. Second, we purposely relied on secondary sources to demonstrate that, by using the same data that others have used, it is feasible to propose an argument that not only challenges their interpretations but, more importantly, reflects more accurately the data available. Or, as Jervis once put it, "The worth of a new approach is often demonstrated by its ability both to show that previous explanations are inadequate and to provide parsimonious and satisfying accounts of a wide variety of events." Jervis, 1970, p. 16. A final note about data and theory: American scholars are truly enamored with data gathering. Needless to say, a theory lives or dies depending on the data. But at the same time we should keep in mind that the theory of relativity was not proposed by an individual who took it upon himself to gather additional data, but by one who relied on his imagination, ability to think logically, and on the data gathered and conclusions arrived at by other analysts.

63. Mefford, 1984, p. 7.

2
Why International Actors Attempt to Achieve Surprise

I t has been argued that surprise is a universal phenomenon sought by any state planning to initiate an act of aggression against one or more adversary. Surprise is sought because it reduces the costs of facing a fully alerted adversary and the chances of being pre-empted.[1]

This generalization, however, is imprecise. There have been instances in which international actors have been willing to face fully alerted adversaries rather than use surprise. Moreover, not all international actors contemplating the initiation of aggression have been concerned about the possibility of being pre-empted.

Two brief examples ought to suffice to support the first objection to the generalization. In 1982, following the Argentinian invasion of the Falkland Islands, the British, upon deciding to retake the islands, gave up surprise as part of the cost of trying to achieve their objectives through coercive diplomacy. Similarly, in 1962, the Americans rejected the idea of launching a surprise attack against the newly installed strategic missiles in Cuba. Like the British in 1982, the Americans in 1962 chose not to take the most drastic step first, hoping to minimize the long-term costs.

With regard to the second objection—that is, that not all international actors engage in surprise to avert pre-emption—two totally different cases ought to make the point. Hitler, in 1941, as he was preparing to launch a surprise attack on the Soviet Union, was well aware that Stalin would not attempt to pre-empt him. Hitler suspected, quite correctly, that the Soviet leader would go to great measures to avert war, and thus would not even consider the possibility of pre-emption.[2] In 1973, Israel concluded that Egypt was on the verge of launching an attack. Israel, however, consciously chose not to pre-empt[3] for fear that such an act would undermine the support of the United States.

Surprise rarely is used indiscriminately. According to Robert Axelrod, a rational international actor should use his surprise resources only when the stakes are large enough to warrant them. If he can achieve what he wishes without resorting to his surprise resources it would be extremely irrational to risk their exposure, since future stakes may be even higher and thus may more genuinely require their use. Axelrod then hypothesizes that attempts at surprise can be expected from any actor when the stakes are very large.[4]

Axelrod's generalization has limited explanatory value. Clearly, in 1973 the stakes for Israel were very high, and yet its decision makers chose not to pre-empt Egypt with a surprise attack. The same argument can be forwarded with respect to the United States in 1962. Before attempting to unearth the conditions under which an international actor will want to resort to surprise it will be necessary to clarify the distinction between two decisions: to go to war and to resort to surprise. At first glance, these two decisions may seem quite different. The decision to go to war entails the comparison of the cost and benefits one is likely to accrue by pursuing various alternatives. The decision to resort to surprise, on the other hand, is generally assumed to spring from a positive decision to go to war. In other words, an actor who chooses to resort to surprise during a war will do so only after having decided that war would be the most viable alternative.

The decision to go to war and the decision to resort to surprise, however, cannot be considered independently by those who are too weak to attain their objectives solely by the overt use of force. For this type of actor, the decision whether to go to war may very well depend on whether he can achieve surprise. Failure to assess whether surprise can be achieved may lead to the initiation of a chain of events that may be impossible to stop, were the originator to discover at some point that surprise is beyond his reach. On the other hand, an actor who is noticeably stronger than his adversary can afford not to assess his chances of achieving surprise, for the costs of failure are likely to be smaller.

Thus, since the main objective of surprise is to provide the user with an advantage he would normally not possess, it can be argued that the incentive to resort to surprise will be great among those who are noticeably weaker, marginally inferior, or marginally superior than their opponents. Conversely, actors who are clearly superior to their opponents are the least likely to resort to surprise.[5]

The decision to resort to surprise is not always a rational one. On occasions, decision makers contemplating the possibility of resorting to surprise have underestimated the potential capabilities of their opponent or overestimated their own, and therefore underrated the risks involved in engaging in a conflict. This means, in effect, that miscalculations can provide an actor with an added incentive for resorting to surprise.[6]

There have been instances, however, in which international actors have resorted to surprise fully aware that the discrepancies in capabilities between themselves and their adversaries were too great to be circumvented by the use of surprise. It is often assumed that when such imbalances are disregarded, the decisions are simply not explicable in rational terms.[7] But to accept this assumption is to overlook the fact that people from different cultures might evaluate alternative courses of action based on different values.[8] In fact, actions that by one standard may seem too risky because of the limited military capabilities of the actor implementing them can be considered less risky if the estimates are performed on a different ranking of values. Furthermore, "rational" decision models sometimes consider only the actor's assessment of utility of undertaking an option, and do not consider the disutility of not undertaking it.[9]

A case in point is the Japanese decision to attack Pearl Harbor in 1941. From a Western perspective, in which winning a war is primary, Japan's decision to attack the United States lacks rationality, since the latter was so much stronger. On the other hand, if protecting status is valued more highly than winning a war, or if submitting to demands from an adversary is viewed as an unacceptable option, then Japan's decision can no longer be perceived as irrational.[10]

Although confronted by the unattractive reality that even the advantages gained from surprise may not be enough to circumvent their country's shortcomings, decision makers need not always be drawn into either accepting the existing status quo or engaging in a surprise strategy. A third choice would be for them to alter their goals and then reconsider the viability of surprise. So far it has been assumed that the principal objective held by the leaders of states remain constant. But, as some students of decision making have suggested, ignoring the possibility that objectives are often altered can lead to misinterpreting choices.[11] For instance, an actor need not be deterred from using a strategy of surprise by the knowledge that its adoption will not be enough to fulfill his most desired objective—if he believes that it can help achieve a lower-ranked, but still very important, objective.

In sum, we have argued that the initial incentive to resort to surprise is the value of the stakes at hand. We then proposed that international actors who are considering the possibility of engaging in aggressive acts against adversaries whose powers are significantly greater or marginally the same will have the greatest incentives to resort to surprise. The argument was qualified by noting that on occasion international actors are bound to misjudge the strengths of their adversaries and therefore have greater incentives to resort to surprise than if their estimates had been accurate. As a second qualification it was proposed that international actors who are fully aware that the achievement of surprise will not be sufficient to help them circumvent their weaknesses may still resort to it if they are convinced that they must do so and can at least attain limited but very valuable objectives.

Having suggested some of the reasons that international actors resort to surprise, we should assess in greater detail the soundness of our arguments. In the process, an attempt will also be made to ascertain the reasons why certain international actors, upon considering surprise as an alternative, chose a different path. In four of the eight cases to be considered, the decisions to resort to surprise will be analyzed in conjunction with the decisions by the would-be surprisers to resort to aggressive means to fulfill their objectives.

Japan's Decision to Resort to Surprise

On December 7, 1941, after months of arduous preparation for war, Japan launched a surprise attack on Pearl Harbor. The interests of the United States and Japan began to clash long before December 1941. During the 1930s, the United States sought three foreign policy objectives in the Far East: (1) to maintain the collective security system founded upon such international agreements as the Washington Conference treaties, the League Covenant, and the Kellogg–Briand Pact, (2) to block any action designed to alter the existing order, by military force if necessary, and (3) to uphold the principle of the "open door," especially in China.[12]

Japan's foreign policy, on the other hand, went through a noticeable transformation during that same period. In the early 1930s, Japan made it very clear that its two cardinal objectives were to ensure that it was recognized as a major power and to guarantee that its security was never threatened.[13] Japan demanded that the Western states gradually abrogate their influence in China and accept Japan's hegemonic position in Asia. In order to assume sole responsibility for maintaining order in the Far East, Japan had to create a military base capable of neutralizing the Soviet Union, its traditional enemy; enforcing its demands on China; and guaranteeing its security against the United States.[14] These imperatives did not indicate, however, that Japan intended to go to war with either the Soviet Union or the United States. Instead, Japan "was committed to a policy which proposed to neutralize the influence of the Soviet Union, the nationalist government of China, and the Anglo–American nations by diplomacy rooted in the efficacy of Japan's military forces."[15]

By 1936, the leaders of Japan had come to the conclusion that in order to fulfill such exacting objectives, drastic new measures would have to be taken.[16] The first step they took was to inform the United States and Great Britain of Japan's intention to abrogate the naval disarmament treaties signed in 1921 in Washington and in 1930 in London.[17] Next, the Japanese proceeded to revamp their economic system. Japan's policy makers realized that under a free economy it would be nearly impossible to meet the requirements of a strong national defense; thus, they proposed a state planning system. They were also aware, however, that for such a new economic system to be able to contribute to the creation of a strong national defense, Japan had to have access to extensive oil reserves. Consequently, the Navy proposed the formation of a fleet with operational capabilities extending into Southeast Asia to protect the free transportation of such resources.[18]

The United States was displeased with Japan's decision to strengthen its naval power. But it did not take retaliatory measures until after August 8, 1937, when Peking was captured by Japan's North China expeditionary forces.[19] Censure of Japan's aggressive behavior against China emanated from several nations, especially the United States. According to European and American policy makers, Western security required that Japan be prevented from achieving victory in China. With this goal in mind, the United States started to send aid and supplies to China's strongman, General Chiang Kai-shek, and initiated a "moral embargo," whereby aircraft manufacturers were informed that the government was strongly opposed to the sale of American planes and aeronautical equipment to Japan. In 1939, the embargo was extended to materials essential to airplane manufacture and the production of high-quality gasoline. Concurrently, in July of that same year, Secretary of State Cordell Hull informed the Japanese ambassador in Washington that the treaties of commerce and navigation signed with Japan in 1911 would not be renewed after 1940.[20]

To counteract some of these measures, Japan launched a major diplomatic offensive to secure a preferential position in the Netherlands East Indies. The United States responded by moving its fleet based at San Diego to Pearl Harbor.[21] This measure did not weaken Japan's commitment to continue its southward expansion. By April of 1940, it concluded a treaty of "friendship" with Thailand. By the end of June, it began to demand: from France, permission for a Japanese military mission to operate in French Indochina; from the Netherlands, a guarantee to continue supplying Japan with raw materials; and from Great Britain, removal of its troops from Shanghai. In response, the United States set up controls over the amount of aviation gasoline and lubricants and the type of oil and scrap metal that American businesses could sell to Japan.[22]

By early 1941, both Japan and the United States realized that their relationship had deteriorated so extensively that it would be prudent for them to examine whether they could solve their differences in an amicable fashion. By July 1941, however, the United States interrupted meetings between Secretary of State Cordell Hull and the new Japanese ambassador to the United States, Admiral Kurusu Nomura, because of Japan's movement of troops into southern and northern Indochina.[23] According to Ambassador Admiral Nomura, Japan had to take such steps to protect vital supplies that might be cut off by Gaullist French agents and Chinese agitators, and to avoid the military encirclement of Japan intended by certain foreign powers. The United States rejected the explanation and added that it had to assume that the invasion of Indochina indicated that Japan was taking the last step before proceeding on a policy of expansion and conquest in the region of the South Seas.[24]

On July 26, President Roosevelt issued an executive order freezing Japanese assets in the United States and bringing under control of the American government all financial and import and export trade transactions in which Japanese interests were involved. Great Britain and the Netherlands took similar measures immediately afterwards.[25] Less than a week later, the United

States tightened the economic squeeze by putting an embargo on the export of oil to Japan.[26]

The joint move by the Americans, the British, and the Dutch shocked the Japanese policy makers. For them, it represented the culmination of years of efforts by the ABCD powers—the Americans, the British, the Chinese, and the Dutch—to deny Japan its rightful place in the Far East by destroying its only available means of self-existence and self-defense.[27] In a sense, as Butow correctly points out, "the whole problem facing Japan had been reduced to a very simple factor, and that was oil."[28] Japan's oil reserves were so limited that, were it to be engaged in a war against both the United States and the Soviet Union, its army could fight for only one year and its navy for only eighteen months. Furthermore, since each day meant an expenditure of another 12 thousand tons of oil, it became imperative that Japan find new oil suppliers.

Fearful that Japan would have to take drastic measures to ensure access to oil reserves and other vital resources, Prime Minister Konoye proposed to his cabinet the idea of meeting with President Roosevelt. Most members supported his proposal, but War Minister Hideki Tojo demanded that Konoye agree to remain in office and lead the country into war if the negotiations failed.[29]

Ambassador Nomura met with President Roosevelt on August 17, and informed him of Prime Minister Konoye's proposal. Following the meeting, the Japanese ambassador informed Tokyo that, although the American president had requested that Japan provide a clearer statement than had yet been furnished as to its attitudes and plans, he seemed positively disposed about the idea of holding a conference involving the heads of state.[30]

By this time, many of Japan's central policy makers were beginning to lose their patience. On September 3, a crucial policy document was presented for discussion to members of the Liaison Group. The document's main point was that, while continuing negotiations with the United States, Japan should also begin preparations for war. The members of the Liaison Group concluded, three days later, that if negotiations were not successful by the last ten days of October, Japan would go to war.[31]

Japan's decision to go to war against the United States has puzzled many scholars. As Roberta Wohlstetter points out, Japan's estimate of the United States' war potential in aircraft manufacture, shipbuilding, and rate of training of its crews was quite accurate for 1941, 1942, and 1943. Wohlstetter also notes that Japan knew it could not keep up with America's production of armaments or aircraft.[32]

Given Japan's accurate knowledge of the actual and potential capabilities of the United States, its decision to engage the United States in war is open to three interpretations. From one point of view, since Japan's decision makers knew that the United States had, in the words of Samuel Morison, "ample resources to stage a comeback,"[33] their decision to take on the United States was an irrational one. Viewed from a second perspective, one could accept Wohlstetter's less caustic judgment that such a decision "is simply not explicable in rational terms."[34] Finally, one could argue that the costs of *not going* to war with the United States might have been perceived by the Japanese decision makers to be even greater than those *of* going to war.

Western analysts have often been inclined to assume that states consider losing a war the worst of all possible outcomes. From this belief it has been inferred that a state that engages in war against an adversary that was known to be stronger was acting irrationally. The problem with such an inference is that it takes for granted the notion that all decision makers across the international arena would invariably rank losing a war as their least desirable outcome. History, however, has repeatedly shown that on certain occasions other outcomes may be more objectionable. Japan's decision to attack Pearl Harbor is a case in point.

Prior to July 1941, the United States had tried to deter Japan's southward move without resorting to coercive measures, hoping to bolster the position of the moderate forces in Japan. Japan's decision makers took a dim view of such acts. And yet, at the same time, they were fully cognizant that they still had ample room to maneuver in their attempts to bring about the results they desired. Things changed dramatically, however, following Japan's actions against French Indochina. It was then that Washington concluded that the only way to convince Japan that the United States would not permit its security interests to be endangered any further was by putting a freeze on Japanese assets in the United States and an embargo on American oil being shipped to Japan. The problem with this action was that it reflected one of the four specific circumstances under which Japan would find it necessary to go to war for its existence.[35] Many of Japan's decision makers were fully aware that engaging in a war with the United States was an endeavor of great uncertainty. Nevertheless, they also felt that losing status and failing in the traditional goal of establishing Japan as the hegemonic force in the Far East was worse than risking the possibility of losing a war. This attitude was probably best voiced by War Minister Tojo when he said, "Sometimes a man has to jump, with his eyes closed, from the veranda of Kiyomizu Temple."[36]

This explanation seems to indicate that Japan's decision makers may have engaged in some form of rational decision-making process by ranking their objectives before deciding whether to attack Pearl Harbor. In order to understand the process fully, Japan's calculations—the likelihood of winning a war against the United States—must be re-evaluated. This explanation is contingent on how the Japanese defined the term *victorious*.

Japan attacked Pearl Harbor not with the hope of defeating the United States militarily, but rather with the more limited objective of eliminating the United States Fleet so it could not interfere with the numerous amphibious operations necessary to conquer the "Southern Strategic Area."[37] Japan's decision makers were aware that, after suffering losses in the initial phase of the war, the United States would rebuild its armed forces in order to retaliate. But Tokyo also believed that in the interim period Japan would be able to secure a strategically powerful position in Southeastern Asia and control the important transportation routes and those areas producing vital materials. Such success would enable Japan to prepare itself for a protracted period of self-sufficiency[38] and establish a strategically impregnable position to retaliate against any American and British attacks.[39] According to this view, Japan did not initiate war against the United States in order to inflict a total military defeat, but to gain access to the necessary material and strategic resources that would enable it to frustrate American attempts to re-establish the old status quo. Such frustration, it was hoped, would force the Americans to agree to end the war on terms acceptable to Japan.[40]

In sum, in considering the pros and cons of going to war, statesmen must ask themselves, "Is this the right time to attack or should I wait?" The time element seems to have played an extremely important role in Japan's decision of *when* to attack. There were three strategic reasons that convinced many of Japan's central planners that it would be counterproductive to delay the war. First, if they waited too long, Japan's oil supplies would dwindle to dangerous levels. Second, delay in initiating the war would give the United States more time to strengthen its military forces. And third, it would be impossible to launch a successful landing operation in the south during the monsoon season or a successful naval strike against Pearl Harbor once winter had begun in the north Pacific. Therefore, if an attack was not launched by December, weather conditions would force a delay until the spring of 1942, the United States would have more time to restrengthen itself; and Japan's oil supply would have reached a perilous point.[41] As pointed out by Navy Chief of Staff Osami Nagano at the Imperial Conference on September 6, 1941:

. . . in the event that a peaceful solution is not attainable, and we have no alternative but to resort to war, the Supreme Command believes, from the standpoint of operations, that we cannot avoid being finally reduced to a crippled condition if we delay for too long. A number of vital military supplies, including oil, are dwindling day by day. This will cause a gradual weakening of our national defense, and lead to a situation in which, if we maintain the status quo, the capacity of our Empire to act will be reduced in the days to come. . . . By the latter half of next year America's military preparedness will have made great progress, and it will be difficult to cope with her. Therefore, it must be said that it would be very dangerous for our Empire to remain idle and let the days by.[42]

The argument forwarded thus far suggests that Japan's policy makers opted for war without considering whether surprise was feasible. Such a conclusion would be premature. Although there is evidence to suggest that the decision to attack Southeast Asia was not dependent on whether or not surprise could be achieved, there is little question that the decision to attack Pearl Harbor was directly linked to the achievement of surprise. More importantly, it was believed quite strongly by certain Japanese policy makers that the success of their operation in Southeast Asia was heavily dependent on a successful strategy of surprise against Pearl Harbor.

Ever since 1909, the Japanese had studied and trained for a decisive fleet counteroffensive against the United States Navy. Such a strategy, however, had one major weakness—it left the initiative in the hands of the Americans.[43] After the United States Pacific Fleet was transferred to Pearl Harbor, Japan's naval officers concluded that, if a successful attack could be launched on Hawaii, the United States would be deprived of the initiative, and its power would be diminished significantly. More importantly, it was believed, especially by Admiral Isoruku Yamamoto, the commander of the Japanese Fleet, that in the event of war with the United States, Japan's prospects of being victorious would be very small unless a crushing blow could be delivered to the United States Fleet in Hawaii at the very outset of the hostilities. Yamamoto made this point very clear in a letter to Navy Minister Admiral Koshira Oikawa by stating that, if the Japanese Navy feared that "such an operation against Hawaii is too risky" and remained in home waters awaiting the Americans, "we cannot rule out the possibility that the enemy would dare to launch an attack upon our homeland to burn down our capital and other cities."[44] Yamamoto's immediate colleagues were not convinced that such a task could be carried out effectively. As explained by Vice Admiral Shigeru Fukudome, who served as Yamamoto's chief of staff from November 15, 1939, to April 10, 1941, most naval officers were originally opposed to the idea because of the operational limitations of Japan's warships.[45]

It was Rear Admiral Takijiro Onishi who was instructed by Yamamoto to find a way to make the impossible possible. By the end of April 1941, Admiral Onishi completed the general plan. The operation consisted of launching an aerial attack on Pearl Harbor. Its success would depend on how well Japan overcame three obstacles. The first problem was that the operation could not be carried out unless Japan could surprise the United States Fleet in Pearl Harbor. The second obstacle was distance; the ships participating in the strike all had to have extraordinarily long cruising ranges to cover a round trip of approximately 65 hundred nautical miles. Finally, there was the problem that the waters of Pearl Harbor had an average depth of only forty-odd feet. This meant that Japan had to design a new aerial torpedo, since none of the existing ones could perform effectively in such shallow waters.[46]

On September 6, 1941, Japan's central decision-making body agreed that if Ambassador Nomura failed to win the concessions being demanded of Washington, Japan would go to war. Thus, preparations for war began in earnest. During this time, members of the Combined Fleet Headquarters, under Yamamoto's leadership, had been designing the general operational plan that Japan would adopt in the event of war. It was not until early October, however, that they informed the Naval General Staff of the plan to launch a surprise attack on Pearl Harbor at the outset of the war. Opposition to the plan was voiced immediately. The Naval General Staff had doubts about the plan's feasibility, and identified five objections. First, it was doubtful that the secrecy necessary to achieve surprise could be maintained because of the scale of the operation. Second, it was argued that, if Pearl Harbor were to be attacked, the blow would have to be of such magnitude as to ensure that the American Fleet would not be able to retaliate immediately. If, on the other hand, the Japanese attack were concentrated solely in Southeast Asia, the United States would not seek a decisive battle, but would first establish advance bases in the Marshall Islands and then attempt an island-hopping strategy. This strategy would give Japan ample time to concentrate all its available strength to repel the American advance.

Third, since 1909 Japan had been relying on ships and planes that had a relatively short radius of action. The implications of this fact for an operation such as the one contemplated against Hawaii were twofold. To begin with, the success of the operation would depend heavily on whether the ships could be refueled at sea. If refueling could not be carried out, not only would the operation against Pearl Harbor fail, but also Japanese naval units taking part in the attack would have been uselessly diverted from other operations. Furthermore, if refueling at sea ran into trouble, radio transmission would be required, which in turn would give the United States warning of the Japanese move.

Fourth, it was considered quite likely that United States patrol aircraft would spot the Japanese Fleet moving toward Pearl Harbor and that this detection would lead to pre-emptive military action. Finally, if the United States were to uncover Japan's intention to attack Pearl Harbor, it would discontinue the negotiations.[47]

Upon learning that the Naval General Staff had objected to the operation against Pearl Harbor, Yamamoto asked members of his staff to return to Tokyo and elaborate on four points:[48]

1. If Pearl Harbor was not attacked, Japan's contemplated new moves in Southeast Asia would immediately be exposed to a serious threat in one of its flanks.

2. In view of the United States–Japanese naval strength ratio, Japan would have no chance of victory unless a serious blow was delivered to the United States Navy.

3. Although the operation against Pearl Harbor would be beset with numerous problems and risks, they could all be overcome with a solid strategy of deception.

4. Unless the operation against Pearl Harbor was executed, Yamamoto had no confidence that he would be able to fulfill his responsiblity.

Yamamoto's points were accepted by the Naval General Staff, and Operation Hawaii became part of Japan's overall operational concept.

To summarize, Japan's decision to initiate a surprise attack against Pearl Harbor was born out of necessity. Japan, according to its decision makers' perceptions, was facing a rival whose unbending behavior was not only preventing Japan from attaining its long-sought goals, but also threatening its livelihood. Faced with this stark reality, Japan's leaders concluded that they had no choice but to move in full force into Southeast Asia no later than December—before their country's oil reserves were depleted to dangerous levels, the monsoon and winter seasons began, and the United States gained an insurmountable naval superiority. Moreover, Japan's leaders eventually accepted Yamamoto's argument that, if they went to war without delivering a serious blow to the United States Navy at Pearl Harbor, the prospect of success in Southeast Asia was going to be very small. Finally, these leaders also agreed with Yamamoto that it was imperative that Pearl Harbor be attacked by surprise. The value of the interests at stake and the superior strength of the United States required that surprise be used.

The argument just presented is in direct contrast to the arguments posited by two other writers. Snyder and Diesing maintain that the Japanese had "no concern for reputation and indeed no clear opinion of how the United States would react to their proposed moves."[49] They then suggest that the Japanese decision to attack Pearl Harbor was undertaken in response to internal needs, with little regard for external realities. Ned Lebow has posited a more sophisticated argument. He proposes that the Japanese leaders were fully cognizant that Japan could hope to win a war against the United States only if it were limited and of relatively short duration. He then adds, "They [the Japanese] convinced themselves, for no other reason than their need to, that the United States would fight such a war."[50] Our analysis, and to a lesser extent Lebow's study, suggest that there is little evidence to support the conclusion arrived at by Snyder and Diesing. The Japanese were very concerned for their reputation; as a point of fact, that was one of the main reasons they went to war. And they were quite aware of the external realities.[51] The fact that the Japanese did not estimate correctly how willing the Americans would be to engage in a protracted war does not mean that they failed to engage in a rational analysis. Rationality, by itself, does not guarantee certainty.

Lebow's argument is of a different nature. When he proposes that the Japanese convinced themselves that the United States would not fight a long costly war "for no other reason than their need to," he is suggesting that, had they analyzed the United States' behavior in the past under similar circumstances, they would have come up with a different conclusion. A more appropriate criticism would be to propose that in the absence of evidence regarding whether the United States would fight a limited war of relatively short duration, the Japanese should have been more cautious. But then it must be kept in mind that international actors differ in their willingness to take risks. As George and Smoke note, weak states with a great deal at stake often are inclined to accept costs and risks that would be unacceptable to more powerful states.[52]

Egypt-Syria's Decision to Resort to Surprise

Following the war of 1967, in which Israel won a decisive military victory and seized vast pieces of territory from Egypt and Syria, there were two major attempts to reach a peace agreement between the main parties. The first attempt was initiated by United Nations Secretary General U Thant, who named Dr. Gunnar Jarring, a Swedish diplomat, as a mediator to promote agreement in the Middle East.

The second peace initiative came from the newly elected American president, Richard M. Nixon. The peace settlement that Nixon proposed shortly after coming into office in January 1969 called for Israel's withdrawal to the pre-1967 borders. Its implementation depended heavily on whether the Soviet Union could convince Egypt to sign a peace agreement and permit Israel passage through the Suez Canal and the Straits of Tiram. By March 1969, the Americans and Soviets had agreed on most major points. But then two obstacles surfaced. First, the Soviet foreign minister, Andrei Gromyko, was faced with the difficult task of selling the plan to Egypt's president, Gamal Abdul Nasser. During his meeting with Gromyko, Nasser rejected the proposal and reiterated two demands: (1) Israeli withdrawal before any talks, and (2) negotiations between the Israelis and the Palestinians. Washington did not lose heart following Nasser's response; instead, it began to formulate a new peace settlement.

In the meantime, while the Americans and the Soviets were trying once again to get the conflicting parties to negotiate, Israel and Egypt began a new shooting war. By the end of 1969, after suffering enormous losses, Egypt could no longer contain Israel's counterstrikes. This new development put the Soviet Union in a predicament, for it was around this time that Washington proposed the outline of a new settlement. Moscow recognized that it could not afford to let Nasser fall, for such an act would have brought a loss of prestige to the Soviets in the Arab world. Thus, Moscow rejected the new American outline, and shortly afterward acceded to Nasser's demands for new and more sophisticated weapons.

The United States did not give up; it called for a new cease-fire. Although both Egypt and Israel, under the pressure of the two superpowers, agreed to the new cease-fire, Nasser took advantage of the occasion to rush the completion of sixteen operational missile complexes. The Israelis, aware that the balance was being tilted away from them, pulled out of the peace talks barely ten days after they had been revived. The United States immediately demanded that they return to the peace talks, and the Israeli government acquiesced.

It was around this time that a major change in the cast of characters took place. President Nasser, who suffered a heart attack and died in September 1970, was replaced by Anwar Sadat, his long-time collaborator. Sadat's ascension to power brought about a dramatic alteration in Egypt's attitude toward the United States' peace initiatives. In February 1971, Sadat announced that he would extend the cease-fire and would accept partial Israeli withdrawal in Sinai; in exchange, Egypt would reopen the Suez Canal. Israel, suspicious of Egypt's sudden turnabout, rejected the proposal. As a final attempt, Dr. Jarring, who once again was acting as mediator, suggested a series of commitments from both adversaries to enter into a peace agreement with one another. Egypt agreed to all of them, including respect for and acknowledgment of Israel's sovereignty, territorial integrity, and political independence. Israel, for its part, agreed to many of the conditions posed by Jarring, including withdrawal to boundaries to be established in the peace agreement, but not the pre–June 5, 1967, lines. In view of Israel's response, Sadat refused, in March 1971, to extend the cease-fire any longer, bringing to an end the diplomatic efforts to reach a peace settlement.

Sadat at this point found himself confronting a major dilemma. On the one hand, he knew that Egypt could not defeat Israel in an all-out war. Thus, he gave diplomacy a chance. As he remarked, "I did have slight hopes of Secretary of State Rogers in 1970 and 1971."[53] On the other hand, Sadat also recognized that his future as his country's new ruler depended on his ability to furnish both the Arab world and his countrymen with a new sense of pride. It became quite apparent to him that the existing arrangement in the Middle East of "no peace, no war" contained the seeds that could destroy what little unity existed among some of the Arab states and could topple him from power. To begin with, both Syria and Egypt, fearful that

Jordan's King Hussein would reach a separate peace treaty with Israel, found it politically necessary to sever relations with the Jordanian monarch. Furthermore, the Egyptian economy could not bear indefinitely the staggering military burden of wavering between a war of attrition and diplomatic postures that did not bring about any rewarding results for Egypt. Finally, it was questionable whether Egypt's social structure could survive much longer the strains imposed by the lack of aggressive initiative from its ruler. Aware that Israel's posture posed a threat to the tenuous sense of Arab unity and to his own domestic power, Sadat concluded that he had to go to war with Israel.

In order to understand what convinced Sadat that a war with Israel would not become an endeavor with catastrophic consequences to his native land, one must look at the problem from two distinct but interrelated perspectives. The first factor that must be kept in mind is that he made his decision to attack Israel almost simultaneously with the decision to design a strategy that would surprise the intended target. Sadat and his advisors were keenly aware that any state that attacks another with greater capabilities without resorting to a surprise attack is likely to be defeated. On March 21, 1973, less than two months after the planning of the attack had begun, General Ahmed Ismail, Egypt's war minister, called for a meeting to settle the first outlines of a complex military and political strategy of deception with which Egypt hoped to achieve surprise.[54]

Although the effective implementation of a strategy of surprise is bound to limit some of the implementer's costs, it is also important to keep in mind that it will not help fulfill the objective for which it was designed if the gap between what the surpriser can achieve and what he wants to achieve is too wide. Hence, what choices does a decision maker have when he realizes that even with the aid of surprise he cannot fully circumvent his country's shortcomings? Under such circumstances, he can choose one of three options.

The first option is simply to tolerate the status quo. This option, however, may not always be politically sound. When the decision maker is prevented from adopting this first choice by the country's internal political atmosphere and the international system, he may decide, instead, to go ahead and attempt to surprise his adversary, fully realizing that the cards are stacked against him and that he is bound to suffer great losses.

A decision maker facing unattractive conditions need not always decide between such unfruitful alternatives. His third choice is to alter his goals and then reconsider the viability of surprise. This was the alternative Sadat chose. He seems to have realized that even with Syria's aid he could not impose a military defeat on Israel, if for no other reason than that the United States would not allow it to happen. As he stated during a meeting with Zeid Rifai, a political adviser to King Hussein of Jordan, "I know I am not Tarzan. I recognize my limitations."[55] Thus, the best solution was not to seek the destruction of Israel, but to get Israel to return the territories that it had seized from Egypt and Syria during the 1967 war.[56]

The achievement of this more limited objective was no longer dependent on Egypt and Syria's ability to defeat Israel and reclaim the territories. Instead, it depended on their ability to destabilize the Middle East to the point where the situation became a threat to American–Soviet detente. Egypt and Syria could thus force the United States to pressure Israel to agree to some of their demands. Although Sadat realized early in the planning stage that Egypt and Syria could not defeat Israel, it was not until June 12, 1973, that he was able to persuade Syria's president, Hafez Asad, to pursue the more limited objective.[57]

In short, the decision to attack Israel was born of necessity. Sadat was confronted with a rival whose unbending behavior was not only dissolving the fragile and limited sense of unity that existed among many of the Arab states, but was also leading his own state to economic and social chaos. Faced with this reality, he believed he had no choice but to attempt to alter the impasse in the Middle East by violent means. To succeed with this task, however, he also had to face and deal with the fact that Israel's military power was mightier than Egypt and Syria's.

Sadat knew that a weaker actor can often offset certain imbalances with surprise. But he was also realistic enough to recognize that Israel was too strong to be brought to its knees. Thus, he decided that Egypt and Syria should go to war not to defeat Israel, but to persuade the two superpowers that if they hoped to build detente on a firm foundation they first had to help redefine the status quo in the Middle East. For this purpose, it would be justifiable to use surprise.

An appropriate question to pose next is: to what extent was the decision by Egypt to resort to surprise engendered by the fact that Sadat was its leader? It has been suggested that two factors—type of political system and leadership style—influence how often surprise is used as an instrument of foreign policy. Furthermore, it has been argued that the political structure most likely to generate surprise is one with a nondemocratic political system and an authoritarian leader.[58] Of these two factors, it is believed that the presence of an authoritarian style of leadership is more important than the nature of the political system.

The explanatory value of the above argument is limited in several respects. First, it is doubtful that the mere presence of a nondemocratic political system with an authoritarian leadership will beget surprise. It may be feasible to propose that under certain domestic and international pressures the disposition to resort to surprise will vary depending on the type of political system and style of leadership. But even this kind of argument is somewhat inappropriate. For example, it is not difficult to envision an instance in which two authoritarian leaders functioning under the same type of nondemocratic political system and facing exactly the same domestic and international pressures will be differently disposed to the use of surprise as an instrument of foreign policy. In other words, it makes very little sense to assume that just because two individuals govern under the same type of political system and have the same leadership style they will share a common attitude toward risk.

Having acknowledged that individuals may differ in their attitudes toward risk taking, we must still confront the question of whether Egypt under a different leader would have resorted to surprise. Needless to say, it would be unreasonable to argue that any other leader would have also resorted to surprise. But in suggesting that Sadat's predilection for risk taking may have been an important influencing factor, we are overlooking the fact that any leader facing the same types of domestic and international pressures would have had to take some major steps in order to survive politically. Stated from a somewhat different perspective, this study is not attempting to suggest that a leader's attitude toward risk taking is irrelevant, but that it is relevant only upon discovering the environmental conditions under which such a leader may find it necessary to resort to surprise.

Germany's Decision to Resort to Surprise

Germany's decision to launch a surprise attack against the Soviet Union in 1941 can be traced, indirectly, to the coming to power of Hitler's regime in the first half of the 1930s. One of Hitler's first acts as the newly appointed chancellor was to reorganize Germany's armament industry. By 1939, the rearmament program had reached mammoth proportions. As Hitler put it, "the warlike equipment of the German people is at present larger in quantity and better in quality for a greater number of German divisions than in the year 1914."[59] Hitler's rearmament policy was guided by two objectives: (1) to alter the European order that had existed since the signing of the Treaty of Versailles in 1919, and (2) to create a Germany that extended beyond the frontiers of 1914.

The nature of these two objectives began to surface following Germany's seizure of Austria and Czechoslovakia, and became fully evident after September 1, 1939, when Poland was invaded by Germany. Prior to the attack of Poland, however, Hitler concluded that it was essential to ensure the neutrality of the Soviet Union so that Germany would not become involved in a two-front war.

After Germany's takeover of Czechoslovakia in March 1939, the British government explored the possibility of erecting a major barrier against Nazi Germany by arranging an alliance between Great Britain, France, and the Soviet Union. Cognizant that the negotiations between the Western powers and the Soviet Union might prove successful, Hitler informed Moscow that Berlin would be willing to formulate some type of political and economic agreement so long as Russia abstained from joining forces with France and Great Britain.[60] The matter was broached to the Soviets at the end of May 1939 by Germany's foreign minister, J. von Ribbentrop, and three and a half months later, on August 23, the signing of a Nazi–Soviet agreement was announced.

The agreement set the stage for the German attack of Poland and, as a consequence, the declaration of war by Great Britain and France against Germany. In the nonaggression pact with Germany, the Soviet Union committed itself to not go to war against Germany and to deliver large amounts of foodstuff and grain, oil, cattle, coal, lead, and zinc. In return, part of Poland went to the Soviet Union—the rest became part of Germany's dominion—and Estonia, Latvia, and Finland were recognized as falling within the sphere of influence of the Soviet Union.[61]

Between September 1, 1939, the day Poland was attacked by Germany, and the summer of 1940, Hitler's success against the West was formidable. During this period, Germany's armed forces routed the Polish, invaded Norway and Denmark, and brought about the collapse of France. Great Britain, although badly wounded, remained unbending in its unwillingness to compromise with the Germans.

Until July 1940, Hitler was convinced that he could persuade the British to reach a peace agreement with Germany. All he wanted from Britain was the acknowledgment that Germany deserved the status of a major power. He made such an appeal in a speech to the Reichstag in July 1940, when he declared that he saw no reason for the war between the two countries to continue.[62] Britain's response, through its foreign secretary, Lord Halifax, was forceful and uncompromising: "We shall not stop fighting until Freedom is secure."[63]

In view of Britain's stand, Hitler was faced with the task of deciding what step to take next. One alternative was to launch a landing operation against England. However, Hitler and his associates soon realized that such a campaign carried the risk of having an adverse effect on the aura of invincibility that Germany had been so successful in building around itself. An invasion of England, they concluded, should be a last-resort maneuver, undertaken only against an opponent who had already been weakened by blockade and air attack.[64]

The question raised by Hitler at this juncture was: Why was Great Britain adopting such an uncompromising position against Germany? Hitler believed that he had the answer. According to his estimates, Great Britain lacked the means to fight a prolonged war against Germany; its hope for survival depended primarily on the Soviet Union's entering the war. As he put it:

Russia is the factor by which England sets the greatest store. . . . If Russia is beaten, England's last hope is gone. Germany is then the master of Europe and the Balkans. . . . Decision: As a result of this argument, Russia must be dealt with. Spring, 1941.[65]

The fact that Hitler suspected that Britain's leaders hoped to persuade the Soviets to fight Germany does not mean that he was seriously concerned that the Soviets would join forces with Britain against Germany. On the contrary, Hitler believed that "even though Moscow is unenthusiastic about Germany's great success, she will nevertheless make no effort to enter into war against Germany of her own accord."[66] In other words, it was not the fear that Stalin would volunteer to forge an alliance with Britain against Germany that led Hitler to attack the Soviet Union, but the belief that what was keeping Britain from reaching a compromise with Germany was the hope that by holding out long enough the Soviets eventually would be drawn into the war.[67]

But there was also another factor that convinced Hitler that it was time to turn east. As he expressed it in *Mein Kampf,* by conquering the Soviet Union, Germany would be restored to its deserved world-power status. In 1932, when explaining his Eastern policy to a group of party comrades, he stated:[68]

I am not thinking in the first instance of economical matters. Certainly we need the wheat, oil and ores. . . . But our true object is to set up our rule for all time, and to anchor it so firmly that it will stand for a thousand years.

Scholars do not fully agree on when Hitler made his decision to attack the Soviet Union. The greatest number argue that from July 1940 on, the invasion of the Soviet Union was firmly on the Nazi agenda.[69] The major dissenting voice is that of James McSherry, who maintains that, although as early as the end of July 1940 Hitler considered the possibility of invading the Soviet Union, his mind was not fully made up until November of that year.[70] For our purposes, it suffices to know that Hitler arrived at his decision between July 31, 1940, and the end of November 1940.

It is generally assumed that the Germans deemed it necessary to surprise the Soviets in order to minimize the costs Germany would have to absorb during the attack and to avert pre-emption.[71] There is no evidence to suggest that Hitler and his generals overlooked the importance of the first factor. It is doubtful, however, that they were ever concerned with the possibility of the Soviets' launching a pre-emptive attack.[72]

Hitler seems to have had two objectives in mind when he designed his strategy of surprise.[73] The two objectives were: (1) to create uncertainty among Britain's high officials as to whether Germany planned to attack Britain or the Soviet Union, and (2) to attract most of the Soviet Army to the western border and take it by surprise when the German troops began to cross the border.

The success of Hitler's European strategy depended on Germany's ability to avoid fighting a two-front war. Hitler reasoned that once the attack against the Soviets was launched, Churchill would exploit the situation and attempt to land forces in Portugal and on the coast of Norway, aid the Soviets through the port of Murmansk, occupy territory north of Gibraltar, and establish air bases in Morocco.[74] The first step taken by Hitler to obstruct the formation of a second front by Britain was to retain thirty-nine divisions in France and the Low Countries, eight in Norway and Denmark, eight in the Balkans, two in Africa, and two in Germany.[75] The second step Hitler took was to keep Britain's top officials uncertain as to which country he planned to attack—the Soviet Union or Great Britain—so they would continue their original efforts to rebuild Britain's defenses instead of working on the creation of a second front against Germany.

The need to keep the British guessing about which country Germany would attack next was closely linked to the belief held by Hitler and his generals that, in a war with the Soviet Union, victory would have to be achieved promptly. This belief was based on an idea developed in the early 1930s and commonly referred to as the *blitzkrieg*. The argument was that in order to avoid fighting a war against a great coalition, Germany had to fight a series of small wars, each designed to win an easily attainable objective in a short, swift, decisive campaign.[76] Germany's strategy against the Soviet Union was designed around this concept.

The German chiefs of staff of the army groups that were to undertake the campaign against the Soviet Union were convinced that it was essential to destroy the Red Army close to the frontier, west of a line between Peipus, Minsk, and Kiev. They believed that this objective had to guide their strategy because the deeper an army penetrated into the hinterland, the wider the front became. Were the Red Army to retreat into the hinterland, Germany would not have enough troops to hold any form of continuous front, the war would drag on well into the winter, the Soviets would be given time to augment their military strength, and Germany could find itself committing a large portion of its troops for a prolonged period of time.[77] This was exactly what Hitler hoped to avoid in order to prevent the British from setting a strong foothold on the continent. As Hitler persistently reminded his generals, the military strategic aim had to be the "destruction of Russia's vital power,"[78] and, for the operation to make sense, the objective had to be attained in a single campaign completed in five months. Therefore, if the vital power of the Soviet Union had to be destroyed near its western border within a period of five months, as agreed by Hitler and his generals, it can be inferred that Germany had to design a strategy that would both attract most of the Red Army to the western border and take it by surprise when the German troops began to cross into the Soviet Union.

To summarize, then, Hitler and his generals had to design a strategy of surprise that would help Germany attain two objectives. On the one hand, there was a need to ensure that Britain's top officials would be unable to predict whether Britain or the Soviet Union would be Germany's next target so that Churchill would be less concerned with the creation of a second front on the European continent than with continuing the efforts to rebuild Britain's defenses. On the other hand, Germany's behavior had to persuade the Soviets that it was imperative that they move most of the Red Army to their western border, but without placing them on full alert, so that Germany could destroy Russia's vital power within a short period of time.

It has been suggested that Operation Barbarossa would not have come to light had a different individual led Germany in 1941. According to Robert G.L. Waite, some of Hitler's actions during his tenure as the leader of Germany were such blunders that they can only be perceived as the result of a strong, unconscious impulse for self-destruction.[79] Waite's argument is based largely on the idea that in 1941 Hitler was closer to victory than at any other time in the course of the war and that circumstances did not require that he send his forces against the Soviet Union.[80] A more appropriate policy, and one that was recommended by Germany's Naval High Command, would have been to launch a major attack in the Mediterranean region.[81]

According to Waite, several personal factors seem to have been at work in Hitler's momentous decision. The first one, suggested by Goring, seems to have been that he could think of military operations only in "continental terms," for he always felt uncomfortable with operations that were carried out at sea. A second factor seems to have been Hitler's personal hope to go into history as the greatest commander of all time. The final, and possibly most important personal factor, seems to have been his inordinate compulsion to punish himself and to fail.[82]

The central flaw in Waite's argument—from which his other errors flow—is rooted in one idea: Hitler did not accept the recommendation of the German Naval High Command to attack in the Mediterranean, but instead attacked the Soviet Union; hence, he was being irrational. This argument would have been persuasive only if—in view of the information available—it had been evident that the campaign against the Soviet Union would have ended in defeat. In other words, to suggest that Operation Barbarossa was not carefully rationalized within the context of the information available, but instead was solely the product of Hitler's pathological desire to self-destruct, is simply to disregard some very important facts.

It cannot be denied that Hitler had a propensity for taking higher risks than most other individuals on his general staff. His inclination to dance on the razor's edge had been challenged in the past by many of his aides, and yet at every stage until 1941 they had been wrong. The invasion of the Soviet Union was a calculated gamble—a gamble, one might add, that would have been perceived as one of the greatest military campaigns in history had it ended in victory.

Hitler's rationale for invading the Soviet Union, aside from his inordinate desire for power, was solid. First, had he in fact succeeded in conquering the Soviet Union, Great Britain would have found it nearly impossible to carry on the war alone. Although Germany eventually fought a two-front war, something that Hitler was quite aware it could not do, this was exactly what he had hoped to avert by invading the Soviet Union while Britain was recovering from its initial losses. Second, Waite is quite wrong in suggesting that the Soviet Union in 1941 was Germany's most valued ally. As we will argue later on, the relationship between the two states had been corroding for some time, and Stalin was contemplating the possibility of attacking Germany if the latter got bogged down in a protracted war with Britain.

By no means do we wish to suggest that there was no measure of self-delusion among Hitler and his associates. The clinching argument for the timing of the attack was the belief by Hitler and his generals[83] that Germany could defeat the Soviet Union completely in a very short time.[84] A couple of external factors contributed to such self-delusion. First, the Finnish–Soviet war had revealed that the Red Army and its leadership were very weak and that the Russian tank forces were not capable of fighting a modern war of movement.[85] And second, German intelligence reports were quite limited in information and for the most part supported the belief that the Red Army was weak.[86]

Possibly the most important personal factor that contributed to Hitler's self-delusion was his racial-political idea. He was convinced that the Russian state, which owed its creation largely to German organizers, had been degenerating since the Jews took over the government following the Bolshevik revolution. The Bolshevik state had been so ineffective since its creation, he thought it would collapse the moment the German troops invaded.

As the data indicate, it is not easy to establish precisely why Germany invaded the Soviet Union in 1941. What makes the situation complex is that Germany could have engaged in a totally different operation. In other words, the domestic and internal pressures it faced in 1941 were not so constraining that Hitler could not have opted for a different policy. Therefore, it would be possible to envision a different leader under the same circumstances opting for a different alternative. But having acknowledged that Hitler's persona was a determining factor is not the same as stating that it was his inordinate compulsion to punish himself and to fail that influenced his decision. Hitler and his associates were faced with a choice; the fact that they chose an alternative that led to defeat does not prove they acted irrationally. In the absence of total information, decision makers risk choosing the wrong alternative.[88]

Having stated that Hitler's choice can be accommodated within the realm of limited rationality, it ought to be also kept in mind that his propensity for taking risks was higher than those of his associates. Moreover, part of the reason he believed that Germany could overpower Russia was that he was convinced that the Bolshevik revolution was a failure and that the Russian government would fall shortly after the invasion. His own racial attitudes notwithstanding, Hitler did not deceive himself that Germany's armed forces would have little trouble defeating the Red Army. The fact that he and his generals placed so much weight on the achievement of surprise attests to the contrary. Hitler himself said it best when he wrote in *Directive No. 21: Case Barbarossa:* "It is of decisive importance that our intention to attack should not be known."[89]

The Decision by the Soviet Union to Resort to Surprise

In 1962, the Soviets reversed a long-standing policy of not placing nuclear missiles outside Soviet territory and deployed a large number of them in Cuba. It has been proposed that attempts to explain the decision can be categorized into five hypotheses.[90] According to Graham Allison, some hypotheses offer more satisfactory explanations than others. He notes also that they are all subject to a common set of difficulties. It is his contention that none of the hypotheses can explain why: (1) there was such a lack of co-ordination between the plan attributed to Moscow and the actual actions; (2) the Soviet premier, Nikita Khrushchev, would want to visit the United Nations in the second half of November, before the intermediate range ballistic missiles (IRBMs) installed in Cuba achieved operational readiness, if his intent were to unveil a fait accompli (American intelligence estimates have indicated that the IRBMs would not have achieved operational readiness until after December 15.); (3) the Soviets failed to camouflage the missile sites; and (4) the Soviets failed to take into account the American U-2 flights over Cuba.[91]

It is Allison's contention that, in order to deal with these unanswered questions, one must look at the Soviet decision to deploy its missiles from a different perspective. The first analytical step is to inquire whether the Soviets might have been misled into believing that the Kennedy Administration would react in a restrained manner to the presence of missiles in Cuba.

Allison maintains that the behavior of certain American officials might have made such a conclusion reasonable.[92]

On concluding that the United States might not react in a forceful manner to the presence of missiles in Cuba, the Soviet policy makers were faced with the task of deciding whether or not to deploy them. It is at this point that Allison parts company with the proponents of the other hypotheses. He contends that the decision to install missiles in Cuba emerged not from grand global planning, but rather "from a process in which a number of different individuals' quite distinct perceptions of separable problems snowballed into a single solution."[93]

According to this hypothesis, the possibility of solving five different problems may have enabled distinct groups within the Soviet decision-making apparatus to agree on a single solution. By installing missiles in Cuba, the Soviets hoped to (1) guarantee the security of Cuba, (2) offset the superior strategic capability of the United States, (3) settle the Berlin question in terms favorable to the Soviet Union, (4) transfer funds away from the military sector and into the industrial sector, and (5) settle some of the domestic differences that had arisen within the Soviet Union.[94]

In sum, Allison's hypothesis differs from the five he discusses early in his book mainly in terms of the number of problems the installation of Soviet missiles in Cuba was supposed to solve. At this juncture it would be appropriate to decide which of the six hypotheses can best explain the Soviet Union's decision to deploy missiles in Cuba. Since we do not possess any additional information that would enable us to arrive at a definite conclusion, we shall pursue a more limited objective. We will assume that each of the five problems described by Allison was taken into account by the Soviet decision-making apparatus and that different groups ranked the importance of the problems differently.[95] Based on these two assumptions, we will ask: What would have been the likelihood of reaching a consensus to install Soviet missiles in Cuba had each of the five problems been evaluated independently, without reference to the remaining problems?

It is clear that as soon as this question is posed, some problems become much less relevant than others. It is quite doubtful, regardless of how badly the Soviets might have misjudged Kennedy's willingness to confront the Soviet Union, that the Soviet military would have agreed to the idea of installing missiles solely for the purpose of eradicating some of the domestic disagreements that had been afflicting the Soviet polity. For the Soviet military, the risks involved could not have been justified by the objectives sought. A similar argument can be advanced with respect to the idea that the missiles were deployed in order to protect Cuba. This is not to say that the defense of Cuba was a negligible matter for the Soviet military. But it is reasonable to assume that if the sole Soviet objective had been to deter an American attack on Cuba, the military leaders would have proposed methods better suited to the task. The presence of a large contingent of Soviet troops, for instance, would have been a more appropriate solution.[96] For that matter, even tactical nuclear weapons could have been deployed more quickly and inexpensively.[97]

If the burden of increases in military expenditure on the Soviet economy had been the only concern, it seems unlikely that the Soviet military would have agreed to install missiles in Cuba.[98] Moreover, as Allison points out, the economic planners probably would not have proposed the installation of missiles as a solution to their problem, but would have benefited from it and supported it if somebody else had proposed it to solve a different problem.[99]

The contention that the Soviets deployed missiles to Cuba in order to use them as a bargaining chip with respect to Berlin has been widely supported and challenged. If the problem is viewed from a bureaucratic perspective, however, there are several reasons why some of the different groups involved in the decision would have opposed this alternative. Two groups in particular are pertinent—the military leaders and the economic planners. The military would have proposed the deployment of weapons that were more symmetrical with the political probe. Even the installation of a few medium range ballistic missiles (MRBMs) in Cuba, as Allison explains, would have been enough to convince the United States that the existing status quo in Berlin was no longer acceptable.[100] Had this proposal arisen, it is likely that the military would have received the support of the economic planners, since the implementation of such a plan would have been much cheaper. Second, the choice of Cuba as a Berlin probe made little sense. Had this been the sole objective, the Soviet military would most likely have calculated that placing pressure on Berlin offered a better chance of success at lower cost, gaining once again the support of the economic planners.

The missile gap is the fifth problem the missiles' installation is purported to have been designed to solve. We think it was the possibility of narrowing the missile gap that enabled the competing Soviet decision-making groups to agree on sending the missiles to Cuba. By narrowing the missile gap, the Soviets would have succeeded not only in fulfilling a long-sought strategic objective, but also in improving the chances of solving the remaining four problems. The economic planners could have supported the missiles' installation as a suitable policy because fewer resources would have been needed to narrow the missile gap. Although narrowing the missile gap would not have been imperative in order to deter an American attack on Cuba, its attainment guaranteed Cuba's territorial integrity.[101] With respect to the Berlin question, it is clear that brining about greater parity in the strategic military threat was not essential to inducing a change in the status quo. But certainly narrowing the gap would have improved the bargaining stand of the Soviets. Finally, very little can be said about what effect the narrowing of the missile gap might have had on the Soviet domestic front. One could speculate, however, that the Soviet leadership would have used it effectively to aggrandize its image and to mollify internal dissenters.

Summing up, it is quite possible that the Soviet Union deployed some of its strategic missiles to Cuba in order to help resolve several problems. And yet it is unrealistic to render the same utility value to the solution of each problem. The prospect of solving four of the five problems considered was in some instances dependent on, and in other cases closely connected to, whether the missile gap was narrowed.[102]

From 1957, following the successful launching of the first sputnik, until near the end of 1961, the Soviets had been proclaiming that the military and strategic balance had significantly shifted away from the United States and toward the Soviet Union.[103] By the summer of 1961, however, American analysts had gathered enough intelligence to conclude that the balance of power had never really shifted away from the United States. Some months later, in November 1961, the United States made this conclusion public.[104]

The Soviets found themselves facing a problem—how to offset the diplomatic disadvantages entailed by the American military superiority. On concluding that the installation of strategic missiles in Cuba would help them alleviate the nuclear gap problem, the Soviets had to decide which would be the most effective way to implement the policy. At the most general level, they must have considered whether or not to conceal the deployment of the missiles until they became operational.

If one accepts Allison's contention that the United States' behavior prior to June 1962[105] indicated that the Kennedy Administration's reaction to the placement of missiles would be minimal, then one can argue that the Soviets could have concluded that surprise would be unnecessary. This conclusion is unwarranted.

Allison refers to four developments that could have misled the Soviets[106]: (1) the hesitant manner in which Kennedy behaved during the Bay of Pigs episode, (2) the view expressed in a speech on the floor of the Senate on June 29, 1961, by Senator J. William Fulbright—whom Kennedy had seriously considered appointing secretary of state—that the national security of the United States would not be endangered further by the placement of missile bases in Cuba,[107] (3) the implication by some officials that the world would be safer if the Soviet Union sought to achieve a more balanced distribution of power with the United States, and (4) the tacit acceptance by the United States of the rearmament of Cuba (since the middle of 1960) with Soviet military equipment.

In looking closely at each of these behaviors, it is difficult to understand why Allison concluded that Soviet leaders could believe that the United States was conveying an inclination to react mildly to the installation of missiles in Cuba. To begin with, although the Kennedy Administration showed a lack of resolution during the Bay of Pigs incident, the threat posed by the presence of an unfriendly regime in Cuba did not even approximate the threat that could have resulted from the presence of Soviet missiles in Cuba. The Soviets had sufficient experience in power politics to be aware of this distinction.

Second, it is difficult to accept Allison's implicit inference that the Soviets would not be sophisticated enough to realize that members of the United States Senate—even those who are close to the president—do not always reflect the president's views. Fulbright's comment that the installation of Soviet missiles in Cuba would not substantially alter the balance of power in the world was not followed by an endorsement from the Kennedy Administration. Furthermore, Allison fails to note that Kennedy's pronouncements during the presidential election expressed a view totally opposite to that advanced by Fulbright.

Another of Allison's points—that some Washington officials favored the Soviet Union's developing a second-strike capability—would give some credence to his argument only if we knew that such officials held high-ranking positions within the Kennedy Administration,[108] and only if we accept Allison's extremely weak excuse that the Soviets did not fully understand that the missiles in Cuba would be useful only for a first strike.[109]

Finally, it makes very little sense for Allison to relate two developments that posed totally different measures of threat. The Kennedy Administration did not obstruct the shipment of conventional Soviet weapons to Cuba partly because those weapons did not seem to pose a direct threat to the United States, and partly because the Administration had been attempting to improve relations with Moscow. Had Washington suspected that the Soviets were deploying some of their strategic nuclear missiles, it would have felt justified in trying to obstruct the deployment.[110]

The argument so far has been that the signals emanating from Washington do not justify the contention that Moscow could have been misled into believing it could deploy its missiles without relying on surprise.[111] To demonstrate why the Soviets decided that they must surprise Washington, it is necessary to re-evaluate what happened in November 1961.

It was in November that Washington informed Moscow that it had evidence of its own missile superiority. In addition to this message, Washington signaled that from then on it would behave in accordance with its true power status.[112]

On deciding to deploy offensive missiles to Cuba, the Soviets had to estimate how much resistance to expect from the United States, and, in particular, how and when this resistance would materialize. Moscow had to be aware that for several years Washington had been unable to translate its strategic superiority into a foreign-policy tool because it had been unsure how its military power ranked with Moscow's. This awareness is likely to have persuaded the Soviets that Washington would be unwilling to relinquish the advantage it had finally established. Washington's determination and ability to maintain its strategic advantage, however, were likely to vary depending on the situation. It was bound to be stronger when the missiles were being deployed than after they became operational.[113] Thus, in order to minimize the obstacles that Washington could erect while the strategic missiles were being transferred and installed, the best alternative would be to not reveal the nature of the policy.

In sum, the Soviets deployed nuclear missiles in Cuba in an attempt to narrow the nuclear advantage held by the United States over the Soviet Union. Moreover, the Soviets sought to achieve surprise for the simple reason that, if they had disclosed their intention, Washington would have tried to block the deployment and installation of the missiles.

Conclusion

The central tenet of this chapter has been that an international actor's willingness to resort to surprise is a function of the value of the interests at stake. In every case considered, the stakes were indeed very high. For Japan it was crucial to deliver a serious blow to the United States Navy at Pearl Harbor in order to increase its own prospects of success in Southeast Asia. Egypt's leader, Anwar Sadat, hoped to revitalize Egypt's political and economic structure and to lengthen his own tenure as president by launching a successful attack against Israel. Hitler seems to have been convinced that a successful attack on the Soviet Union would reduce the risks of having to battle in the future a two-front war against two powerful adversaries. And finally, Nikita Khrushchev seems to have calculated that by installing Soviet strategic nuclear missiles in Cuba he would be able not only to narrow the nuclear advantage held by the United States, but also to solve a myriad of other political and economic problems. In each instance, the achievement of surprise was critical.

This general proposition can be further substantiated by looking at two cases in which surprise was considered, but rejected. In 1973, as the prospects of an attack by Egypt and Syria became clearer, Prime Minister Golda Meir and her closest advisers considered pre-empting the Arabs with a surprise attack of their own. Meir, with the full support of her minister of defense, Moshe Dayan, rejected the idea. The decision not to pre-empt the Arabs was, for all practical purposes, a political decision.[114] On the one hand, Meir and Dayan were very much concerned about world public opinion. They did not want Israel to be accused of starting a war, as it had been in 1967 in the aftermath of the Six-Day War. As Meir put it:

> I regret not launching it [an interceptive strike] because there is no doubt that the [military] position would have been much better. I do not regret [the decision] . . . because at least we do not have the argument with the world.[115]

The Israeli decision makers were also worried about the possibility that if they pre-empted the Arabs, the United States would not be able to assure the future flow of arms to Israel. Meir articulated this view very clearly when she stated:

> Had the situation as to who began hostilities not been clear beyond the shadow of a doubt, I question whether the vital equipment we received in the course of time would have flowed as it did, as it still continues to flow.[116]

In view of Meir's statements, it can be inferred that for her it was more important not to be condemned by world opinion and not to jeopardize Israel's military relationship with the United States than to gain certain immediate military advantages via a pre-emptive surprise attack.

In 1962, the United States was also placed in the position of having to decide whether to launch a surprise attack. President Kennedy's advisers, on learning that the Soviets were installing strategic missiles in Cuba, considered the costs and benefits of launching a surprise surgical air strike against the Soviet missiles in Cuba.[117] This alternative was rejected for three reasons. First, the air force warned that the destruction of all the missiles could not be guaranteed. To assure their destruction the United States would have to mount not a surgical strike, but rather a massive air attack of at least five hundred sorties. Second, an attack of this magnitude could have resulted in the death of Russians, thus pressuring the Soviets to retaliate. The third and chief flaw stemmed from the question of whether the United States could justify a "Pearl Harbor in reverse." Not only was there the belief by some of Kennedy's advisers that the United States had to abide by its heritage of never launching an unannounced attack, but also there was concern as to how NATO and Latin America would respond to the action. In short, the Kennedy Administration calculated that the costs of engaging in a surprise attack were likely to outweigh the benefits.

The argument that an international actor will resort to a surprise attack only when the benefits of such an action outweigh the costs is incomplete. It is also important to try to understand the conditions under which the benefits of relying on surprise would outweigh the costs. The cases considered in this study indicate that this might be so under a variety of conditions. One condition, however, was found to be common among the four cases.

Japan in 1941, and Egypt–Syria in 1973, knew that their chances of defeating the United States and Israel, respectively, would have been almost nonexistent had they not sought to achieve surprise. The Soviet Union in 1962 engaged in a strategy of surprise because it knew that it would not be able to overcome American resistance if the intention to install Soviet nuclear missiles was disclosed. And, finally, Germany in 1941 sought to surprise the Soviet Union for fear that if the intention to attack was disclosed, the Soviets would counteract with a strategy that might prolong the war. In each of these cases the aggressor seems to have calculated that the benefits of relying on surprise outweighed the costs largely because surprise was considered essential to compensate for his weaknesses.

This conclusion is substantiated by Israel's decision to forego a surprise attack in 1973. Prime Minister Meir was much concerned about how the world in general, and the United States in particular, would react if Israel pre-empted the Arabs. Her decision not to pre-empt, however, took into account other factors besides world opinion. On three occasions Meir asked the chief of staff, General David Elazar, and the commander of the Israeli Air Force, General Benjamin Peled, whether Israel's survival would be placed in jeopardy or whether there would be long-range military disadvantages if Israel did not pre-empt.[118] Each time both questions were answered in the negative.

Meir's decision to reject a pre-emptive surprise attack, therefore, came only after she had been assured that Israel possessed the military strength not only to defeat the would-be attackers, but also to control the costs Israel would have to absorb for not taking the initiative. In other words, the value of not being challenged by world public opinion and of ensuring the continued support of the United States was perceived to be greater than that of launching a pre-emptive surprise attack only because Israel's policy makers believed that Israel was strong enough to retaliate without endangering its security or incurring excessive costs.

It is possible to arrive at a similar conclusion by analyzing the decision by the Kennedy Administration not to launch a surprise air strike against the Soviet missiles in Cuba. President Kennedy and his advisers estimated that the naval blockade, despite its limitations, sufficed to communicate firmness of resolve while at the same time enabling the United States and the Soviet Union to avoid direct military confrontation. The blockade was a way of signaling Washington's determination to take more severe steps if Moscow did not agree to remove its missiles from Cuba.

This last point is very important to the current argument. Kennedy was able to opt for a midcourse alternative between inaction and attack because of the military superiority of the United States in the region. As Graham Allison put it:

> American local superiority was overwhelming: it could be initiated at a low level while threatening, with high credibility, an ascending sequence of steps

short of nuclear threshold. All that was required was for the United States to bring to bear its strategic and local superiority in a way that demonstrated American determination to see the missiles removed, while at the same time allowing Moscow time and room to retreat without humiliation.[119]

The propensity by an international actor to forego surprise when he is convinced that his strength is significantly greater than that of his adversary is further substantiated by the Israeli War of Independence (1947–1949). "The overwhelming Arab military capability," writes Michael Handel, "and numerical superiority in every possible aspect completely eliminated their incentive to launch a carefully planned surprise attack in the opening phase of the war."[120]

At this juncture it may be tempting to conclude that an international actor will resort to surprise only when he must compensate for some weakness. According to Klaus Knorr, this argument cannot be substantiated—international actors who were clearly superior to their adversaries have also resorted to surprise. Knorr supports this argument by noting that in 1967 Israel launched a surprise attack against a noticeably weaker adversary.[121]

Knorr's contention does not invalidate our argument. To substantiate our initial position further, we will show that the pre-emptive surprise attack by Israel in 1967 was not against an inferior target, and compare the 1967 crisis with the 1973 crisis. In addition, to strengthen the argument that international actors who are significantly more powerful than their adversaries are less likely to resort to surprise, we will analyze two cases in which the incentives for resorting to surprise were apparently high, and yet surprise was by-passed. The two cases are (1) the invasion of Guatemala in 1954, and (2) the attempt to invade Cuba in 1961.

The details of the Six-Day War are well known and need not be retold here.[122] It suffices to note that the unanimous agreement to launch a surprise attack against Egypt's air force during the early hours of June 5, 1967, came only after it had been clearly established that Israel was on the verge of being the target of a powerful united Arab attack. Until June 1, when Jordan and Egypt signed a defense pact similar to that which existed between Syria and Egypt, there was disagreement among the Israeli leaders as to whether to solve the existing crisis via diplomatic means or to resort to war. But, as Israel's Foreign Minister Abba Eban, one of the initial supporters of a diplomatic solution to the crisis, noted:

The Egyptian–Jordanian agreement made it plain that we would probably have to fight on three fronts. . . . Arab unity, which seemed an unsubstantial mirage a few days earlier, was now becoming impressive.[123]

The belief that Israel had to strike first via a surprise attack in order to ensure victory was also forwarded by newly appointed Defense Minister Moshe Dayan. According to Dayan:

> If we took the enemy by surprise we would knock out at least one hundred of their warplanes out of action. . . . The first shot would determine the side which would suffer the heaviest casualties and would assuredly change the balance of forces. . . . Considering the situation in which we found ourselves, with hundreds of enemy tanks poised on each of the axes leading into Israel from the Egyptian bases in Sinai, together with the last minute preparations they were making, it would be fatal for us to allow them to launch their attack.[124]

Finally, there was the question of whether Israel's economy could maintain full mobilization for an extended period of time. During a military crisis, Israel's economy is completely paralyzed, for every male citizen between the ages of 18 and 55 is called to service. An extended crisis could have led to Israel's economic collapse.[125]

The arguments posited by Knorr and this study can be further tested by engaging in what is commonly referred to as a *crucial-case study* test. According to Harry Eckstein, it is possible to "test" a theory by focusing inquiry on "most likely" or "least likely" cases—cases that ought, or ought not, to invalidate or confirm theories.[126]

In 1967, Israel, upon concluding that it would be the target of an attack, chose to launch a pre-emptive surprise attack; six years later, upon arriving at the same conclusion, Israel made a conscious decision not to repeat its behavior. Israel was a democracy both in 1967 and 1973. The structure of the decision-making body did not vary dramatically during the interim period, nor did its composition.[127]

In his study of the two crises, Michael Brecher argues that war-induced stress narrowed the range of alternatives Israel's decision makers perceived to have open to them.[128] In view of Brecher's argument, it could be inferred that as war-induced stress increases and the range of alternatives is narrowed, the tendency to resort to war will be greater. The problem with this generalization is that it does not account for the perceptions of the decision makers with respect to their own capabilities and those of their adversaries.[129] In 1967 the Israelis became convinced, upon concluding that they would be attacked, that the only alternative left to them was a pre-emptive surprise attack; and yet in 1973, under similar circumstances, they opted for a different path. The main difference between the two crises was that in 1967 Israel questioned its ability to overcome a pre-emptive joint Arab attack; such doubt did not recur in 1973. The level of stress induced by the approaching wars was significantly lower in 1973 than in 1967 largely because during the second crisis Israel felt more confident of its ability to retaliate against an Arab attack.[130]

The comparison of the two Middle East wars also gives us reason to propose that an actor's propensity to take risks may not be as critical as initially assumed. One can acknowledge that, in each of the four major cases considered here, the states that opted for surprise had leaders known for their inclination to take risks. Thus, if one were to use these cases as a sort of theoretical foundation, it could be inferred that one of the reasons Israel launched a surprise attack on Egypt in 1967 was because Israel's decision makers had a genuine passion for risk taking. But this conclusion would clearly be challenged if the 1967 war were to be compared with the 1973 war in view of the fact that the composition of the Israeli decision-making body did not change noticeably from one period to the other. In other words, before concluding that a decision maker's propensity to take risks will have an impact on whether or not he resorts to surprise, it is imperative to define the conditions under which he must make such a choice.

The major weakness of the counterarguments presented so far is that the cases considered involved instances in which decision makers were engaged in the assessment of whether or not to resort to a *pre-emptive* surprise attack. It could be argued that the conditions preceding the consideration of a surprise attack might differ from the conditions preceding the consideration of a pre-emptive surprise attack. To test for this possibility, two additional cases were included in the analysis of why international actors resort to surprise. In 1954 and 1961, the United States organized and financed the invasion of two international actors that were measurably weaker: Guatemala and Cuba. Although in both instances the United States implemented covert measures to deceive its international targets, in neither case did it attempt to achieve surprise. On June 18, 1954, a small number of troops led by Castillo Armas, a Guatemalan national, invaded Guatemala. The intent behind the operation, which had been organized and financed by the United States, was to overthrow the government of Jacobo Arbenz Guzman. A similar operation against the newly established government of Fidel Castro was initiated by the United States seven years later.

The decision to overthrow each government was arrived at only after U.S.–owned property had been nationalized. This is not to say that the United States' covert activities were triggered by the belief that American investments abroad were sacrosanct. This perception may have been part of the impetus, but, more importantly, expropriation generally was perceived as a sign that the government engaging in such activity was opening the path to a communist takeover, hence posing a challenge to U.S. control.

In June 1952, Guatemala's National Assembly unanimously enacted a radical agrarian reform bill. By May 1953, the government of Guatemala had redistributed 740,000 acres from 107 farms. Approximately 400,000 acres of the redistributed land belonged the the U.S.-owned United Fruit Company. That same summer, President Eisenhower, Secretary of State Dulles, and his brother, Allan Dulles, the Director of the CIA, agreed that it was imperative to intervene in Guatemala in order to avert a communist takeover. This sentiment was best expressed by John Foster Dulles:

> If the United Fruit matter were settled, if they gave a gold piece for every banana, the problem would remain just as it is today as far as the presence of Communist infiltration in Guatemala is concerned. That is the problem, not United Fruit.[131]

The pattern repeated itself seven years later. In May 1959, Cuba passed its own agrarian reform law. Less than a year later, Richard Bissell was authorized by the Eisenhower Administration to produce "A Program of Covert Action Against the Castro Regime."[132] The decision, once again, was arrived at only after Cuba had nationalized several American-owned cattle ranches and banks.[133] The objective was no different from that sought in 1954—to avert a communist takeover.

The second factor that is common to each intervention is that the United States' covert activities were generally accompanied by economic policies designed to create economic disarray in the targeted countries and/or military policies conceived for the purpose of diminishing the ability of the targeted governments to defend themselves against an overthrow attempt. During early 1954, the Arbenz government, convinced that an invasion of Guatemala was only a matter of time, requested of the United States that it lift the embargo it had imposed in 1944. The Eisenhower Administration refused, pushing Arbenz to solicit assistance from the Soviet Union. In late 1959, the United States refused to lift the embargo of weapons it had imposed on Cuba in May 1958, during the Batista regime. This action was accompanied by pressure on the British government not to sell jet fighters to Cuba. Moreover, in mid-1960, the Eisenhower Administration persuded U.S. oil refineries in Cuba not to process Soviet crude oil, cut the Cuban sugar quota by 700,000 tons, and prohibited U.S. exports to Cuba. Each of these economic steps was taken with the intent of augmenting Cuba's economic woes, which, it was hoped, would weaken Castro's popular support.

In comparing U.S. actions against Guatemala and Cuba, the geographical location of these two states can be expected to have had an impact on the pattern of U.S. intervention. In March 1954, just over three months prior to the invasion of Guatemala, the United States submitted at the Inter-American Conference held in Caracas a proposal titled: "Declaration of Solidarity for Preservation of the Political Integrity of American States Against Total Communism."[134] The intent of this proposal was twofold: to isolate Guatemala, and, possibly, to forward a formal justification for its eventual action. The United States adopted a similar strategy against Cuba in late 1960. Pressured by the United States, the Organization of American States, meeting in San José, Costa Rica, adopted a resolution condemning intervention by an *extracontinental* power and any attempt by Moscow or Peking to exploit the Latin American situation.[135]

Finally, U.S. covert activities in both instances, rather than attempting to overthrow the targeted governments with superior force, relied primarily on deception. When the invasion against Arbenz began on June 18, 1954, Castillo Armas was heading a force consisting of 150 agents already in Guatemala and 150 troops with little military experience. Had Arbenz known how weak his adversary was, and had he chosen to fight, there is little doubt he would have emerged victorious. To counter Arbenz's superior military strength, the United States relied on false information to give the impression that Castillo Armas was leading a large insurrection force, with the United States waiting in the wings to intervene if necessary. Planners of the strategy did not assume that the armed forces and the population would desert Arbenz because of anticommunist fever, but because of fear of Castillo Armas's superiority. This strategy was borrowed from the recent success in Iran. As told by Immerman, the CIA used propaganda in both instances to prepare the population for "a military operation so that it would interpet any sign of force as the beginning of a massive effort."[136] On April 17, 1961, Cuba was invaded by 1,500 forces financed and trained by the United States with the intent of bringing down the Castro regime. Success of the strategy was predicted on the assumption that, although Fidel Castro had the potential power to obliterate the challenge, he would suffer the same loss of nerve as Arbenz. The majority of the Cuban population and armed forces would perceive the invasion as the beginning of a massive antigovernmental effort and would thus turn their allegiance away from Castro. The invasion came to an unexpected end not so much because Guatemala was the wrong analogy, but because Cuba learned from Guatemala's mistakes.[137]

The two events just discussed add strength to the argument that interventional actors that are measurably superior to their intended targets generally need not risk exposure of their limited surprise resources. In its actions against Guatemala and Cuba the United States made sure its targets were well aware ahead of time that an invasion was forthcoming. Two purposes structured the willingness to sacrifice surprise. First, it was hoped that both targets would recognize the determination of the United States to succeed in the fulfillment of its objectives and, as a result, would acquiesce fully to its demands prior to the launching of the invasions. If this aspect of the strategy failed, then the United States hoped that, by making clear its intent to support the invading forces, the leaders of the targeted states would mount a less forceful resistance. In other words, by *not* attempting to surprise them, the United States hoped both to enhance its chances of succeeding and to minimize the costs likely to be accrued during the attempted takeovers.

The decision to rely on surprise is not always based on an accurate estimation of capabilities. The Germans in 1941 underestimated the strength of the Soviet armed forces. The central danger faced by would-be surprisers who make this type of mistake is that their miscalculations are bound to provide an incentive for wanting to rely on surprise. In other words, had the Germans accurately estimated the power of the Soviet Union, they might have been less determined to launch a surprise attack.

The extent to which this argument applies to Japan is not entirely clear. There are indications that the Japanese might have been aware of the potential capability of the United States to revitalize its military power. This realization, however, did not prevent the Japanese leaders from concluding that Japan had no other choice than to resort to a surprise attack. This feeling seems to have arisen from the belief that Japan had to establish itself as the dominant military and economic power in Southeast Asia.

It should also be noted that not every international actor who resorts to a suprise attack against a superior adversary and who is aware that even with the aid of surprise he cannot overcome all his weaknesses pursues this path determined to risk total defeat. In 1973, Egypt–Syria launched an attack against Israel fully aware that they could not expect to defeat it. Accordingly, they sought an objective that was compatible with their own capabilities, such as getting Israel to return the territories it had seized from them during the 1967 war.

Notes

1. Whaley, 1973.

2. As I will argue later on, Barton Whaley misinterprets Hitler's rationale for resorting to surprise against the Soviets. See Whaley, 1973a.

3. Later in this chapter I will discuss extensively the reasons why the United States in 1962 and Israel in 1973 did not engage in surprise attacks.

4. Axelrod, 1979, p. 224.

5. Klaus Knorr has suggested that there are no noticeable differences regarding incentives between would-be surprisers. Part of the problem with his argument is that he fails to discriminate between acts of surprise that precede war or lead to war and those initiated during the actual war. The two types of cases cannot be properly compared, for they are at different levels of analysis. See Knorr, 1983, p. 179.

6. Numerous factors contribute to miscalculations. For an incisive discussion of the subject, see Lebow, 1981.

7. Wohlstetter presents this argument regarding the decision by Japan to attack Pearl Harbor. See Wohlstetter, 1962, p. 352.

8. Wasserman, 1960, pp. 156–164.

9. Handel, 1976, p. 24.

10. See Russett, 1967, p. 90.

11. March, 1977.

12. Kinhide, 1966, p. 180.

13. Ishii, 1930, pp. 220–229.

14. Crowley, 1966, p. 190.

15. Ibid., p. 195.

16. Ibid., p. 299.

17. The 1921 treaty was the Washington Conference Treaty System; the 1930 treaty was the London Naval Treaty.

18. Iriye, 1971, p. 125.

19. Butow, 1961, p. 99.

20. U.S. Congress, 1946, Document 244, p. 7.

21. Butow, 1961, p. 189.

22. Ibid., pp. 190–191.

23. For an extensive and detailed analysis of the meetings, see U.S. Congress, 1946, Document 244, pp. 14–17.

24. Ibid., pp. 16–17.

25. Ike, 1967, p. 112.

26. Ibid., p. 112.

27. Butow, 1961, p. 223; Ike, 1967, p. 118.

28. Butow, 1961, p. 236.

29. Ike, 1967, p. 124; Butow, 1961, p. 244.

30. U.S. Congress, 1946, Document, 244, pp. 300–303.

31. Ike, 1967, p. 129.

32. Wohlstetter, 1962, p. 352.

33. Morison, Vol. III, 1951, p. 81.

34. Wohlstetter, 1962, p. 352.

35. United States Armed Forces, Far East and Eighth United Army, pp. 11–12 and 14–16.

36. Cited in Hosoya, 1971, p. 93.

37. Morison, 1951, Vol. III, p. 32.

38. Ike, 1967, p. 247.

39. Ibid., pp. 207, 226.

40. Ibid., pp. 247–249.

41. Butow, 1961, p. 248.

42. Ike, 1967, pp. 138–139.

43. Fukudome, 1969, p. 5.

44. Ward, 1952, p. 1272; U.S. Congress, Document 244, 1946, p. 53. Quoted in Prange, 1980, p. 17.

45. Fukudome, 1969, p. 5.

46. Ibid., p. 6. For a detailed account of Admiral Onishi's proposal, see Prange, 1980, pp. 9–29.

47. Fukudome, 1969, p. 6–8.

48. Ibid., p. 8.

49. Snyder and Diesing, 1977, p. 301.

50. Lebow, 1981, p. 274.

51. On this last point the reader should refer to note 32, also in this chapter.

52. George and Smoke, 1974, p. 221. Evidently, Yamamoto was, by nature, a risk taker. As noted by one of his staff officers, "In all games Yamamoto loved to take chances just as he did in naval strategy." (Quoted in Prange, 1980, p. 13.) Moreover, Yamamoto seemed to have had enough political clout to persuade his superiors to adopt the Pearl Harbor plan by threatening to resign if they did not. As inconceivable as this idea may seem, one must keep in mind that "Yamamoto's position and influence in the Japanese Navy were unique. He was in truth a leviathan among men." (Quoted in Prange, p. 300.) Neither of these two challenges, however, undermine our initial point. Regardless of how predisposed an individual may be to take risks, the likelihood that he will take them will not be random, but conditioned by the value of the interests at stake and his range of options.

53. Insight Team of *The London Times,* 1974, p. 47. An anonymous reviewer has been critical of our "heavy" reliance on the Insight Team of *The London Times* as a data source. According to such reviewer, the Insight Team is not a reliable source of information. Without becoming involved in the merits of this opinion, it ought to be noted, as it will become evident in chapter 3, that the data extricated *solely* from *The London Times* make up only ten percent of the data used to build the argument. Moreover, even if one were to challenge the veracity of such data, the argument built in that portion of the chapter would remain unaltered. The reader must keep in mind that the intent of this book is to propose a different perspective by relying on data used extensively by other analysts.

54. Ibid., pp. 67–68.

55. Ibid., p. 81.

56. Heikal, 1975, p. 25; Dupuy, 1978, p. 388; Insight Team, 1974, p. 72.

57. Insight Team, 1974, p. 73; Handel, 1976, p. 31.

58. Handel, 1981.

59. "The Nuremberg Judgment—Victor's Verdict: Blunder Thrown Out of Court," 1962, p. 2.

60. Langer and Cleason, 1953, p. 14.

61. Seaton, 1971, p. 9.

62. McSherry, 1970, Vol. 2, p. 140.

63. Quoted in McSherry, 1970, Vol. 2, p. 140.

64. Leach, 1973, p. 51.

65. Quoted in Warlimont, 1964, p. 114.

66. Quoted in McSherry, 1970, Vol. 2, p. 141.

67. It should be acknowledged, however, that Hitler did not trust Stalin and feared that, if he did not attack in 1941, the Soviet leader might decide to move against Germany once the Soviet industrial build-up was completed. See Irving, 1977, p. 181; Rich, 1973, p. 209.

68. Quoted in Leach, 1973, p. 11.

69. See Dallin, 1957; Leach, 1973, p. 51; Seaton, 1971, p. 36; Fugate, 1984, chapter 2.

70. McSherry, 1970, Vol. 2, chapter 20.

71. This argument is advanced by Whaley, 1973.

72. We address this point later on.

73. Our argument concurs with Leach's (1973) and Fugate's (1984) detailed analyses of Hitler's overall strategy to attack the Soviet Union.

74. Leach, 1973, pp. 159–168.

75. Ibid., p. 168.

76. Ibid., p. 13.

77. Seaton, 1971, pp. 57–58. As stated by Fugate, "The consensus in the Quartermasters Branch seemed to be that the Red Army would have to be brought to battle and defeated west of the Dnieper line or else the German forces, spreading out in a fan shape into the interior of the Soviet Union, would lack the density to defeat the Russians." Fugate, 1984, p. 72.

78. Quoted in Leach, 1973, p. 100.

79. Waite, 1977, p. 481.

80. Ibid., p. 484.

81. Ibid., p. 484.

82. Ibid., p. 486.

83. This belief was shared by many statesmen from other countries, including Winston Churchill. See Hinsley, Vol. 2, 1979, p. 482.

84. Rich, 1973, p. 210. See also Fugate, 1984, chapter 2.

85. Warlimont, 1964, p. 145.

86. Ibid., p. 145. Moreover, as reported by Fugate, German military intelligence was unsuccessful in estimating the actual military strength of the Soviet armed forces. Fugate, 1984, pp. 61–65.

87. Rich, 1973, p. 210.

88. Fugate makes a similar point when he notes that "in retrospect one should not attempt to fault here with either Hitler or the generals for believing too strongly in their own technical and tactical superiority." Fugate, 1984, p. 74.

89. Cited in Trevor-Roper (ed.), 1964, p. 94.

90. Allison, 1971, p. 42. The five hypotheses are:

1. The "bargaining barter" hypothesis argues that the missiles were deployed for use as a bargaining tool in a summit meeting or United Nations confrontation with President Kennedy.

2. The "diverting trap" hypothesis proposes that the missiles were installed in Cuba to incite a violent response from the United States, which in turn would fuel a wave of anti-Americanism in Latin America.

3. The missiles were placed in Cuba to avert an attack on Cuba by the United States.

4. The missiles were installed to undermine the credibility of the United States' commitments to other states, for it was assumed that it would act indecisively.

5. The missiles were introduced in an attempt to narrow the missile superiority held by the United States.

91. Ibid., pp. 55–56.

92. Ibid., p. 232. The content of these signals will be discussed in more detail in chapter 5.

93. Allison, 1971, p. 237. It should be acknowledged that Allison advances three somewhat different explanations. It is clear, however, that he favors the one just posited.

94. Ibid., pp. 238–244.

95. Allison's five problems are quite similar to those considered by the different proponents of the five hypotheses.

96. Allison, 1971, p. 49.

97. Ibid., p. 49.

98. As soon as we discuss the last problem it will become evident why the Soviet military would not have agreed to install missiles in Cuba only to help the Soviet economy.

99. Allison, 1971, p. 243.

100. Ibid., p. 52.

101. Khrushchev, in his memoir, contends that his two principal objectives for installing the missiles in Cuba were to ensure Cuba's territorial sovereignty and to compensate the balance of power. It is interesting to note that, although he begins his justification for deploying the missiles in Cuba by arguing that he was greatly concerned for its security, the greatest portion of his justification is dedicated to explaining how the presence of strategic missiles in Cuba would have heightened the strategic standing of the Soviet Union vis-a-vis the United States. See Khrushchev, 1970, pp. 493–494.

102. Roger Hilsman said it best when he noted that "the motive for the decision was strategic in the broad sense that a general improvement in the Soviet military position would affect the entire political context . . ." Hilsman, 1967, p. 164.

103. Hilsman, 1967, p. 161.

104. The news came in a speech given by Deputy Secretary of Defense Roswell Gilpatric. Hilsman, 1967, p. 163.

105. Most analysts agree that the decision to install the missiles in Cuba could not have been made later than June 1962.

106. Allison, 1971, pp. 231–232. Allison mentions five signals, but the last one could not have affected their decision because it came after the decision to deploy the missiles had been made.

107. Fulbright stated: "I suppose we would all be less comfortable if the Soviets did install missile bases in Cuba, but I am not sure that our national existence would be in substantially greater danger than is the case today. Nor do I think that such bases would substantially alter the balance of power in the world." Fulbright, June 29, 1961, p. 11704.

108. Allison does not provide any information as to who the officials were.

109. See Allison's note 227 for chapter 6. Allison, 1971, p. 325.

110. That Khrushchev was aware that Kennedy would have taken every reasonable measure to obstruct the shipment of missiles is supported by his statement

that: ". . . if we installed the missiles *secretly* and then if the United States discovered the missiles *were there after they were already poised and ready to strike,* the Americans would think twice before trying to liquidate our installations by military means." (Emphasis added.) See Khrushchev, 1970, pp. 493–494.

111. It must be pointed out that Allison never claims that the Soviets attempted to install the missiles without concealing their intentions.

112. See Hilsman, 1967, p. 163.

113. Had the missiles become operational, the Soviets would have been able to exercise their own counterdeterrence. See Horelick and Rush, 1966, p. 148.

114. See Brecher, 1980, p. 177.

115. Quoted in Brecher, 1980, p. 177.

116. Quoted in Brecher, 1980, pp. 177–178.

117. The United States considered six alternatives. Launching a surprise surgical air strike or setting up a blockade became the two most prominent alternatives. See Allison, 1971, pp. 58–61.

118. Brecher, 1980, p. 178.

119. Allison, 1971, p. 57.

120. Handel, 1983, p. 112.

121. Knorr, 1983, p. 179.

122. See Stein and Tanter, 1980; Brecher, 1980.

123. Quoted in Stein and Tanter, p. 219.

124. Ibid., p. 237. See also Handel, 1983, p. 133.

125. Handel, 1983, p. 131.

126. Eckstein, 1975, p. 118. Here we do not presume that this test will validate the initial argument. We can only hope that it will strengthen its degree of acceptability.

127. See Brecher, 1980, pp. 407–413.

128. Ibid., p. 248.

129. Another problem with Brecher's argument is that it infers the proposition from two situations that are not the same. The comparison is between the range of perceived alternatives *just prior* to the 1967 war and those during the *first three days* of the 1973 war. Had the comparison been between the two periods just prior to the wars, he might have concluded that the levels of war-induced stress were different.

130. Brecher acknowledges that in 1973 the Israelis felt much more confident regarding their own capabilities vis-a-vis the Arabs than in 1967.

131. Quoted in Immerman, 1982, p. 165.

132. May 17, 1960.

133. For a period of time, U.S. Ambassador Philip W. Bonsal did not object forcefully to the seizure of U.S.–owned property. The trend was reversed by January 1960.

134. This was a critical step in the overall propaganda campaign initiated by the U.S. in 1954.

135. Immerman, 1982, p. 145.

136. Ibid., p. 162.

137. On the use of analogies to arrive at the decision by the U.S. to intervene, see Hybel, 1985.

3

Surprise with Respect to Target and Time: Pearl Harbor, 1941, and Yom Kippur, 1973

S urprise, we have argued, largely depends on whether the would-be
surpriser can control his victim's perception of threat. Ideally, the best
strategy would be one in which the would-be surpriser controls his
victim's sense of vulnerability, concern over the areas where the surprise will
be staged, and degree of tension and mistrust. However, it is unreasonable
to expect a would-be surpriser to possess the ability to affect all three components. Therefore, before choosing a strategy, an international actor must
carefully assess the kind of environmental constraints he must overcome in
order to achieve surprise, and determine whether he has the means to surmount them.

To develop a general understanding of how environmental constraints
can condition a would-be surpriser's choice of strategy, it will be helpful to
separate the four major cases considered in this study into two categories:
those in which the would-be surprisers did not try to achieve surprise with
respect to their intentions, and those in which they did. Cases in the first
category can be further divided into instances in which the would-be surpriser sought to achieve surprise with respect to his target, and instances in
which time was the principal dimension of surprise.

This chapter will analyze the steps taken by Japan in 1941, and Egypt–
Syria in 1973, to achieve surprise with respect to target in the first instance,
and time in the second. In chapter 4 an attempt will be made to ascertain
the extent to which the strategies chosen by Japan and Egypt–Syria contributed to the achievement of surprise (if in fact surprise was achieved), or the
reason that the would-be surprisers failed to bring about their intended objectives. In chapter 5 we will analyze the strategies of surprise selected by
Germany in 1941 and the Soviet Union in 1962. In each instance the would-
be surpriser sought to achieve surprise primarily with respect to its intention.
The same question addressed in chapter 4 will be considered in chapter 6,
but with regard to Germany and the Soviet Union.

Japan's Target Strategy of Surprise

In mid-August 1941, Japan's military leaders decided that war preparation
should go hand in hand with diplomatic efforts and that, if Japan failed to

obtain satisfaction of its demands via the latter means, it would open hostilities immediately against the Americans, the British, and the Dutch.[1] On September 20, at a liaison conference, Premier Konoye and his cabinet accepted the demand from the chiefs of the Army and Navy General Staff that a "suspense" date be established.[2] The suspense date marked the time when Japan would shift from military preparations to the final troop movements and fleet dispositions necessary for the launching of hostilities.

Japan did not take any precautionary measures to conceal its intent to resort to war if diplomacy failed. Via the media and speeches, and through the deployment of troops and equipment, Japan repeatedly expressed its intention to employ force to achieve its objectives. Of these two means, only the first one will be discussed now.

According to Otto Tolishus, a veteran American journalist stationed in Japan, Japan's "armed diplomacy" swung into full action on October 22, 1941. On that date, the *Japan Time Advertiser* published an editorial written by Japan's Foreign Office. One of the points emphasized by the editorial was that Japan was ready to fight the United States, if necessary, to defend its interests.[3] A few days later, on October 26, the new Japanese prime minister, Hideki Tojo, while speaking in Osaka, announced that "wars can be fought with ease. Nothing can surprise me. No international pressure can disturb me. The unit that makes Japan one and whole will solve all problems."[4] On November 17, in an address before the seventy-seventh session of the Diet—the first such address ever to be broadcast in Japan—Prime Minister Tojo stated: "The Empire now stands at a crossroads of destiny unparalleled in its 2,600 year history. The government is resolved to fulfill with all its power the responsibilities of assisting the throne."[5] Following Tojo's address, Foreign Minister Shigenori Togo added that Japan was conducting negotiations with the United States, but that "there is a limit to our conciliatory attitude," and that there was "no necessity of spending much time on them hereafter."[6] From that day on, Tojo and other members of his cabinet continued to urge the Japanese people to unite and prepare for war, to expand war material production, and to reduce consumption.[7]

Japan's message did not go unnoticed among American policy makers. By the first week of December 1941, the United States had learned that Japan had been carrying on for some time a major program designed to expand its military capabilities. Furthermore, it had become quite evident in the United States that Japanese nationals were being warned of the imminence of a major crisis and were being asked to unite and to be willing to sacrifice for the glory of Japan. American leaders had little problem concluding that Japan would resort to war. However, they had difficulty accepting the idea that Pearl Harbor would be a target. Much of their initial reluctance was born of their low sense of vulnerability.

Japan relied on two methods to maintain the United States' sense of

vulnerability at a low point. The first was to extend a blanket of secrecy
over changes being made with respect to its navy. Within this particular
means, three major steps were taken. The first step was to change Japan's
naval doctrine. As we have noted already, ever since 1909 the Japanese Navy
had accepted defensive operations against the United States as its fundamental policy. In October 1941, however, following Japan's decision to begin
war preparations, the Naval General Staff agreed with Admiral Yamamoto's
assessment that the accomplishment of the overall mission assigned to the
Japanese Navy depended on whether a decisive surprise attack against Pearl
Harbor was launched at the earliest possible time.[8] What this agreement
meant, for all practical purposes, was that the Japanese Navy decided to
replace the strategy that kept carriers and battleships near home waters for
protective measures with a much riskier one that dictated that they be used
to facilitate the launching of an aerial attack against an enemy thousands of
miles away.

The Japanese Navy, however, had to change in two other important
respects before it could even attempt to launch a surprise attack against Pearl
Harbor. It was common knowledge that the waters of Pearl Harbor had an
average depth of only forty-odd feet and that no known torpedo could perform effectively in them. It was not until September or October 1941 that
Japanese naval research institutes were able to perfect a stabilizing device that
made aerial torpedoes operable in Pearl Harbor's shallow waters. The fur-
nishing of an adequate supply of the new model torpedoes to the planes to
be used to attack Pearl Harbor was not completed until the very eve of the
fleet's departure.[9]

The second crucial problem the Japanese Navy had to overcome had to
do with the cruising range of its ships. Because the Japanese Navy had designed its strategy around the assumption that its ships would battle in a
defensive war against the United States, their radius was generally short. Of
the six aircraft carriers involved in the Hawaiian operation, three lacked
adequate cruising range, as did all the destroyers. It was hoped that the ships
could be refueled at sea on the outward voyage, weather permitting, but
thereafter they would be in an operational status and thus would be on their
own as far as fuel supplies were concerned. To overcome this problem, two
steps were taken. First, refueling was delayed until the very last possible
moment, and, second, each ship had its normal supplies supplemented by as
many additional drums as it could possibly load.[10]

Japan did not rely on secrecy alone in its attempt to maintain the United
States' sense of vulnerability at a low point. The second means it utilized
during the final weeks before the attack was negotiation. Opinions about
whether negotiation was used as a deceptive measure by the Japanese vary.
On the one hand, Robert Butow contends that the government was not using
negotiation as a blind behind which to complete preparations for the at-

tack.[11] On the other hand, scholars such as Wohlstetter, Morison, Ike, and Whaley argue that negotiation was used by the Japanese to provide a thin screen to give the American leaders a false impression that the war was somewhat further off.[12] Both arguments are partly correct, depending on the period under investigation. It must be said, however, that Japan's reliance on negotiation as a means of deception was very limited.

From the day Ambassador Admiral Nomura began to meet on a regular basis with President Roosevelt and Secretary of State Hull until September 6, 1941, Japan's sole purpose for negotiating was to attempt to attain its objectives without having to resort to war. As Butow put it, "Tokyo was hard-headed enough to realize that a victory achieved through Japanese diplomacy would be as satisfactory, in terms of results, as one garnered through war. It would also be far less costly . . ."[13] On September 6, 1941, however, because no result had been attained through negotiation, it was agreed at a liaison conference that, although negotiation should proceed, Japan would simultaneously prepare for war.

Does this mean, then, that from September 6 on, Japan used negotiation merely as a cover? In order to answer this question, it is necessary to divide the period between September 6 and December 7 into two subperiods, before and after November 29.

On September 6, after it was decided that negotiation with the United States and war preparations would continue hand in hand, Japan's naval chief of staff, Admiral Nagano, stated: "Our Empire must exert every effort to overcome the present difficult situation by peaceful means."[14] Nagano's view was in full accordance with those presented by Prime Minister Konoye, Army Chief of Staff General Sugiyama, and Foreign Minister Toyoda. By November 1, the view among members of the Liaison Conference that Japan could not continue postponing the decision to initiate hostile actions against the United States had broadened. At that time, it was decided that war would begin on December 1, but that negotiation would continue until November 30. If diplomacy were successful by that deadline, the war would be called off.[15]

On November 29, 1941, at the Seventy-Fourth Liaison Conference, two major decisions were made. In view of the fact that negotiation with the United States had failed to bring about the results sought by Japan, the decision to go to war was formally sanctioned. The second decision arrived at was that negotiation with the United States should continue solely for deceptive purposes. It became evident that negotiation would be used as a deceptive measure when Foreign Minister Togo, after inquiring whether the Japanese diplomats in Washington should be informed about the decision to go to war, received the following answer from Prime Minister Tojo:

Our diplomats will have to be sacrificed. What we want is to carry on diplomacy in such a way that until the very last minute the United States will continue to think about the problem, we will ask questions, and our real plans will be kept secret.[16]

Foreign Minister Togo agreed by responding: "I will tell our representatives to exert their efforts in diplomacy so that the United States will continue considering the problem . . ."[17] The cabinet meeting was followed by an announcement to the press that Japan would continue to negotiate with Washington in an effort to induce the latter to reconsider its decisions.[18]

To summarize, then, Japan began to use negotiation as a tool of deception only after November 29, when its policy makers became fully convinced that Washington could not be persuaded to change its stand via peaceful means.

One of the deceptive means often used by would-be surprisers to maintain a low sense of vulnerability in their opponents is the cry-wolf method. This method is generally employed by a would-be surpriser who wishes to signal to his intended victim that, although he would like to employ aggressive means to attain his objectives, he lacks the capabilities to do so effectively and can only resort to empty bluff. Sometime in January 1941, the American ambassador in Japan, Joseph Grew, was informed by the Peruvian Embassy that the Japanese intended to launch a massive surprise attack on Pearl Harbor. Moreover, when Japan moved into French Indochina later that year, some of the rumors circulating were that Pearl Harbor would be the next target. The fact that neither set of signals was followed immediately by an attack could lead one to speculate that the Japanese might have purposely initiated them to dull the effect of subsequent warnings.

Regardless of how persuasive this argument may seem at first glance, it does not hold very well when one takes into account Japan's overall naval strategy during the first seven months of 1941. Although Admiral Yamamoto had begun to plan a surprise attack on Pearl Harbor early in January 1941, it was not until October, after overcoming stiff opposition from numerous sources, that Yamamoto was able to persuade the Naval General Staff that a surprise attack on Pearl Harbor was both necessary and possible if Japan intended to go to war against the United States. One could speculate that Yamamoto, aware that Pearl Harbor had to be attacked by surprise to increase Japan's chances of winning the war (if Japan decided to go to war) took it upon himself to send the false signals. That Admiral Yamamoto would have made such a decision seems quite unlikely for two reasons. First, he was well aware of the negotiation process going on between the United States and Japan, and it is unlikely that he would have initiated anything that might have endangered its success. One may point out that an individual who was against negotiating with the United States could have relied on the "cry-wolf" syndrome not only to create a false sense of assurance among the Americans, but also to sabotage the negotiation. This is possible, although it seems unlikely that both effects could be achieved simultaneously. Nevertheless, to sustain this argument one would have to disregard the second rationale for contending that Yamamoto would not have initiated the false alarms on purpose. Yamamoto firmly believed in the need to attack Pearl Harbor by surprise if Japan decided to begin hostile activities against the Philippines, Malaya, and other areas in Southeast Asia. But he was equally opposed to the idea of engaging in a war against the United States because of his belief that in the long run Japan would be defeated. He expressed this belief very clearly to Prime Minister Konoye when he stated that "should the war be prolonged for two or three years, I have no confidence in our ultimate victory."[19]

So far, the argument has been that:

1. Japan vocalized its willingness to resort to violent means to attain its objectives.

2. Japan sought to keep the United States' sense of vulnerability low with respect to Pearl Harbor by concealing the adoption of a new naval strategy and the elimination of certain vexing technological problems.

3. Japan tried to control Washington's concern with respect to Pearl Harbor via negotiation.

4. Japan did not rely on the cry-wolf method to keep Washington's sense of vulnerability low.

By displaying its efforts to launch aggressive acts against several targets in Southeast Asia, Japan was employing a sophisticated strategy to deceive the United States about its intention to attack Pearl Harbor. Moreover, the strategy was partly contingent on the United States' knowing when Japan intended to initiate such attacks.

Roberta Wohlstetter has addressed the first part of the argument in an indirect manner. She contends that the basic Japanese plan called for a carefully timed series of surprise blows aimed not only at Pearl Harbor, but also at the Philippines, Guam, Wake Island, and the British and Dutch holdings in the Far East.[20] From Wohlstetter's argument it could be inferred that Japan could not have used its move south as a means to divert American attention from Pearl Harbor, because in order to implement such an operation Japan would have had to sacrifice the part of the plan that called for a series of surprise blows in Southeast Asia. This inference cannot be fully justified. The first factor that must be taken into consideration is the extent to which Japan's planners took special precautionary measures to protect the plans to attack to the east and the south. With respect to the plan to attack Pearl Harbor, the number of individuals who knew about its existence was limited to those who had been involved in designing it, members of the Naval General Staff, the chief of the army general staff, the navy and war ministers, the foreign minister, and the premier.[21] Furthermore, when the time for its execution drew near, its content was communicated verbally only to those individuals who were going to play essential roles in directing the operation.[22] On the other hand, they distributed seven hundred copies of the plan to go south, giving full details of the attacks that would be launched against the Philippines, Malaya, and the other southern regions.[23]

Second, it is necessary to compare the types of precautionary measures taken by the Japanese to conceal their final preparations, specifically, the movement of vessels, troops, and military equipment that would be involved in the execution of both missions. In order to conceal the existence of the Pearl Harbor Task Force, the Japanese attempted to create the impression that the vessels, sailors, and soldiers that were part of the task force were in the Inland Sea. To this end, they eliminated all direct radio communication between vessels of the task force as they began to move out from their bases in the Inland Sea. The thirty-two ships secretly slipped out one by one beginning November 10, and navigated north to Hitokappu Bay in the remote Kurile Islands, where they remained until November 25. During their stay at Hitokappu Bay, they kept complete radio silence, prohibited the throwing of garbage, and canceled all shore leaves.[24] The second step taken was to simulate the volume of the entire task force by padding the radio traffic between the vessels remaining in the Inland Sea. To reinforce this measure, a significant portion of the men at the Yokosuka Naval District were sent on leave to Tokyo and Yokohama.[25] The final, and probably the most critical, step of the strategy was to conceal the movement of the fleet as it left Hitokappu Bay and sailed toward Hawaii. This was not an easy task, since it required keeping secret the location of six carriers carrying 432 aircraft, as well as nine destroyers, two battleships, two heavy cruisers, one light cruiser, and eight tankers. After considering several alternative routes, it was decided that the best way to avoid detection was to sail east to the meridian of Midway Island before turning on a southeasterly course toward the Hawaiian Islands. On reaching the meridian of Oahu, at a point about 490 miles north of the island, the fleet would turn south in order to approach Pearl Harbor form the north. This particular route was thought to be the most secure because it was well off shipping lanes and out of range of American aerial patrols.[26]

In contrast, the Japanese took few measures to conceal the movement of troops and equipment to either Formosa or Cam Ranh Bay to be used in the southern operation. They were shipped in huge convoys that could be easily spotted, since they had to sail through areas commonly traveled by merchant ships.[27] As General Koichi Shimada put it, the scores of transport vessels heading south seemed to him "an almost unmistakable tip-off that a large-scale amphibious move to the South impended."[28] General Shimada's point is reinforced by the fact that the volume and proportion of messages being directed southward increased dramatically without any effort to camouflage the traffic.[29]

Additional evidence supports the contention that Japan was not overly concerned about concealing its intention to move south. At the Liaison Conference held on November 5, Tojo, while explaining to the other participants why he believed negotiation with the United States still had a chance to succeed, stated: "They [the Americans] will learn how determined Japan is from the deployment of our troops, which we will carry out on the basis of the present proposal."[30] Prime Minister Tojo's statement indicates quite clearly an intention to use the deployment of forces as a means to persuade the United States that Japan would resort to war, if necessary, in order to fulfill its objectives. There are several reasons for believing that he was referring to the operation south and not the operation east. First, and most important, it is exceedingly unlikely that Tojo would have alluded to the Hawaiian operation in the presence of individuals who had not yet been informed about the plan to attack Pearl Harbor. Second, Tojo would not have used the Hawaiian operation to coerce the Americans, for such an action would have provided President Roosevelt and Secretary of State Hull with the necessary justification to end the negotiations. Finally, it is questionable whether Admiral Yamamoto and the Naval General Staff would have consented to the use of the Hawaiian forces as a means to show Japan's determination, in view of the fact that the success of the mission depended on Pearl Harbor's being attacked by surprise.

The thrust of the latter part of our argument seems to imply that Japan was unconcerned about attaining surprise in Southeast Asia. Such an inference would be quite misleading. To support this point, it is necessary to discuss only briefly some of the steps taken by Japan to attain surprise in the Philippines and in Malaya.

The principal step taken to surprise the American forces in the Philippines was the initiation of the air attack on Manila from air bases in Formosa. At one time, during the planning stage, Japanese strategists considered using some of the carriers not employed against Pearl Harbor as a way of reducing the distance the attacking Japanese planes would have to travel to targets in the Philippines. After extensive debate it was decided that use of the carriers for this purpose would be more of a hindrance than an asset. Carriers would increase the risk of forewarning the Americans, since the ships would have to be maneuvered within the range of possible observation in order to launch the Zeros for the opening attack. Furthermore, the carriers would have to observe strict radio silence as they approached their target in order to conceal their whereabouts from the Americans. But the available carrier-based fighters were insufficient for the operations against the Philippines; the mission also required the use of the bombers based in Formosa. This meant that, if the carriers maintained radio silence, the necessary coordination of the attack on Manila between the Formosa-based bombers and the carrier-based fighters far off at sea would have had to be sacrificed.[31] Given the unpredictability of weather conditions, Japanese strategists concluded that coordination of the two-pronged air attacks on Manila would be necessary. But since this conclusion meant that radio silence could not be maintained, the decision was made to launch the air attack solely from bases in Formosa.

The Japanese also hoped to achieve some form of surprise on their expedition against Manila. The Japanese expeditionary force left Hainan early in December 1941. Two days later, after reaching the Gulf of Siam, the fleet sailed into the gulf as if it intended to move toward Bangkok. The objective behind this maneuver was to give the British the impression that the expeditionary force was sailing toward Siam rather than Malaya.[32]

Briefly summarized, then, it seems quite clear that, with respect to Southeastern Asia, the Japanese followed two paths. On the one hand, they took special precautionary measures to conceal their actual targets. It ought to be recognized, however, that although the Japanese might have hoped to catch their adversaries totally unprepared, they were aware that their chances of doing so were going to be impaired by the earlier attack on Pearl Harbor. The second path the Japanese followed was to take few precautionary measures to disguise their *general intention* in Southeast Asia. It would be very neat and precise to rationalize that Japan's sole purpose for disclosing its overall intention in Southeast Asia was to use the operation as part of a feint of the move east. But this argument would overlook one important factor— necessity. As soon as the Japanese planners began to organize the move south they realized that it would be nearly impossible to hide the movement of such an enormous force through heavily traveled shipping lanes.[33] Aware that their overall strategy depended heavily on achieving surprise at Pearl Harbor, the Japanese war planners might well have decided to accept the fact that surprise for the southern operation was problematical and to make the best of that reality by converting the movement of forces south as part of a deception plan for the all-important eastern mission.[34]

Going beyond the recognition that Japan did not attempt to disguise its hostile intention, how did Japan signal the time that it intended to go to war? Japan, by deploying its forces to the south in a very open manner, was signaling to its adversaries not only the intention to use them, but also the *approximate time when* it intended to use them. It can be argued that such evidence is never fully clear. An actor may simply wish to signal a threat or create the appearance of indecisiveness by deploying forces, with no intent of actually launching the attack. But it must also be taken into consideration that Japan resorted to numerous other means besides the deployment of its forces to express its intention to go to war. Thus, although Japan's leaders could have rescinded their decision to attack, Japan's overall behavior signaled the time framework within which the attack was planned to take place. What Japan's leaders did not disclose was the exact time and targets of the attacks of the southern operation. In other words, Japan was willing to surrender strategic surprise, but hoped to retain tactical surprise.

Earlier in this chapter it was noted that, in an attempt to create the impression that the Pearl Harbor task force had not sailed from the confines of the Inland Sea, the Japanese naval authorities padded the radio traffic between the vessels remaining in the Inland Sea and sent on leave to Tokyo and Yokohama a large number of sailors stationed at the Yokosuka Naval District. The Japanese Navy, however, may have also had another objective in mind when it took such steps—to persuade the Americans that Japan had not altered its traditional naval strategy.

During July 1941, when Japan sent its ultimatum to France with respect to French Indochina, it kept the carriers near the coastline to protect the home waters in case the United States decided to take counteractive measures. Such a move was consistent with Japan's strategy that, in a war against the United States, Japan's carriers would be used only for defensive purposes. While keeping the carriers near the coastline, the Japanese Navy followed two procedures used four months later, both of which were noted by the Americans. The first procedure was to switch the communication of the carriers to low-frequency short-range wavelengths to ensure that the Americans could not pick them up.[35] The second procedure was to grant the sailors of the carriers liberty.[36]

There is no available evidence that, in July 1941, these two steps were undertaken with the intention of conveying the impression that Japan, in a move south, would invariably keep its carriers near the coastline to protect its home waters. But it seems clear that, in November 1941, when the Japanese cut all communication between the carriers, padded the radio traffic between the remaining vessels, and sent a noticeable number of sailors on liberty, they did so not only to hide the carriers' true whereabouts, but also to signal that they remained within the confines of the Inland Sea for protective purposes as the move south became evident.

In sum, Japan's central objective was to achieve surprise regarding its most important target: Pearl Harbor. Japan opted for this strategy because it believed it could control the United States' concern over the possibility of Pearl Harbor as one of the targets. Japan counted on controlling the concern of the United States by disclosing its intention to direct its aggressive acts against targets in Southeast Asia. But Japan could rely on such an action only because the Hawaiian Islands were not in the vicinity of Japan's other targets, and because Washington believed that Japan lacked both the military might to fight two major wars simultaneously[37] and the technological capability to overcome Pearl Harbor's natural barriers.

To carry through its strategy, Japan also had to conceal its rationale for attacking Pearl Harbor. In other words, Japan could not afford to disclose its rationale that, to succeed with its amphibious operations in Southeast Asia, it first had to eliminate the only force with the power to interfere: the U.S. Fleet anchored at Pearl Harbor. This meant that in order to achieve surprise with respect to its target and rationale, Japan had to preserve the sense of vulnerability of the United States at a low level; this goal, in turn, required that it achieve surprise with respect to its military capability and doctrine. To realize these various objectives, Japan sought to conceal: (1) the rate at which it produced and refined its military equipment, including its attempts to render its aerial torpedoes operable in Pearl Harbor's shallow waters and its attempts to improve the cruising range of its carriers and destroyers, and (2) the adoption of an offensive naval strategy.

Egypt–Syria's Time Strategy of Surprise

The predicament faced by Egypt and Syria in 1973 was in some ways similar to that confronted by Japan some thirty years earlier. The two Arab states had been trying to pressure Israel to return the territory it had occupied following its victory during the Six-Day War in 1967. Israel, however, had no intention of giving in to their demands without receiving in return some major guarantees, including the recognition of Israel as a sovereign state.

Aware that the war of attrition they had been conducting against the Israelis would not bend them, Egypt and Syria began to rebuild their respective military forces with help from the Soviets. The flow of Soviet weapons to Egypt increased dramatically after February 1973, and Syria, after May of that same year, began to receive a complete air defense system of SAM missiles plus another forty MIG-21 fighters. The clearest indication that the Arab states would resort to war to achieve their objectives, however, came from Sadat's own public pronouncements. In 1971, the Egyptian president warned the Israelis that it would be the "year of decision." Initially, Israel paid little attention to the threat for it recognized that it was dissent within Egypt that forced Sadat to view the necessity of war in specific terms. But, by the end of March 1973, just a month after the flow of Soviet weapons into Egypt had taken an upturn, Sadat made several remarks that left very little doubt of his intentions. In an interview with Arnaud de Borchgrave of *Newsweek,* Sadat stated, "Everything in this country is now being mobilized in earnest for the resumption of the battle—which is now inevitable."

Furthermore, he made it clear that Egypt would have the means to fight because the Soviets were "providing us with everything that's possible to supply."[38] He reiterated his intention to go to war just a week before the fateful act took place. On September 28, during a speech commemorating the third anniversary of Nasser's death, he stated that the liberation of the Egyptian territories occupied by Israel remained the foremost goal of his Government.[39]

Israel did not take these new pronouncements lightly. During mid-April 1973, for instance, Minister of Defense Moshe Dayan ordered a partial reserve mobilization and military alert along the Suez Canal in response to major military mobilization and war exercises held by Egypt. On May 21, Dayan issued a memorandum to Israel's general staff warning of the possibility of war during the second half of the summer. And finally, on September 13, Israel prepared itself for the possibility of a large retaliatory attack from Syria following an extensive air battle between the two rival states.

All things considered, however, the prevailing attitude among Israel's leaders was that Egypt and Syria would not attack because they were still too weak. An actor's disposition to feel threatened depends primarily on whether he believes that he is stronger or weaker than his opponent. Israel perceived its own capabilities to be considerably greater than those of Egypt and/or Syria. "The total balance of forces," explained Moshe Dayan, "is in our favor . . . ."[40] From this belief it was inferred that the Arabs would not engage in war against Israel in the near future. As explained by Dayan, the favorable balance "outweighs all other considerations and motives, and puts a break on the *immediate renewal* of hostilities."[41]

Israel had good reason for not feeling vulnerable. Its military doctrine was designed around two central assumptions. The first assumption was that Egypt would refrain from attacking so long as its air force lacked the power to dominate the skies.[42] Israel was well aware that Egypt had been receiving massive shipments of weapons from the Soviet Union and was attempting to increase its air power. But, for the first time in history, Israel itself was beginning to feel sufficiently well equipped.[43] Following the war of attrition with Egypt, Israel began to receive large quantities of modern weapons from the United States. Many of its old fighter bombers were being replaced by planes with a longer combat radius, and new and better tanks were enlarging the tank corps. Also, Israel believed that Egypt would have trouble learning to operate efficiently and quickly its new complicated weapon systems and integrating them into its armed forces. Furthermore, Israeli intelligence analysts were convinced that it would take at least until 1975–1976 to retrain and prepare a new generation of soldiers.

The second assumption that dictated part of Israel's military doctrine was that Syria, because it was too weak militarily, would not dare to launch a full-scale attack against Israel without Egypt's involvement.[44] Syria, like

Egypt, had been receiving massive shipments of weapons from the Soviet Union. But it was likely to run into the same type of difficulties that Egypt faced in its attempt to assimilate the new weapon systems into its armed forces. It was thus inferred that, since Egypt had no intention of attacking Israel until it had rebuilt its air strength, there was no reason to fear a Syrian attack. In addition, Israeli intelligence analysts thought it very unlikely that the Egyptians and Syrians would agree on a common strategy to launch a coordinated two-front attack against Israel.[45] In short, the Israelis did not feel vulnerable.

Egypt was very well aware of Israel's attitude. As Herzog points out, the Egyptians "noted with satisfaction the overconfidence in Israel, its faith in the ever-growing technological and cultural gap between itself and the Arab countries and its conviction of the inability of the Arab leadership to make a decision to attack, not to mention the lack of unity in the Arab world."[46] Egypt and Syria's central task was to ensure that, as they augmented their capabilities, Israel's sense of vulnerability would remain constant.

On April 1, 1973, at a secret meeting, representatives of both Egypt and Syria agreed on an outline for military cooperation. By keeping secret the nature of their agreement, Egypt and Syria were, in fact, strengthening their overall capabilities without increasing Israel's sense of vulnerability. To protect further the nature of the agreement reached, and to reinforce Israel's belief that Egypt and Syria would have great difficulty in formulating a common strategy against Israel, the chiefs of staff of both states announced three weeks later, at a well-publicized meeting, that some military and political problems remained unresolved and were obstructing a joint Syrian–Egyptian action.[47] Israel's decision makers never questioned the veracity of this statement and, until the final hours before the attack, assumed that Egypt and Syria had yet to agree on a common strategy.

Egypt and Syria's second major precautionary measure was to disguise the real nature of the objectives they hoped to achieve vis-a-vis Israel. For years, as already noted, the predominant objective of the two Arab states had been to deprive Israel of its existence. Both states, however, lacked the resources to fulfill this objective. In contrast, the resources required to destabilize the situation in the Middle East and, as a consequence, to threaten the atmosphere of detente that the United States and the Soviet Union had been so eager to build were more limited. Agreement on this new objective was reached during a secret meeting between Sadat and Assad on June 12, 1973. And, once again, the two Arab states succeeded in concealing the nature of their agreement from Israel's intelligence analysts.

The third precautionary measure taken by Egypt and Syria to control Israel's sense of vulnerability was to conceal the true rate at which their respective armed forces were improving their military capabilities. Although the Israelis were aware that the two Arab states were receiving shipments of weapons, Egypt and Syria attempted to conceal how well they were being integrated into their armed forces. Their deceptive tactic was to leak stories about the unsatisfactory quality of Russian military equipment, the low maintenance level of anti-aircraft missile batteries, and the shortage of spare parts.[48] This deceptive step had the intended effect. The Israelis continued to believe that their opponents would fail to integrate the newly acquired weapons into their armed forces or to develop a maintenance program sophisticated enough to keep them in operation.[49]

Another step taken by the Arabs to improve their capabilities without alerting the Israelis was to design a new technique to cross the Suez Canal. The canal is a major barrier. Due to the steepness and irregularity of its banks, amphibious vehicles cannot descend into or ascend out of the canal without preparation of a path. To reinforce such a barrier, the Israelis had piled up a sand embankment thirty to sixty feet high and had constructed a line of strong points along the eastern part of the canal that came to be known as the Bar Lev Line. The presence of these obstacles led Moshe Dayan to calculate that it would take the Egyptians at least twelve hours to set up the bridges necessary to cross the canal and that the available Israeli troops along the Bar Lev Line could contain the attack until additional troops could be mobilized and transported to the front.[50] To counteract the presence of the aforementioned obstacles and to surprise the Israelis, Egyptian engineers secretly developed a technique that would enable Egyptian troops to cross the canal and master the steepness of the banks and their irregularities in half the time estimated by Dayan.[51]

Finally, aware that Israel's defense strategy depended on the destructive powers of its planes and tanks, Egypt and Syria concluded that they had to alter their military doctrine to rob Israel of part of its military superiority. To counterbalance Israel's air power, Egypt and Syria began to deploy large quantities of their latest Soviet anti-aircraft missiles and to mount the Egyptian attack along the length of the canal to dilute Israeli air power against any single troop concentration or bridge.[52] Furthermore, to neutralize the superior power of Israel's tanks, Egypt transformed every unit of infantry in the first wave across the canal into tank destroyers.

So far, the argument has been that Egypt and Syria relied on conventional means to conceal the improvements they had achieved with respect to their capabilities in order to control Israel's sense of vulnerability. The purpose of sending false signals is to obscure the signals that may herald the advent of the real crisis.[53] It is not possible to ascertain whether the two Arab states purposely engaged in a cry-wolf stratagem to mislead the Israelis. However, by looking closely at Israel's reaction to the false alarms, one cannot help but speculate that Egypt and Syria indeed may have designed their actions to promote the development of a cry-wolf syndrome.

Of the three major warnings that Israel received between the end of 1971 and May 1973, the last one, received during April–May 1973, was the most costly.[54] After closely examining the signals emanating from Egypt, Israeli intelligence analysis predicted that the Egyptians would once again come short of launching an attack. Moshe Dayan and Chief of Staff David Elazar, however, rejected the analysis and ordered partial mobilization. War did not break out, and Israel had to pay a heavy price—10 million dollars—for the failure of its top governmental officials to accept the intelligence estimate of their subordinates. Dayan, cognizant of his mistake and of the fact that his military intelligence analysts had been accurate in all of their previous estimations, decided that it was time to listen closely to what they had to say.[55] In concurrence with this sentiment, Israel believed that its military strength was having a powerful deterrent effect on Arab willingness to attack.[56] This meant that, in order to reinforce Israel's estimation that Egypt and Syria lacked the means and resolution to attack, Egypt–Syria had to behave as though they wished to attack, but were unable to do so. In due time, Israel found it not only very difficult to trust the credibility of the warnings, but also unbearably expensive to react to every possible warning of war with a mobilization of its own. In the words of Coral Bell, "The unfulfilled threats of the two previous years had left a prevasive impression of military irre- solution."[57]

Another deceptive means Egypt may have used was negotiation. Ac- cording to Avi Shlaim, the Arabs, in an attempt to create a misleading impression concerning their capabilities, plans, and intentions, welcomed Secretary of State Henry Kissinger's peace initiative in September 1973.[58] Michael Handel also acknowledges that Egypt used diplomacy in an attempt to deceive Israel.[59] Neither writer, however, attempts to explain *how* Egypt used diplomacy to mislead Israel.

Sadat seems to have used diplomacy to deceive the Americans, not the Israelis. A state preparing for war often must be concerned about the pos- sibility of drawing a pre-emptive strike.[60] Sadat was fully aware that Egypt and Syria were going to find it very difficult to conceal their imminent ag- gressive intentions during the days just prior to the attack. Furthermore, he knew that Israel's overriding military strategy had always been the pre-emp- tive strike. Therefore, it seems quite reasonable to speculate that part of Sadat's strategy would have been geared to minimize the likelihood of an Israeli pre-emptive attack. If one combines this concern with the fact that Israel's freedom of action was highly constrained by the regional and global interests of the United States, it is not difficult to comprehend why President Sadat might have wanted to mislead the Americans into believing that he still had hopes for a peaceful settlement.[61]

To find out whether there is some truth to this argument, one must look closely at the negotiations that went on between Egypt and the United States, on the one hand, and between Israel and the United States on the other hand. Upon his appointment as secretary of state, Henry Kissinger met with several Middle Eastern foreign ministers between September and the beginning of October 1973. By then, Kissinger had become concerned about the possibility that oil might be used as a weapon against the United States if a new war against Israel ensued.[62] During his meetings, Kissinger asked the foreign ministers whether they would welcome an attempt on his part to deflate the tension in the Middle East. All the foreign ministers, including Mohammed Zayyat from Egypt, responded that his involvement could bring about some positive results.[63]

Kissinger's reaction to the meetings was enthusiastic. He concluded that Egypt wanted not a new round of war but a new round of negotiations. He communicated this impression to Abba Eban, Israel's foreign minister, and also communicated Zayyat's willingness to return to Washington in November to work out the necessary procedures. Eban agreed that November would be a good month to meet since, as Kissinger put it, "Nothing dramatic can happen in October."[64]

Kissinger was so convinced that Egypt wanted to engage in negotiations that he took special precautionary measures to constrain Israel from launching a pre-emptive attack. On one occasion, he told Israel's ambassador to the United States, Simcha Dinitz, "If you fire the first shot, you won't have a dogcatcher in this country supporting you."[65] The intensity of Kissinger's pressure on Israel gained force as the threatening signals from Egypt began to increase. After receiving a cable reporting on the growing tension in the Middle East from Kenneth Keating, the American ambassador in Israel, Kissinger once again warned Abba Eban not to pre-empt. He repeated the warning to Mordechai Shalev, the charge d'affaires at the Israeli Embassy in Washington, and he instructed Ambassador Keating to pass the same message on to Meir.[66]

Kissinger's message was loud and clear. On October 5, General Elazar, after having been notified that troops along the Egyptian and Syrian borders had swung into offensive formation, warned his staff that a call-up of the reserves was quite likely. On the following morning, after being informed by the military intelligence chief, General Eliahu Zeira, that Egypt and Syria would strike that day at 6:00 P.M., Elazar urged Meir to launch a pre-emptive attack.[67] With Dayan's backing, Meir vetoed the plan. Her rationale was that, if Israel struck first, it would be extremely difficult to persuade the world, and especially the United States, that such a step was not simply a rerun of 1967. "How many friends," she asked, "would we have if we did that?"[68]

To summarize, although there is no direct hard evidence that can link Egypt's attempt to deceive the United States via negotiations with the pressure exerted by the latter on Israel not to pre-empt, our speculation is rooted in four well-acknowledged facts. First, via his foreign minister, Anwar Sadat did attempt to mislead Secretary of State Kissinger about Egypt's willingness to negotiate. Second, as a result of his meetings with many of the Arab diplomats, Kissinger became convinced that Egypt wanted to negotiate, not go to war. Third, Kissinger exerted a great deal of pressure on Israel not to pre-empt. And, finally, Israel considered the viability of pre-empting, but rejected the idea for fear of losing America's support.

The conventional and deceptive means considered so far would not have been sufficient to mask *when* Egypt and Syria planned to attack as both states began to implement the final stages of the first phase of the attack. Early in the planning stage, Egyptian officials estimated that Israel would learn about Egypt's preparations fifteen days prior to the assault.[69] To avoid meeting the full brunt of Israel's regular army and mobilized reservists, Egyptian planners concluded, based on the assumption that it would take Israel from five to seven days to mobilize its troops fully,[70] that they had to cut down Israel's learning period to four or five days. To fulfill this task, the Egyptians relied on two types of maneuvers, both well known by the Israelis, to camouflage the deployment of their forces. The first maneuver they took advantage of was to prepare the deployment of Egyptian troops as part of Egypt's annual autumn military operation, under the code name *Liberation 23*.[71] Second, since Egypt had been carrying on large- and small-scale maneuvers or command post exercises near the Suez Canal since November 1972, the new deployment of forces was executed to fit such a pattern.[72]

The reliance on these maneuvers was accompanied by a series of smaller misleading acts. First, although the imminence of an attack was obvious to most senior Egyptian and Syrian officers, the specific date and time of attack were known by only a very small group of individuals. Egypt's central planners were so concerned about keeping the date and time a secret that they did not even inform members of the cabinet during the regular Wednesday meeting, or Mohammed Zayyat, who had been negotiating with Kissinger in New York.[77] Second, to conceal the actual number of troops stationed by the canal and to give Israel the impression that those forces were there only in training, a brigade would be moved in that direction during the day, but only a battalion would return to its departing point at night.,[74] To reinforce the notion that troops were sent to the canal solely for training purposes, two other steps were taken. One was to send home some of the reservists called up in September so that they could be back at work by October 6, and the other was to place a small news item in *Al Ahram* newspaper announcing that officers could take leave to perform the Moslem *omrah*.[75] Finally, to prevent the Israelis from becoming suspicious about the new equipment that was being stored near the canal, deep trenches were dug to cover the trucks and the water-crossing equipment, and special crates were constructed to camouflage other equipment.[76]

The steps undertaken by Syria to mislead Israel just prior to the final assault were much simpler than Egypt's. Such lack of complexity may be explained by the fact that, since Israel believed Syria would never attack on its own, Syrian planners had a more limited need to mask the movement of their troops.

Syrian policy makers, like their Egyptian counterparts, took advantage of a pattern fully known by Israel. Because of its geography, Syria had to maintain a fully mobilized army on an emergency footing during the greater part of the year concentrated in the area stretching from the cease-fire line back to Damascus.[77] Although these forces were rarely reduced except during the winter, early in the summer of 1973 they were thinned out substantially. This reversal in procedure, however, came to an abrupt end during the first week of September, when the lines began to thicken once again.[78] Shortly thereafter, on September 13, Syrian and Israeli planes fought an air battle in which thirteen Syrian planes and one Israeli plane were shot down. Syria used the air battle to justify the further increase of forces on its border with Israel.

On September 26, in a routine press release, Syria announced the concentration of troops for annual maneuvers. Less than a week later, it began to move its tanks and heavy artillery from their rear positions to deployments opposite the Israeli outposts.[79] The Syrian tanks, however, were positioned "hull-down," dug in to resist an assault rather than to launch one, and the medium artillery was placed back to protect Syrian territory. In other words, Syria mobilized in a *defensive* formation.[80] The Syrians justified this maneuver by contending that it was intended to stop an anticipated Israeli retaliatory attack following the hijacking of the train carrying the Soviet Jews from Moscow to Vienna.[81]

In sum, three factors contributed to Egypt and Syria's decision to opt for a time-type strategy of surprise. On the one hand, they were aware that, because of the past relationship and geographical proximity of the three countries, it would be senseless to conceal their intention to attack and their target of attack. On the other hand, Israel's low initial sense of vulnerability enabled Egypt and Syria to opt for a strategy designed to maintain that low vulnerability, a factor that helped them to disguise *when* the attack would be initiated.

Egypt and Syria implemented the strategy by:

1. Concealing that they would attack jointly;
2. Concealing that they intended to pursue a more limited objective than the one expected by Israel's policy makers (in other words, attempting to achieve surprise regarding their rationale for the attack);
3. Concealing the adoption of more sophisticated military strategies and misleading the Israelis, via the press, about the true qualitative state of their newly acquired weapons and their armed forces in general;

4. Promulgating the belief among Israel's policy makers via the cry-wolf method that, although they would like to attack, they still lacked the resources necessary to engage in a major war;

5. Ensuring that the threatening signals coming from the northern and southern fronts were counterbalanced by signs showing that there was no cause for concern.

Target and Time Strategies of Surprise

Neither Japan in 1941 nor Egypt–Syria in 1973 tried to achieve surprise with respect to their intentions. In both instances the aggressors left few doubts about their determination to resort to war to achieve their objectives.

Several factors prevented Japan from pursuing an intention-type strategy of surprise. The Japanese leaders seem to have reasoned that, as the relationship between the United States and Japan deteriorated, it would become more and more difficult for Japan to conceal its intention to resort to force. Egypt–Syria faced a similar predicament. Both states had been demanding the return of the territory that Israel had occupied following the Six-Day War in 1967. Their demands had often been accompanied or followed by limited hostile acts. Also, on several occasions the leaders of both states had proclaimed their determination to launch a major attack. It could be inferred, therefore, that would-be surprisers are unlikely to opt for an intention-type strategy of surprise when their relationships with their victims have been uncharacteristically conflictual.

The fact that both Japan and Egypt–Syria chose not to conceal their intentions does not mean that they opted for the same type of strategy. Japan opted for a target-type strategy of surprise, while Egypt–Syria chose a time-type strategy of surprise.

To conceal its decision to make Pearl Harbor its primary target, Japan relied on two circumstances: the tendency by American high officials to downgrade Japan's military strength, and the vast distance that separated Japan's two general targets—Southeast Asia and the Hawaiian Islands. Japan recognized that the United States was convinced that Japan did not possess the capability to launch simultaneously two large and exceedingly complex attacks against targets located thousands of miles apart. In an attempt to reinforce this American perception, Japan followed two paths. On the one hand, by disguising both the rate at which and the extent to which Japan's military capabilities were being augmented, its policy makers tried to avoid aggravating Washington's sense of vulnerability. At the same time, they did not attempt to hide Japan's intention to launch attacks against targets in Southeast Asia, but did conceal the deployment of Japanese carriers toward Pearl Harbor.

Egypt–Syria also seem to have relied heavily on their victim's belief that its adversaries were not strong enough to launch an effective attack. The leaders of both Arab states were aware that Israel's policy makers were convinced that (1) a major Egyptian attack was unlikely until Egypt's armed forces, its air force in particular, had been substantially strengthened; and (2) Syria was too weak to mount a large-scale attack on its own. Moreover, the leaders of Egypt–Syria knew that Israel's policy makers believed that a major Arab attack would be guided by one goal—the defeat of Israel. These two Israeli beliefs enabled the Arab leaders to engage in a strategy whereby they would try to control Israel's sense of vulnerability by disguising the rate at which they were augmenting their countries' capabilities.

Egypt–Syria, however, did not have the geographical advantage possessed by Japan. Any mobilization on their part was bound to signal that, if they went to war, Israel would be the target. The sharing of boundaries with Israel and the hostile atmosphere that had permeated their relationships prevented the leaders of Egypt–Syria from attempting to convey the impression that they would direct their aggression against other targets.

Apart from these differences, the strategies of Japan and Egypt–Syria shared three dimensions of surprise. In each instance the would-be surprisers sought to control the sense of vulnerability of their victims by concealing the rate at which they were augmenting their military capabilities and the fact that they had altered their military doctrines and, thus, the strategies implicit in them.

The final dimension of surprise sought by both Japan and Egypt–Syria concerned the rationale for their attacks. This dimension played a critical role in the strategies of both aggressors. Japan's policy makers reasoned that in order to succeed in Southeast Asia, they first had to eliminate the American fleet anchored in Pearl Harbor. Clearly, therefore, if Japan hoped to disguise the fact that Pearl Harbor was its principal target, it could not afford a disclosure of the rationale for attacking it. The structure of Egypt–Syria's problem was somewhat different. It was common knowledge that Israel's policy makers believed that Egypt–Syria would not launch a major attack until they regained the strength to inflict a major defeat on Israel. But Egypt–Syria would not launch a major attack until they regained the strength to inflict a major defeat on Israel. But Egypt–Syria were also aware that, so long as Israel maintained a close relationship with the United States, it would be nearly impossible to defeat it. Thus, a more reasonable rationale for attacking Israel would be to intensify the conflict in the Middle East so that both the United States and the Soviet Union would want to intervene in order to preserve the new atmosphere of detente that they had been building so carefully. Given this new rationale, the two Arab states did not need the resources to inflict a major defeat on the Israelis; they could launch an attack that had more limited objectives than those anticipated by Israel. Egypt–

Syria's time-type strategy of surprise, therefore, was in part dependent on whether they could also diguise their rationale for the attack.

In accordance with the argument presented thus far, would-be surprisers who are significantly weaker than their adversaries are in an enviable position. These actors can often tolerate disclosure of some evidence of their hostile intentions without noticeably augmenting their adversaries' resolve to pre-empt. These same international actors, however, are not always free to choose randomly from the remaining strategies of surprise. Japan's decision to rely on a target-type strategy of surprise and Egypt–Syria's decision to forego it provide evidence for two general arguments. First, it could be argued that would-be surprisers will be inclined to opt for a target-type strategy of surprise under these conditions: when they cannot conceal their intention, when they believe they can control their victims' sense of vulnerability, and when they can act as though their actions will be directed against actors other than their adversaries. Finally, it could be proposed that would-be surprisers are likely to adopt a time-type strategy of surprise when they cannot conceal their intention and target, but can, at minimum, control their victims' sense of vulnerability.

Notes

1. Butow, 1961, p. 247.
2. Ibid., p. 262.
3. Tolischus, 1943, p. 279.
4. Ibid., p. 281.
5. Ibid., p. 297.
6. Ibid., p. 297.
7. Ibid., pp. 302–303.
8. Fukudome, 1969, p. 8.
9. Ward, 1952, p. 1282. For an insightful discussion of how Japan went about designing and testing the new aerial torpedoes, see Prange, 1980, Chapter 19.
10. Ibid., p. 1282.
11. Butow, 1961, p. 242.
12. Wohlstetter, 1962, pp. 200–203, 349, 393; Morison, Vol. III, 1951, pp. 64–79; Ike, 1967, pp. 199–260; Whaley, 1973b, p. A-248.
13. Butow, 1961, p. 242.
14. Ike, 1967, p. 138.
15. Ibid., p. 200.
16. Ibid., p. 262. The decision to use negotiation as a means of deception, however, was made on September 6—long before November 29. At that time it was decided that diplomatic negotiation during the days prior to the launching of the

attack had to be continued with a view toward "facilitating the switchover from political to military methods."

17. Ibid., p. 262.

18. Tolischus, 1943, p. 314.

19. Quoted in Wohlstetter, 1962, p. 350.

20. Ibid., pp. 339–340.

21. Fukudome, 1969, p. 9.

22. Whaley, 1973b, p. A-251.

23. Ibid., p. A-251.

24. Ibid., p. A-256.

25. Ibid., p. A-253.

26. Collier, 1969, p. 97; Whaley, 1973a, p. A-256. The advantage of choosing such a treacherous route was best voiced by Commander Minoru Genda when he told Vice Admiral Chirichi Nagumo, the newly appointed commander of the First Air Fleet, "If you think the northern route is bad, then you must remember the American admirals will think the same." Quoted in Prange, 1980, p. 220.

27. Manchester, 1979, p. 222.

28. Wohlstetter, 1962, p. 361.

29. Whaley, 1973b, p. A-259; Prange, 1980, p. 362.

30. Ike, 1969, p. 238.

31. Shimada, 1969, pp. 31–32; Prange, 1980, p. 230.

32. Morison, Vol. III, 1951, pp. 187–188.

33. Prange, 1980, p. 282.

34. Our argument is indirectly supported by Prange. At one point he notes that the Japanese placed little communications security around the forces to move south, just as they had never concealed their intention to dominate Southeast Asia. Later on in his study he adds that it was the sweeping offensive southward that served as a camouflage to the task force navigating toward Pearl Harbor. Finally, he notes that the pattern of deception involved the sending of the same messages time and again by the ships navigating south. See Prange, 1980, pp. 326, 354, and 435.

35. Morison, Vol. III, 1951, p. 130.

36. Wohlstetter, 1962, p. 111.

37. Japan would have to have been more than blind not to know that the United States held the capabilities of Japan in utter contempt. The American attitude was voiced with great precision by Congressman Charles I. Faddis of Pennsylvania when he noted that the Japanese "will not dare to get into a position where they must face the American Navy in an open battle. Their Navy is not strong enough and their homeland is too vulnerable." Prange, 1980, p. 36.

38. *Newsweek,* April 9, 1973.

39. *The New York Times,* September 29, 1973.

40. *Jerusalem Post,* August 11, 1973.

41. Ibid. (Emphasis added.)

42. Handel, 1976, p. 23.

43. Ibid., p. 44.

44. Agranat Commission of Inquiry, April 1974.
45. Insight Team, 1974, p. 68.
46. Herzog, 1975, p. 32.
47. Insight Team, 1974, p. 68; Handel, 1976, p. 20.
48. Herzog, 1975, p. 68; Handel, 1976, p. 30.
49. Handel, 1976, p. 45.
50. Insight Team, 1974, p. 139.
51. Baker, 1974, p. 40.
52. Herzog, 1975, p. 33; Handel, 1976, p. 58.
53. Handel, 1976, p. 54.
54. Ibid., p. 54.
55. Agranat Commission of Inquiry, 1974, p. 47.
56. Handel, 1976, p. 30.
57. Bell, 1974, p. 534.
58. Shlaim, April 1976, p. 355.
59. Handel, 1976, p. 59.
60. Whaley, 1973a, p. 59.
61. According to Heikal, Foreign Minister Zayyat was purposely kept in the dark as to when the attack would take place so as not to put him under too much strain during his meeting with Kissinger. See Heikal, 1975, pp. 25.
62. Herzog, 1975, p. 25.
63. Ibid., p. 38.
64. Quoted from Kalb, 1974, p. 460.
65. Quoted from Kalb, 1974, p. 460.
66. Ibid., pp. 459–461.
67. Insight Team, 1974, pp. 121–122; Herzog, 1975, p. 52; Kalb, 1974, p. 457.
68. Insight Team, 1974, p. 122.
69. Heikal, 1975, p. 15.
70. Ibid., p. 16.
71. Ibid., p. 16; Insight Team, 1974, p. 90.
72. Dupuy, 1978, p. 319.
73. Heikal, 1975, p. 25; Herzog, 1974, p. 39; Dupuy, 1978, p. 391.
74. Heikal, 1975, pp. 16–17; Herzog, 1974, p. 36; Dupuy, 1978, p. 392.
75. Heikal, 1975, p. 32.
76. Herzog, 1974, p. 36.
77. Handel, 1976, p. 57.
78. Ibid., p. 60.
79. Insight Team, 1974, p. 106.
80. Ibid., p. 106; Dupuy, 1978, p. 392.
81. Heikal, 1975, p. 17; Insight Team, 1974, p. 101.

4

Why Were the Americans and Israelis Surprised in 1941 and 1973, Respectively?

Surprise at Pearl Harbor

Most intelligence analysts who have looked closely at the Pearl Harbor case share Wohlstetter's view that it was unreasonable for the United States not to have given greater weight to the likelihood of a Japanese attack on Pearl Harbor.[1] In this section we intend not so much to challenge Wohlstetter's argument, but to offer an alternative explanation. We will propose, instead, that in order to have seriously considered such an eventuality, it would have been necessary that American policy makers have at least one piece of critical information. They lacked that one piece. Furthermore, we contend that American foreign-policy makers were unable to find that piece of critical information because Japan's strategy of surprise was designed to provide to the United States only with information that would reinforce the preconceptions of its policy makers.

From the moment Japan's leaders concluded that diplomacy would not elicit the results they desired, they expressed their willingness to resort to war, if necessary, in several unambiguous ways. American leaders had no difficulty in deciphering this aspect of Japan's intention. What American policy makers had to consider carefully was: *Where* did Japan plan to attack?

To understand how the United States addressed this problem, it is necessary to grasp the type of inferences American decision makers were deriving from their own assumptions and Japan's actions. Midway through October 1941, the United States Army and Navy held different views about the prospects of a Japanese attack against the United States. The army believed that, in view of the United States' existing and potential strength in the Philippines, Japan would resort to every means available to keep Amercia out of the war.[2] Confidence in the immunity of the United States from Japanese aggression was partly bolstered by the underestimation of production rates and performance of various Japanese vehicles and equipment. Army intelligence for instance, believed that Japan's air power was significantly weaker than it turned out to be. It estimated that Japan was producing only 200 aircraft per month for both the army and the navy, when the actual rate was 426 planes per month.[3] In addition, army intelligence calculated that the Japanese Zero single-engine fighter could fly only 800 miles, when its actual range was 900 miles, and that it could reach a maximal speed of 250 statute miles per hour, when in fact it could reach 300 miles per hour. Finally, it estimated that America's pilot training was superior to Japan's, although Japanese pilots actually flew a significantly greater number of hours. As a result, the army argued that the best way to prevent the spread of hostilities in the Pacific area was to use forceful diplomacy and apply increasing military and economic pressures on Japan.[4]

The navy did not share the army's confidence. Although it also underrated Japan's capabilities in many ways,[5] it believed that—due to the ever increasing stringency of the embargo placed by the United States, Great Britain, and the Netherlands East Indies—Japan would attempt to strike out and get the goods it needed by force.[6]

By early November 1941, the United States' view of Japan's intentions had changed somewhat. State Department officials continued to feel confident about the ability of the United States to defeat Japan in a military action of a few weeks.[7] This sense of confidence was not fully shared by members of the Joint Army–Navy Board. Aware that the main involvement in the Far East would be naval, they became very concerned about the facts that the navy was involved in the Atlantic and that time would be required to strengthen the Pacific Fleet. For this reason, the Board recommended that the American government not take any drastic measure against Japan.[8] At the same time, however, its members believed that, because of the existing strength of the United States Army Air Forces in the Far East, Japan would not dare risk taking action against the Philippines or moving toward the south.[9] Briefly summarized, then, the overall view by the beginning of November seems to have been that the American military presence in the Far East was impressive enough to have a deterrent effect on Japan.

By late November 1941, it had become quite evident that Japan had set itself a deadline for the negotiations. Moreover, the news of massive war preparations and of actual Japanese military advances along the coast of Southeastern Asia convinced many American policy makers that the likelihood of averting a war was quite small. At the weekly session of the War Council, held on Wednesday, November 25, President Roosevelt expressed the view that Japan was likely to begin launching surprise attacks as soon as the forthcoming Monday.[10] The consensus reached was that the Japanese were likely to attack Siam, Malaya, or the Dutch East Indies, but not the Philippines.[11]

By November 27, after learning that a large expeditionary force was sailing south from Shanghai, President Roosevelt and Secretary of State Hull were no longer willing to discard the possibility of an attack on the Philippines. General Marshall disagreed. He believed that Japan would refrain from attacking because it knew how costly an attack on the Philippines could turn out to be.[12] Such a belief, however, did not prevent Marshall from ordering General MacArthur in the Philippines to be alert for a possible attack.

In the meantime, Pearl Harbor also was being warned of what was transpiring in Southeast Asia. On November 24, Admiral Kimel was informed that a surprise aggressive movement in any direction, including an attack on the Philippines or Guam, was a possibility.[13] Three days later, Admiral Kimmel received another dispatch stating that there were indications of an amphibious movement against the Philippines, the Thai or Kra Peninsula, or possibly Borneo.[14]

On November 28, at another War Council meeting, Secretary of State Hull re-emphasized the need to assume that Japan might make surprise a central point in its strategy.[15] Part of the rest of the meeting centered on whether the expeditionary force that had left Shanghai would attack the Philippines, Thailand, Singapore, Kra Isthmus, Rangoon, or the Dutch Netherlands or would simply land in Indochina.[16] But, as Secretary of War Henry Stimson noted later, "the possibility of an attack on Pearl Harbor was not discussed at the meeting, since our thoughts were focused on this movement toward Southeast Asia which indicated a crisis in that direction."[17]

The next major meeting of members of the War Council took place on December 6. By then it had become quite evident that Japan had no intention of relying any longer on diplomacy. Furthermore, it had been learned that Japan had placed over 100,000 troops in Indochina; that there were large concentrations of Japanese naval forces in Cam Ranh Bay, Saigon, and the Hainan–Formosa area; and that three Japanese convoys were entering the Gulf of Siam.[18] Based on this evidence, the War Council expected war to break out at any time between Great Britain and Japan, and, since the United States was going to support Great Britain, it also meant war with the United States.[19] In other words, the United States estimated that Japan would go to war in Southeast Asia, either on the weekend of November 30 or of December 7, and might attempt to conduct acts of sabotage against Pearl Habor, but a major attack on Pearl Harbor was not expected.

Two factors seem to have contributed to the feeling that Pearl Harbor was not vulnerable to a Japanese attack. The first, and probably most important, was the belief among military men that Japan was incapable of undertaking more than one major operation at a time.[20] As it became clearer that Japan intended to move southward, the threat to Hawaii was assumed to have receded enormously.[21] The second factor that played an important role was the attitude of many American officials toward Pearl Harbor. Although certain military men contended, as will be explained shortly, that a surprise attack against Pearl Harbor might be achieved without any warning whatsoever, the predominant belief seems to have been that such an action would be very difficult to carry out. Vice Admiral W.S. Pye, for instance, maintained that the Japanese could not get close to Pearl Harbor without ten minutes' warning, and that ten minutes was all the time the Americans needed to get to their positions to man their guns.[22] An even more optimistic view was expressed by General Marshall's aide, who noted:

> The Island of Oahu, due to its fortifications, its garrison and its physical characteristics, is believed to be the strongest fortress in the world. . . . With this force available a major attack against Oahu is considered impracticable.[23]

The physical characteristics of Pearl Harbor bolstered the sense of invulnerability felt about Hawaii. In March 1941, Major General F.L. Martin, commander of the Hawaiian Army Air Corps, and Rear Admiral Patrick Bellinger, commander of the Hawaiian Based Patrol Wing, had concluded that a Japanese declaration of war might be preceded by an air attack on Oahu, which most likely would be launched from one or more carriers less than three hundred miles away from the central target.[24] This line of thinking, however, did not find much support among other officials of the armed forces in Hawaii. Midway through February 1941, Admiral Husband Kimmel, commander of the Hawaiian Fleet, had been assured that "a minimum depth of water of seventy-five feet may be assumed necessary to successfully drop torpedoes from planes."[25] Since the depth of the water in Pearl Harbor was thirty feet or less—except in the channels, where it was forty feet—one could infer that such information would have convinced Admiral Kimmel that a torpedo attack on Pearl Harbor had little or no chance of success. Some months later, after a new reassessment had been conducted, the aforementioned estimation was altered to read:

> While no minimum depth of water in which naval vessels may be anchored can arbitrarily be assumed as providing safety from torpedo plane attack, it may be assumed that depth of water will be one of the factors considered by an attacking force. . . .[26]

Although there was a noticeable shift from a statement of unfeasibility to the assumption that water depth would be one of the factors taken into account by the adversary, the fact of the matter is that an overall sense of invulnerability persisted. On the basis of the available information, Admiral Kimmel and his staff concluded that "the danger of a successful torpedo attack on Pearl Harbor was negligible."[27]

In short, then, there seems to be little question that, in view of their perceptions of Japanese capabilities, the Americans, both in Washington and in Honolulu, did not feel very vulnerable with respect to Pearl Harbor. This sense of invulnerability *was not founded* on the notion that Japan would recognize its inferior status as a world power and, thus, come to the logical conclusion that a war with the United States would be a self-defeating endeavor. To be sure, this belief had been held for a period of time by some of Washington's decision makers, especially within the army and the State Department. However, as it became clearer that the negotiations would not bear any positive result and that Japan had no intention of abandoning its objectives, such an opinion was replaced by the view that, if the Philippines were attacked, the threat on Pearl Harbor would recede because Japan lacked the capabilities to undertake more than one major operation at a time. In addition, it was assumed that the shallow waters at the harbor would have discouraged any incentive that may have remained among Japan's strategists to launch a major attack against Pearl Harbor.

According to Roberta Wohlstetter, the main reason the United States failed to avert surprise was that it did not ask itself whether Japan could risk striking Great Britain (by attacking one of its colonies) without striking at the United States, in view of the Anglo–American alliance.[28] She adds that the Japanese Imperial Council had discussed at length such a question before adopting the Pearl Harbor attack plan, and so had the Americans earlier in 1941. If such was the case, and we agree that it was, then why did the Americans fail to raise the same point later on?

The answer is quite simple. To begin with, as already noted, United States leaders operated on the premise that an attack on British possessions by Japan would bring United States military forces into the war. But in the United States' view, Japan's knowledge of this would *not* lead Japan to attack Pearl Harbor, because it was thought that Japanese leaders shared the United States' view of the military infeasibility of such an attack. American leaders did not come across any type of information that would have challenged their low sense of vulnerability with respect to Pearl Harbor. To begin with, the United States Army and Navy never found out how successful Japan had been in augmenting its naval and air power, and in improving the quality of the operating personnel.[29] Second, the United States had long been aware that Japan's naval strategy had been defensive. Therefore, when American Naval Intelligence lost track of the four Japanese carriers during the three weeks preceding December 7, navy intelligence analysts continued to assume that the carriers were staying near the home waters to provide air cover, and were communicating on low-frequency short-range wave-lengths, just as they had done during the French Indochina ultimatum.[30]

It is essential to keep in mind that the analyses conducted early in 1941 with respect to the likelihood of an attack on Pearl Harbor were, as Wohlstetter puts it, "theoretical projections of possible methods of enemy attack."[31] To gain credibility and acceptance among members of the American intelligence circle, it would have to have been demonstrated that the Japanese had the means to implement such a hypothetical attack. In other words, had the Americans learned that Japan had succeeded in overcoming technological problems with respect to its aerial torpedoes and that its navy had switched from a defensive naval strategy to an offensive one, it is reasonable to speculate that their sense of vulnerability with respect to Pearl Harbor would have increased substantially. Moreover, one can assume that more active and energetic efforts would have been made to scout thoroughly the western waters of the Pacific.

It is worth noting that, although Wohlstetter is very critical of the American estimates of Japanese intentions with respect to Pearl Harbor, she concedes on numerous instances that the United States lacked the data that would have induced its leaders to take seriously the possibility of such an attack. For instance, she concludes her review of the information available to Commander Edwin Layton, Admiral Kimmel's fleet intelligence officer, with the observation that it *justified a prediction* that the major Japanese effort would be directed at Great Britain, particularly in Malaya, and not at the United States.[32] At another point, while summarizing the information that intelligence officers had been able to gather via MAGIC, Wohlstetter acknowledges that there was nothing in it that established clearly that Pearl Harbor was to be included in the Japanese plan of attack.[33] She reaffirms this impression when she notes that during the final week in November the president and his closest associates did not receive any information that would have suggested any change in their perception that Japan planned to pursue a course of expansion in Southeast Asia without coming into direct conflict with the United States via Pearl Harbor.[34] Finally, in her summary, Wohstetter adds that, although American decision makers had an impressive amount of information, they had neither a complete list of Japan's targets in Southeast Asia nor accurate knowledge of its capabilities or its willingness to accept very high risks.[35]

It should also be noted that even after conducting one of the most thorough analyses of the events that preceded the attack on Pearl Harbor, Gordon Prange is unable to support his argument that the United States should have been able to avert surprise. Prange contends that "all the American failures and shortcomings that contributed to the Japanese victory at Pearl Harbor stemmed from the root disbelief that the Japanese would undertake the risky venture."[36] Prange has overstated his argument. He is correct in noting that the United States was convinced that Japan would not engage in such a risky venture, but he fails to point out that the Japanese went out of their way to ensure that such disbelief would remain constant. He acknowledges this point indirectly in two instances. First, he agrees that the wind codes intercepted before December 7 would not have added anything to what it was already known regarding the critical character of the relations between the United States and Japan.[37] Second, while discussing the public attitude in the United States regarding developments in the Far East, Prange notes that the American public was "not warned of the danger approaching Hawaii for the simple reason that *nobody in Washington knew or suspected it.*"[38]

We have already established that, although the Japanese sought to deceive the Americans during the final phase of their strategy by continuing negotiations, the United States was successful in inferring that this was their intended objective. Before moving to the last point in this section, however, it will be helpful to ascertain whether the signals coming from the European theater helped Japan camouflage its own threatening signals.

According to Wohlstetter, the United States was less attentive to what the Japanese were planning partly because the signals coming from Europe regarding the threat to Great Britain and the Soviet Union were announcing danger more frequently and more specifically than those coming from the Far East.[39] Although Wohlstetter is right, it is quite unlikely that the Japanese leaders intentionally used the war in Europe to camouflage their own activities. Japan wanted to attack Pearl Harbor in December, not because it thought the Americans would be more attentive to developments in Europe than in Asia, but because it was running out of oil, was concerned about the weather, and was aware that by delaying the attack it was facilitating the strengthening of the United States navy. It is possible, however, that the Japanese leaders decided to exploit the situation in Europe after making the decision to attack Pearl Harbor. In order not to compete with the threats coming from the European theater, Japan had to ensure that its signals would announce danger less frequently and less specifically than those originating in Europe. By keeping the American policy makers' sense of vulnerability low, Japan was, in fact, keeping its signals from competing with those from Europe.

All in all, the United States was surprised not because its information processing was hindered by groupthink[40] or because of the initial predisposition of the American decision makers to believe that Pearl Harbor would not be attacked.[41] The United States failed to avert surprise because Japan chose a strategy of surprise that was successful in exploiting the image the American leaders had of Japan's capabilities, behavioral style, and approach to calculating political action.

Surprise on Yom Kippur, October 1973

For the most part, intelligence analysts agree that Egypt and Syria surprised Israel. Disagreement centers on whether the two Arab states were successful in misleading Israel. On the one hand, scholars such as Brecher, Shlaim, and Handel argue that Israeli policy makers misled themselves because of their strict adherence to the *Concept*. These analysts are reiterating mainly the conclusions arrived at by the Agranat Report. On the other hand, Major

General Chaim Herzog claims that, although there were numerous indicators that should have given rise to concern, they were offset by perhaps twice the number of signs showing that there was no real cause for alarm. Our stand lies between these two arguments. We will try to demonstrate that Israel was surprised not so much because of its adherence to the *Concept,* but because the two Arab states succeeded in reinforcing the specific images held by Israel's decision makers.

Crucial to Egypt–Syria's strategy of surprise was the amount of time it would take Israel to mobilize fully its regular and reservist forces. The goal of any international actor attempting a *time* surprise attack is to minimize his target's warning time. A would-be surpriser's main concern is not so much to ensure that his target will not learn *when* he will be attacked, but that he will not learn early enough to be able to have his forces fully mobilized by the time the attack takes place. To avoid meeting the full brunt of Israel's regular army and mobilized reservists, Egyptian planners concluded that they had to cut down Israel's learning period to four or five days.[42]

Did the two Arab states succeed in surprising Israel with respect to the time of the attack? In a spectrum between zero warning and full alert, Israel was partially surprised in the sense that its military forces were not fully mobilized when the attack took place.[43] There is very little question that in view of the information available, Israel could have broadened its warning time. It is quite doubtful, however, that they could have concluded before October 1 that a joint Arab attack would soon ensue.[44]

On September 24, Israeli intelligence reported the concentration of more than six hundred Syrian tanks, over one hundred artillery batteries, and three infantry divisions along the border. Major General Yizhak Hoffi, the commander of Israel's northern front, voiced his concern about Syria's new deployment of troops at a general staff meeting. General Zeira, the Israeli chief of military intelligence, reassured the members at the meeting that Syria was merely conducting its annual maneuvers. Dayan, however, was worried enough to order the addition of a brigade and some heavy artillery units in the Golan Heights.[45]

A few days later, a critical event took place. Intelligence analysts in any one day receive an abundance of signals coming from a variety of foreign sources and must decide which should be given priority. Although a highly organized bureaucracy is able to handle more than one important set of signals simultaneously, it is clear that on some occasions decision makers will be so concerned with one set that they might overlook others. On September 28, 1973, two Arab gunmen held up a train carrying Soviet Jews from Moscow to Vienna, took five Jews and one Austrian customs official as hostages, and demanded that Austria close a transit center in Vienna called Schonau Castle, which was being used by Soviet Jews on their way to

Israel. It is not fully known whether the Syrians or the Egyptians were behind this act, but, because the group that executed the operation was based in and controlled by Syria, it is difficult to discard the argument that the Arabs might have had something to do with the designing of the plan for the purpose of distracting the attention of the Israeli government. Insofar as Israel was concerned, there is no question that from September 28 until the morning before the war broke out Israel and its government were obsessed by the Austrian incident.[46]

In the meantime, Israeli intelligence continued to monitor Egypt–Syria's military activities. On Monday, October 1, Israeli intelligence reported the deployment of Syrian tanks and heavy artillery from their rear positions to locations just opposite the Israeli outposts. It was also noticed that some units that had been previously stationed on the Jordanian frontier had been moved to Golan. Israel's intelligence analysts did not alter their earlier estimations. To begin with, they pointed out, Syria still had its forces in a defensive formation. Furthermore, they added, the movement of troops away from the Jordanian border was simply a gesture of good will toward Jordan.[47]

The Israeli intelligence community had also been following with great concern the deployment of Egyptian troops. With the commencement of the Egyptian maneuvers, a significant increase in the degree of activity by the canal was noted. More important, it was noticed that the maneuvers were the biggest that Egypt had ever carried out. Nevertheless, not much was made of this deployment, because the size of the maneuvers had been increasing every year. The United States Central Intelligence Agency, however, pointed out that this was the first time in several years that the Egyptians had maneuvered in formations as large as full divisions, and that they had hooked up a very complex field communications network. The Israelis were informed about these new developments and asked whether they indicated that Egypt was getting ready for an assault. Israel's intelligence analysts gave little credence to the concern voiced by the Americans, but as a precaution put the army on its southern front on alert on September 26.[48]

On October 1, Israeli intelligence reported the beginning of an extensive Egyptian military exercise. It also reported earth-moving activity, the clearing of mine fields along the approaches to the canal, and preparations of areas for bridges and pontoons. Israeli intelligence noticed that Egyptian troops, in conjunction with maneuvers, set new mines at other points and closed many of the old descents to the water. Israel's response was to put its navy on full alert.[49]

On October 3, two major meetings took place among members of Israel's government. In the earlier meeting, held between Meir and her closest associates, Dayan and Elazar voiced their concern that Egyptian and Syrian maneuvers were coordinated. Brigadier Aru Shalev, the assistant to the director of military intelligence, rejected the possibility of an Arab attack because as he put it, "there has been no change in the Arab assessment of the balance of forces in Sinai such that they could go to war."[50] That same evening Meir convened a cabinet meeting. Most of the discussion centered on the Austrian incident and Meir's failure to persuade Austria's Prime Minister Bruno Kriesky to reconsider his decision to close the transit center.[51]

On the following day, the partial alert that had been in effect for some days at the Southern Command was relaxed by special order of the general staff.[52] That same night, however, Major General Shmuel Gonen, commander of the Southern Command region, was informed that through the night the Egyptians had been carrying on unusual earth-removal operations along the northern sector of the canal.[53]

In the early hours of Friday, October 5, Syria redeployed its heavy artillery from the northernmost sector of the Syrian line to the south to cover the length of the Israeli front. Along with its heavy artillery, Syria concentrated 900 tanks and 140 artillery batteries. That same morning a meeting of Israel's general staff was called. Several of the parties present became extremely concerned about the new developments along the Suez Canal. It was noted that Egypt had fifty-six batteries of artillery, bringing the total in the forward areas up to 194. Moreover, it was reported that all five infantry divisions were fully deployed, that all five concentration areas for bridging and crossing equipment were partially filled up, and that the ramps were occupied by platoons of tanks along the entire canal.[54] Participants at the meeting were informed also of the evacuation of Soviet advisers and technicians from Egypt and Syria. Although it was not clear why the Soviets were evacuating their advisers and families, evidence that Egypt and Syria might be getting ready to attack was abundant. General Zeira, however, still believed that the probability of an Arab attack was very low.[55] In view of these developments, the Israeli Army and Air Force were placed on a high state of alert and leaves were cancelled, but the mobilization of reserves and additional measures were delayed until the intelligence picture became clearer.[56]

Finally, on October 6, at 3:00 A.M., Israeli intelligence concluded that an attack was imminent and that it would take place around 6:00 P.M. of that same day. The general mobilization of Israel's reserve units began six hours after the definitive information on the approaching war had been received. At 2:00 P.M., four hours earlier than predicted, Egyptian and Syrian forces opened fire along the entire front line.

The development of events from September 24 on indicates that Israel could have justified ordering a full mobilization just after October 1. What Israel lacked was a piece of critical information that would have supported an earlier full mobilization. The precautionary measures a state will take to protect itself from a potential aggressor is largely a function of how vulnerable it feels. If Israel did not take greater precautionary measures earlier, it is mainly because it did not feel very vulnerable. Israel was unaware that Egypt and Syria intended to seek a joint limited objective. Moreover, Israel's principal leaders did not know that the Arab states had dramatically improved their overall capabilities. For instance, it was not until Monday evening, two and a half days after the war had begun, that Israel's high command came to realize that the SAM-6s used by the Egyptians were being fired at a density much greater than in any other conflict. As Moshe Dayan put it: "I doubt whether there is another place in the entire world that is protected by such a dense array of modern missiles."[57] Moreover, very little was known about the effectiveness and performance of such missiles along with the SAM-7s and the radar-controlled anti-aircraft 2SU23-4 gun.[58] With respect to Egypt's decision to arm its first way across the canal with antitank weapons, Moshe Dayan indicated Israel's ignorance when he stated, "Our effort to bring up the tanks to the canal to prevent the erection of the bridges cost us very dear. We hadn't anticipated that [the missile attack by the first wave]."[59]

The fact that Dayan was surprised with respect to Egypt's military power and doctrine does not, in and by itself, prove that Israel's surprise can be attributed to Egypt's strategy. To be sure, Israel had no way of knowing that Egypt–Syria had decided to seek a more limited objective nor that they had dramatically altered their military doctrine. But, as is made clear by Handel, the quantities and performance of antitank and antiaircraft missiles (including the SAM-6) were known by Israeli military intelligence and the air force, tank corps, and other headquarters.[60] Thus, from this perspective it could be suggested that, had the Israelis used this information to reassess their vulnerability, they would have concluded that its low value could no longer be justified and that additional security measures had to be taken.

The problem with this line of argument is that it does not take into consideration the attempts by Egypt–Syria to misinform Israel with respect to their ability to incorporate the new weapons into their own military structure.[61] Not only did the Israelis accept the view that the two Arab states were trying to project, but, more importantly, this forced perception led them to conclude that there was no need to reassess their sense of vulnerability, at least in the short run.

In short, Handel's argument that the technological surprise suffered by Israel was not inevitable because the information regarding the military capability of Egypt–Syria was available to its intelligence analysts is not entirely accurate. Israel, from the outset, was convinced that its two Arab rivals would have problems incorporating their newly acquired weapons into their military structure. But Israel's willingness to adhere to this assessment of its opponents was not independent of the information available to its intelligence analysts. Israel was surprised because Egypt–Syria managed to disguise how quickly their troops had learned to use the Soviet weapons effectivey.

In addition, during the time that Egypt and Syria were deploying their forces, their leaders never attempted to reduce the concern of the Israeli policy makers regarding the possibility that Israel would be their target by proclaiming that they had some other target in mind. Past behavior and geography precluded such a means of deception. However, Israel might have centered its attention more on the developments on the northern and southern fronts had its attention not been drawn by the kidnapping of the Soviet Jews in Austria.

One must also bring into the picture the role that negotiation and the cry-wolf syndrome played in constraining Israel's freedom of action. History made it impossible for Sadat to use negotiation to moderate the level of tension and mistrust Israel felt toward Egypt. The evidence, however, supports our speculation that the Egyptian leader sent his foreign minister to Washington hoping to persuade Kissinger that Egypt would rather negotiate than engage in a new round of war so that the American secretary of state would find it very difficult to justify aid to Israel if it decided to pre-empt. Israel acquiesced to the demand and paid a price much higher than it had ever imagined.

Finally, even if Israel had wanted to mobilize, it could not have afforded to respond fully to another false alarm; the memory of the costs accrued during the last false alarm was very fresh in the minds of its policy makers. In this context, therefore, one could argue that the cry-wolf syndrome was wisely exploited by the Arabs. On the one hand, it reinforced Israel's belief that it had no reason to feel vulnerable; on the other hand, it made it very costly for Israel to respond to unclear signals with a full mobilization.

Conclusion

The two cases just discussed indicate quite clearly that the target and time strategies of surprise selected by the initiators of the attacks were heavily dependent on the initial preconceptions of their respective victims. To acknowledge this fact, however, is not the same as stating that the victims were surprised because of their refusal to reassess their own preconceptions. This kind of linkage can be argued only after it has been established that the victims had enough information to warrant the taking of such a step. Neither the United States in 1941 nor Israel in 1973 had the type of critical information necessary to trigger a thorough re-evaluation. Both victims failed, in large measure, because their respective adversaries went to great lengths to ensure that the initial preconceptions would remain intact. Japan in 1941 and Egypt–Syria in 1973 resorted to a series of deceptive measures to reinforce the impression held by their respective adversaries that they had little reason to feel vulnerable. Moreover, in the case of Israel, its two attackers took numerous steps to constrain Israel's determination and ability to pre-empt a major Arab attack.

Thus, it could be proposed that, if an international actor attempts to achieve surprise with respect to target or time, his chances of being successful are inversely related to his victim's sense of vulnerability and directly related to his own ability to estimate and control his victim's sense of vulnerability. Finally, an international actor who hopes to achieve surprise specifically with respect to his target must not only estimate correctly his victim's sense of vulnerability and control it, but also must persuade him that he is not one of the intended targets.

Notes

1. Wohlstetter, 1962, p. 55. See also Morison, Vol. III, 1951; Jervis, 1976, p. 412; Janis, 1982, chapter 4; and Prange, 1980, chapters 75 and 80. A note on Prange's book *At Dawn We Slept* is appropriate at this point. This book is undoubtedly the most detailed and precise analysis of the decisions made during the period preceding December 7, 1941. It should be of special interest to students who wish to broaden their understanding of the rationale behind the Japanese decision to attack Pearl Harbor and how the decision makers interacted while the strategy was being formulated.

2. Wohlstetter, 1962, p. 153.
3. Hearings, part 14, 1946, p. 1380.
4. Ibid., p. 1347.
5. Wohlstetter, 1962, p. 337.
6. Ibid., p. 157.
7. Hearings, part 14, 1946, p. 1064.
8. Ibid., p. 1064.
9. Ibid., p. 1064.
10. Wohlstetter, 1962, p. 239.
11. Ibid., p. 241.
12. Watson, 1950, p. 450.
13. Hearings, part 39, 1946, p. 339.
14. Ibid., p. 339.
15. Ibid., part 2, p. 440.
16. Ibid., part 2, p. 440.
17. Trefousse, 1958, p. 193.
18. Wohlstetter, 1962, p. 272.
19. Ibid., p. 273.
20. Morison, Vol. III, 1951, p. 128.

21. Collier, 1969, p. 105

22. Hearings, part 22, 1946, p. 540.

23. Ibid., part 15, p. 1635.

24. Ibid., part 22, p. 350.

25. Ibid., part 33, p. 1283. Paradoxically, at this time the Japanese would have agreed with the estimate received by Admiral Kimmel. But, as noted by Prange, the Japanese were determined to overcome the many technological problems that were obstructing the effective implementation of an aerial attack against the Amercian ships anchored at Pearl Harbor. Prange, 1980, p. 159.

26. Ibid., p. 1318.

27. Ibid., part 6, p. 2509.

28. Wohlstetter, 1962, p. 277. Jervis and Prange present similar arguments when they note that, the moment the United States concluded that Japan would go to war, it should have reconsidered the possibility of Pearl Harbor's being one of the intended targets. Jervis, 1976, p. 412; Prange, 1980, chapter 81.

29. Wallen, 1968, p. 65. Also, as noted by Prange, "Washington lacked a special spy ring in Japan working independently of its official representatives to provide a steady flow of military information and to ferret out startling rumors like the one of a possible attack on Pearl Harbor." Prange, 1980, p. 32.

30. Morison, Vol. III, 1951, p. 130. Moreover, as noted by Admiral Kimmel, in the six months before the attack, "there existed a total of 134 days—in 12 separate periods—each ranging from 9 to 22 days, when the location of the Japanese carriers from radio traffic analysis was uncertain." Hearings, part 6, p. 2523.

31. Wohlstetter, 1962, p. 23.

32. Ibid., p. 55.

33. Ibid., p. 225.

34. Ibid., p. 275.

35. Ibid., p. 387.

36. Prange, 1980, p. 730.

37. Ibid., p. 361.

38. Ibid., p. 371 (emphasis added).

39. Ibid., p. 193.

40. Janis is the principal defender of this position. See Janis, 1982, chapter 4.

41. Jervis is the main proponent of this argument. See Jervis, 1976, p. 145.

42. For a more detailed discussion of this point see chapter 1, p. 25. The Israeli government had been promised a warning time of at least forty-eight to seventy-six hours. See Handel, 1983, p. 137.

43. See Handel, 1983, note 67, p. 145.

44. October 1, or five days before the attack, marked the maximal warning time Egypt–Syria calculated they could afford for Israel to have.

45. Handel, 1976, pp. 30–31; Brecher, 1980, pp. 70–71.

46. Handel, 1976, p. 32; Herzog, 1974, p. 49.

47. Handel, 1976, p. 34

48. Insight Team, 1974, p. 92. It should be remembered that on that same date Dayan placed Israeli troops in the Golan Heights on alert.

49. Handel, 1976, p. 33; Herzog, 1974, p. 45.

50. Insight Team, 1974, p. 108.

51. Ibid., p. 107.

52. Handel, 1976, p. 35.

53. Herzog, 1974, p. 46.

54. Ibid., p. 47.

55. Handel, 1976, p. 37.

56. Insight Team, 1974, p. 116

57. Insight Team, 1974, p. 189.

58. *Aviation Week,* March 16, 1975, p. 15.

59. Insight Team, 1974, p. 142.

60. Handel, 1983, note 69, p. 146.

61. We discussed this tactic earlier in this chapter. See also Handel, 1983, p. 137.

5

Surprise with Respect to Intention: Barbarossa, 1941, and the Cuban Missile Crisis, 1963

I n direct contrast to the two cases considered previously, both Germany in 1941 and the Soviet Union in 1962 sought to achieve surprise with respect to their intentions. Moreover, neither actor tried to include in its strategy the factors of time or target. However, the circumstances that led each actor to opt for a strategy of surprise with regard to intention were quite different.

Germany's Intention Strategy of Surprise, 1941

Hitler's strategy of surprise was quite complex. Initially, the strategy was designed to persuade Stalin that Great Britain, not the Soviet Union, would be Germany's next major target. As time went by, it became evident that this strategy could not work. The major problem faced by Hitler and his generals was geographical. They seem to have realized that it would be nearly impossible to persuade the Soviets that they planned to attack Britain when the bulk of Germany's armed forces was facing east.

Confronted with this dilemma, Hitler seems to have reasoned that the only way he could get the Soviets to deploy their forces to their western border, but not put them on full alert, was to encourage them to believe that, although he was dissatisfied with the state of German–Soviet relations, he did not want to resort to force to remedy the existing problems. A second objective was to prevent the Soviets from grasping the rationale for a German attack. To understand Hitler's strategy, one must consider Stalin's sense of vulnerability, the type of relationship the Soviets and the Germans had had since the signing of the nonaggression pact, Hitler's judgment of Stalin's risk calculations, and the manner in which Hitler relied on his perception of Stalin's risk calculations to exploit their relationship.

During the twelve months that preceded June 22, 1941, numerous Soviet officials had expressed the view that Hitler would not attack Russia until after he had defeated Britain. The view was founded on the premise that Germany was dependent on Soviet natural resources and lacked the means to battle a two-front war. Part of this belief was explained by Stalin to the

British ambassador to Moscow, Sir Richard Stafford Cripps, not long after the German attack. So long as the British blockade and the war continued, Stalin explained, Germany was dependent on the Soviet Union for its raw materials.[1] Stalin added that he had assumed that Hitler had deployed his forces on the eastern borders for the purpose of augmenting Germany's bargaining stand. The second aspect of the Soviet rationale was explained by Maxim Litvinov, the Soviet ambassador to the United States, on December 13, 1941. On that occasion he maintained that the Soviet leaders had not taken seriously the warnings about Hitler's intention to attack because they had assumed "that it would have been madness on his part [Hitler's] to undertake war in the East against such a powerful land as ours, before finishing the war in the West."[2]

One of the clearest indications of Stalin's conviction that Hitler would not attack in 1941 was provided by the type of economic plan he approved on June 6, 1941. The plan, which was a detailed schedule for the shift-over of Soviet industry to war production, called for the conversion of a large number of civilian plants to military purposes and the construction of defense facilities to be completed by the end of 1942—a year and a half after the German invasion of the Soviet Union was to begin.[3] As the Soviet economist G. Kravchenko put it after a careful examination of the Soviet economic plans of that period, "Stalin underevaluated the real threat of war against the Soviet Union from the side of Fascist Germany and did not believe in the possibility of attack on the USSR in the summer of 1941."[4]

Hitler's strategy of surprise was founded largely on his perceptions of the Soviet leader. He was convinced that Stalin was not an adventurist and thus would not move against a superior adversary.[5] But Hitler also believed that Stalin would always attempt to maximize Soviet gains and thus would abide by the Soviet–Nazi Pact only so long as he considered it to be in the interest of the Soviet Union.[6] Hitler's own words expressed these perceptions very clearly when he noted:

> Stalin, Russia's master, is a clever fellow. He will not take an open stand against Germany, but it must be expected that he will increasingly create difficulties in situations which are difficult for Germany. He wishes to enter upon the inheritance of impoverished Europe, is in need of success, and is inspired by the *Drang nach Westen*. Also, he is perfectly aware that after a complete German victory Russia's position would become very precarious.[7]

From these perceptions, Hitler concluded that, although Moscow was unenthusiastic about Germany's great success, it would not attack until it became stronger and Germany found itself in trouble with the West. Furthermore, he also decided that so long as Germany was the more powerful state of the two and its actions signaled a threatening intention, Stalin would go out of his way to make sure that Germany's leaders did not get the impression that the Soviet Union was planning to attack Germany.

In order to comprehend fully how Hitler must have come to decide that Stalin hoped to appease him and how Hitler exploited this realization in order to deceive Stalin, it is essential to follow closely how both leaders reacted to each other's actions. On April 29, 1939, the German chancellor gave an important speech on the subject of Danzig. The most relevant aspect of the speech was the absence of Hitler's usual tirade against Bolshevism, the Soviet Union, and Stalin. His omission served as the basis of the Soviet–Nazi Pact signed four months later.[8] Thereafter, until sometime in December 1940, Hitler sought to conceal any thought he might have had about breaking the nonaggression pact between Germany and the Soviet Union for fear that Stalin would exploit Germany's ongoing struggle with the West. Thus, when Hitler and his generals began to ponder the viability of launching an attack on the Soviet Union and to take steps to prepare for the event, they also took several precautionary measures to conceal the preparations.

From the moment it began to move its troops east until just before attacking, the German government dispersed the rumor that Great Britain would be Germany's next target.[9] From this action it could be inferred that Hitler used Britain as a false target in order to mislead Stalin and keep low his sense of vulnerability. The problem with this interpretation is that it does not account for the fact that the number of German troops moved east during that period and the style in which they were deployed should have increased Stalin's sense of vulnerability.

The redeployment of German troops to the east began sometime in August 1940. The rumor released to explain the move, as just noted, was that Germany was preparing for the invasion of Britain, and the troops were being transferred to hold training maneuvers out of the range of British bombers and reconnaissance aircraft.[10] To give greater credibility to the story, most of the German units were ordered to lay well back from the eastern frontier, were widely dispersed, and were engaged in training programs.[11]

With time, as the concentration of troops increased, the Soviets not only started to question the veracity of the German story but also, as a precautionary measure, began to redeploy their own troops toward Russia's western frontier.[12] To deflate some of the Soviet fear, on February 15, 1941, the Germans began to tout the operation to the Russians as a "deception diversion" to mislead the British about *Sea Lion*. The Germans dispatched a series of secret notices from Berlin to military attachés in several German embassies, including the one in Moscow, informing them that some eight divisions would soon be withdrawn from the Russian border and that the rumors of war were false. These notices were sent with the expectation that the information would be leaked to Soviet intelligence.[13]

Although Germany's cover stories were intended to control Stalin's sense of vulnerability, it is difficult to imagine that Hitler would have expected this strategy to succeed, particularly if one takes into account that in January 1941 the number of German divisions facing the Soviet Union was thirty-four, but by April 5 it had grown to forty-six. Furthermore, the redeployment of the forces during that same period was carried out in an obvious and aggressive manner. The German Air Force, for instance, intensified its program for the construction of airfields by building a continuous chain of aerodromes along the railway line from Poland to Lodz and, by the end of March 1941, began reconnaissance flights over Soviet territory.[14]

At first glance, Hitler's strategy seems to make very little sense. On the one hand, he was attempting to conceal his aggressive intentions vis-a-vis the Soviets by voicing his plans to attack Britain; on the other hand, he was disclosing his intention to attack the Soviets by moving his troops closer and closer to the eastern border in a very threatening fashion. But before reaching such a conclusion, one must recall the original argument as to why Hitler believed that the Soviets had to be surprised.

In order to defeat the Soviet Union, Hitler and his generals calculated that Germany had to attract the Red Army to the western border, disperse it along the border, and take it by surprise once the attack was launched. Their central concern was that, once the German attack had begun, the Soviets would attempt to retreat into Russia's hinterland. To minimize this possibility, it was proposed that the Russian front be pierced by armored spearheads, encircled from the rear, and liquidated.[15] Hitler confirmed this view on January 9, 1941, when he stated that the attack:

> should on no account turn into a frontal pushing back of the Russians. Therefore the most brutal break-throughs are necessary.[16]

It seems reasonable to infer, therefore, that a surprise attack would minimize the initial Soviet resistance and increase Germany's chances of thrusting through the Soviet resistance and encircling from the rear.

To implement this strategy, Hitler had to fulfill two potentially contradictory objectives simultaneously. On the one hand, he had to increase Stalin's sense of vulnerability to the point that the latter would deem it necessary to deploy the core of his forces close to the western border. On the other hand, he had to ensure that Stalin would not place his deployed forces on full alert. How he sought to fulfill the second objective is the topic of our next discussion.

The relationship between Germany and the Soviet Union following the signing of the nonaggression pact in September 1939 and during most of 1940 was not without disagreements; the pact, however, was never in danger of being dissolved. The main impetus behind the attempt to keep the relationship from faltering came from Hitler. During late 1940, just as he was considering the pros and cons of attacking the Soviet Union, Hitler was also contemplating quite seriously the idea of asking the Soviet Union to join Germany, Italy, and Japan in a grand coalition against Britain. Hitler asked Molotov, Russia's foreign secretary, to visit Berlin to discuss the conditions under which the Soviet Union would be willing to become a member of such an alliance. Molotov arrived in Berlin around the middle of November 1940. Two weeks after the meeting, the Soviet foreign secretary informed the German government that the Soviet Union would join the grand coalition under four conditions. The Soviets demanded the withdrawal of German troops from eastern Germany, the acceptance by Hitler of a mutual-assistance pact between the Soviet Union and Bulgaria to assure Soviet security in the Balkan area, the recognition of the area in the general direction of the Persian Gulf as the center of Soviet aspirations, and the renunciation by Japan of concession rights for coal and oil in Sakhalin.[17]

It is unlikely that any of the conditions set by Stalin would have placed a heavy burden on Germany or that they would have precluded Hitler's reaching a compromise if he had wanted to. By then, however, Hitler had decided that the Soviet Union would be Germany's next victim, and thus he never bothered to respond to Molotov's proposal. On December 17, Molotov informed the German ambassador to Moscow, Friedric Warner Schulenburg, that "the Soviet Government was astonished that it had not yet received from Germany any answer to its settlement of position of November 25."[18]

The events that transpired between the time Molotov visited Berlin and his communication with the German ambassador to Moscow are relevant for two reasons. First, the events marked the last time, at least until the outbreak of the war, that the Soviets would approach the Germans with a set of demands. Second, Hitler's original proposal for a grand coalition and his subsequent refusal to acknowledge the Soviet response might have helped Stalin to rationalize, as the threats from Germany intensified, that the German leader had no intention of attacking, but was simply increasing the pressure so that the Soviet Union would abandon, or at least moderate, the conditions under which it would join Germany to fight Britain.

Negotiations between the Soviets and the Germans with respect to the division of territory were equally affected by Hitler's change in behavior. According to one of the secret protocols of the Nazi–Soviet Pact of 1939, Germany was to receive a portion of Lithuania once the Soviet Union had annexed it. In July 1940, however, Molotov informed Germany that the cession of the area would be extremely inconvenient for the Soviet Union and requested an agreement that would leave the territory in question permanently with Lithuania. Germany responded that it would be willing to consider the request if the compensation were adequate. The Soviets offered 3,860,000 gold dollars, or the equivalent in goods, delivered within two years. On September 9, Germany responded that the offer was not acceptable, but that Germany was still willing to negotiate and would soon propose a counteroffer. The counteroffer was not made until more than three and a half months later, on December 28. At that time, Germany asked that the Soviets pay as compensation raw materials worth 13 million gold dollars. Hitler extended the offer against the advice of his chief trade negotiator, Karl Schnurre, who had argued that it was unreasonable for Germany to ask for raw materials that the Soviet economy could scarcely provide. The Soviets finally agreed to deliver double their original offer and at a more accelerated pace.[19]

Trade negotiations also became a test of wills between the Soviets and the Germans. By September 1940, the delivery of goods from Germany to the Soviet Union had fallen substantially. Concerned about the possibility that the trend would continue, Moscow warned Berlin that, if it did not augment the deliveries, the Soviet Union would have to suspend its exports to Germany. Hitler's reaction was swift. Aware of the importance of Soviet raw materials to Germany's war economy, he immediately directed that Soviet orders be given top priority.[20] By the beginning of March 1941, the roles had been reversed; it was the shipment of goods from the Soviet Union to Germany that was behind schedule. The reduction in the delivery of raw materials reflected Stalin's dissatisfaction with Germany's aggressive behavior in southeastern Europe. However, two weeks later, as rumors of a pending German attack on the Soviet Union began to intensify, Stalin became more cautious and ordered the immediate increase of deliveries to Germany.[21] In the meantime, Hitler was ordering exactly the opposite. For instance, late in 1939 the Soviets had purchased from Germany an unfinished cruiser, the *Lutzov*. As part of the agreement, German specialists would help finish the cruiser, and Germany would supply the rest of the parts necessary to complete it. By April 1941, however, parts were arriving late, and the German specialists were starting to return home. By the end of May, out of the several hundred specialists assigned to help build the *Lutzov*, only twenty remained at the shipyard; none was left by June 15. A similar trend became noticeable with respect to German cargo ships on Soviet waters; by June 16, they had all left.[22]

The way in which Hitler meddled in the affairs of states that were of great strategic value to Moscow also changed noticeably. Prior to the invasion of the Soviet Union, Hitler concluded that to carry out the operation effectively, Germany first had to consolidate its power in the Balkans. With respect to Rumania, Hitler was aided greatly by Stalin's greed. On March 6, 1940, Germany and Rumania reached a provisional agreement whereby Rumania would receive armaments from Germany in exchange for petroleum. The Soviets, in the meantime, had their own plans with respect to Rumania. On June 23, 1940, Molotov made it clear to the German ambassador in Moscow that the Soviet Union would resort to force if Rumania did not relinquish control over Bessarabia and Bucovina and that it expected Germany to support the Soviets in their action. After intense negotiations and numerous new threats from the Soviets, the Germans succeeded in persuading the Rumanians to acquiesce to all of Moscow's demands. On June 28, 1940, Rumania gave in and relinquished the territories demanded by the Soviet Union.[23]

Stalin's desire for new territory was not satisfied. At the end of October 1940, certain Danube islands located within Rumania's frontiers were occupied by Soviet troops. Hitler, not wanting to antagonize Stalin, ruled out any strong language or behavior against such action.[24] Stalin won both rounds, but in the process he increased Rumania's antagonism.

It did not take long for Hitler to test how far the Rumanians were willing to go to get back at the Russians. On December 13, 1940, Hitler issued *Directive No. 20: Operation Marita.* The directive spelled out his plans in the Balkans. In order to prevent the Soviet Union and Great Britain from joining forces in the Balkans when Germany turned east and to facilitate the massing of German troops for the offensive against the Soviet Union, Hitler believed that he had to have control over northern Greece.[25] The operation called for the build-up of German troops in southern Rumania which would subsequently advance through Bulgaria—with its full authorization—to attack Greece.[26]

Hitler was aware that such action would alarm the Soviets, but he went ahead with the plan.[27] In fact, he went beyond his initial decision to attack Greece. During the early part of 1940, Germany had been making extensive concessions to secure Yugoslav accession to the Tripartite Pact. By the middle of March, Yugoslavia's leaders decided that they had to accept Hitler's terms or risk the consequences of his wrath. Two days after Yugoslavia had become a member, however, its government was toppled by a coup d'etat. Stalin, who also had been attempting to secure the cooperation of the Yugoslavs, did not waste any time. He renewed his past attempts by proposing that his government and the new Yugoslavian administration sign a friendship and nonaggression treaty. Stalin's perseverance came to a successful end on April 6, 1941, when both parties reached an agreement. But it was a short-lived triumph. On that same day, while German troops started to march into Greece, German bombs began to fall on Belgrade.[28] Stalin, fully aware that Hitler had gained the upper hand, refrained from criticizing the action and did not even acknowledge that his country and Yugoslavia had signed a friendship treaty.[29]

By April 1941, Stalin's fears about Hitler's intentions had increased substantially. The Soviet leader ordered that new troops be moved to the western border.[30] But he also directed that no military measure be taken that might be construed by the Germans as being provocative.[31] The need to be prepared for a possible German attack and to make sure that the Soviet Union would not provoke Germany to attack were emphasized until the very final hours prior to the attack on the morning of June 22, 1941.[32]

The month of May brought more of the same. Hitler had no intention of easing Stalin's mind, and Stalin continued with his attempt to persuade the Germans that the Soviet Union would not initiate any hostile action. On May 4, 1941, during a major speech to the Reichstag, Hitler discussed Germany's campaigns against Greece and Yugoslavia and its intentions in the Balkans, but did not utter a single word about the Soviet Union. His silence once again managed to unsettle Stalin. On May 7, the Russian leader took an unprecedented step; he became the new Soviet premier. The action was unprecedented because Stalin had always preferred to remain in the background while exercising complete power. As reported by Schulenburg, the German ambassador to Moscow, Stalin's main hope was that by assuming formal leadership he would be able to shorten the Soviet chain of command in order to improve, via his personal efforts, Soviet–German relations. The appearance of Stalin at the head of the Soviet government was followed immediately by two other precautionary measures. On May 9, *Pravda* published a lengthy article denying that the movement of Soviet troops was for aggressive purposes. On that same day, the delegations of Norway, Yugoslavia, and Belgium were informed that, since they had lost territories over which they exercised national sovereignty, their missions in the Soviet Union would no longer be recognized.[33]

In concurrence with these steps, Stalin ordered in May that the extension of any proposal, demand, or propaganda likely to irritate Hitler be avoided. Two cases are worth mentioning. Since February 1941, the Soviets and the Germans had been negotiating the marking of the northern part of the Soviet–German boundaries. A few weeks after the negotiations had begun, Molotov claimed that the frontiers originally laid out in 1923 had been marked unfairly and that the Soviets could not accept such injustice. By May, however, the Soviets waived their earlier claim and agreed that no change should be made in the existing frontier.[34] A similar attempt at conciliation could be witnessed in terms of Soviet propaganda. Between January and March 1941, the Comintern, via the *World News and Views,* a British communist journal, praised the Communist Parties in Germany, France, and Austria for working ceaselessly to overthrow the Nazis. In May, however, the journal subdued its tone and simply published greetings from the Communist Party in Germany, calling for a just peace and blaming the millionaires, not the Nazis, for the ongoing war in the West.[35]

Finally, as the month of June began, Stalin took one last, desperate, conciliatory step. On June 13, at seven o'clock in the evening, just when the crowds were returning home from their jobs, a major announcement was blasted into the streets of Moscow via strategically placed loudspeakers. In the announcement it was denied that war between the Soviet Union and Germany was imminent and that the mobilization and training of the re-servists of the Red Army indicated that the Soviet Union was getting ready to attack Germany.[36] Stalin's objective was to rob the Germans of any pre-text of aggression. He wanted them to realize that he knew of their prepa-rations along the border, but had no intention of responding in form. Having expressed his future course of action, Stalin waited for Hitler to reveal his plans.

Hitler, however, had no plan to disclose his intention, not when Stalin was acting just as he hoped he would. By deploying almost three times as many divisions eastward as were deployed facing the west, by taking a tougher negotiating stand than he had during 1940, and by pursuing a highly ag-gressive military policy against states in the Balkans, Hitler managed to incite Stalin's sense of vulnerability to the point that the Russian leader deemed it necessary to order the fortification of Russia's western border. To avoid the possibility that Stalin might go further and place the Red Army on full alert, and to ensure that it would be taken by surprise by an attack from Germany, Hitler did what he could to encourage Stalin's belief that the German mili-tary build-up was for diplomatic bargaining purposes. Aware that Stalin was not ready to go to war yet and that he would attempt to deny Germany of any justification to attack, Hitler covered his intention with a blanket of silence. Hitler's hope seems to have been that, as Stalin realized that Ger-many was dissatisfied with some of the agreements it had reached in the past with the Soviet Union, he would begin to transmit signals indicating that the Soviet Union wanted to reach an amicable solution to their differ-ences. An unalerted Red Army was the main behavior sought by Hitler, and the main appeasing signal he hoped the Soviet leader would transmit.

In sum, Hitler sought to conceal his intention in a clever and complex way. He did not attempt to keep Stalin's sense of vulnerability low. Initially, the German leader sought to ensure that Germany's eastern borders would not be threatened so that he could freely commit his armies to the west. Hitler appeased his eastern adversary by acquiescing to many of his de-mands. On accepting the possibility that a confrontation with Britain on its own territory could be very costly and could tarnish his newly gained aura of invincibility, Hitler decided that it was time to render powerless the Rus-sian bear.

This task required a great deal of finesse. Hitler, aware of Germany's inability to engage in a protracted war simultaneously with Britain and the Soviet Union, concluded that in order to prevent this problem he had to disguise his true intentions from his two rivals. All in all, the task of mis-leading the British was the least complicated aspect of Hitler's strategy. Hitler sought to convey the impression that Britain could be his next target by deploying close to fifty German divisions throughout Western Europe and by spreading the rumor that Germany's eastwardly deployed troops were on training maneuvers, far from Britain's reach, preparing for its invasion.

The strategy to mislead the Soviets had to accomplish two distinct but closely connected objectives. On the one hand, Stalin had to be persuaded to deploy the Red Army to the west. On the other hand, it was essential that the Russian leader not feel threatened to the point that he would accelerate the rebuilding of his country's defenses and place his forces on full alert. The fulfillment of the two objectives was deemed necessary by Hitler and his generals because they believed that, if Germany fought the Soviet Union before defeating Britain, the war had to be won in a short period of time near the Soviet western border. One of the main fears of the German leaders was that Germany would be engaged in a protracted war in Russia's hinterland and that Churchill would exploit the situation by launching an invasion of Western Europe.

Hitler erected his strategy of surprise around two beliefs. First, he argued that the Soviets were convinced that it would be detrimental for Germany to attack the Soviet Union before defeating Britain in view of the fact that Germany was highly dependent on Soviet natural resources and lacked the means to battle a two-front war. Second, Hitler speculated that Stalin, regardless of how unenthusiastic he might be about Germany's great military success, had a great deal of respect for its power and thus would make great efforts to persuade the German leaders that he had no belligerent intention if threatened by them. Based on these two beliefs, Hitler altered the east-west distribution of German troops so that the number of German divisions facing east was almost three times greater than the number pointing west, took a tougher negotiating stand against the Soviets than he had during the year immediately after the signing of the Moscow Pact,[37] and pursued a highly aggressive military policy against states in the Balkans that were of great strategic value to the Soviet Union.

Finally, so that Stalin would refrain from accelerating the build-up of his country's defenses and from placing his forces on full alert, Hitler sought to keep the Soviet leader's sense of vulnerability at a manageable level.[38] Thus, Hitler continued to promulgate the view that Britain might still be his forthcoming victim and covered his intentions with a blanket of silence. Hitler expected that Stalin would interpret his unwillingness to respond to any of the proposals forwarded by the Soviets as an indication that the door for conciliation remained open, but that Germany expected more from the Soviet Union. Furthermore, Hitler hoped that Stalin, fearful of engaging in a war against a better-prepared adversary, would take advantage of the assumed opportunity to avert war and would express his nonhostile disposition by keeping his deployed troops on a peace status and by not accelerating the reconstruction of his country's defenses.

Moscow's Intention Strategy of Surprise, 1962

One of the first things that Moscow must have realized early in its decision to install missiles in Cuba was that the only reliable option it had was to adopt an intention-type strategy of surprise. Moscow could not settle for a target-type of surprise. Having been Cuba's major supplier of weapons since 1960, Moscow was aware that any disclosure of its determination to install strategic missiles outside the Soviet Union would have elicited a dramatic increase in the surveillance of Cuba by the Americans. Moreover, any attempt to confine surprise simply to the *time* of such a move would have prompted a similar reaction.

The shortest and most reliable path to surprise by any international actor, when it is available, is to do what his adversary is convinced he will not do. Moscow had a solid understanding of this dictum. Since 1949, when the Soviet Union conducted its first successful atomic test, Moscow had never placed strategic nuclear weapons outside Soviet territory, not even in other Soviet-bloc countries. Moscow's long adherence to this policy had a noticeable effect in the United States. The consensus among Kremlinologists was that the Soviet Union would not station offensive nuclear missiles in Cuba. These experts relied on three arguments to support their conclusion. Their fundamental thesis was that the Russians had been extremely careful in the past not to station strategic missiles outside their own territory.[39] Second, they contended that, if Khrushchev were to alter Moscow's long-standing policy, Cuba would not be his testing ground for two reasons. To begin with, the distances to be traversed by air and sea between the Soviet Union and Cuba made the deployment of missiles vulnerable to American interception. Furthermore, it was thought that the Castro regime was too unstable to be trusted either as the recipient of strategic weapons or as the host of strategic weapons that remained under Soviet control.[40]

The third argument presented by the Kremlinologists was that Khrushchev would not introduce missiles in Cuba because he was a rational man.[41] The implication was that only a lunatic would risk discovery by the Americans while deploying the missiles and/or placing such dangerous weapons in a country as unstable as Cuba.

In brief, Moscow's long-standing policy of not installing strategic nuclear weapons outside Soviet territory seems to have prejudiced Washington to expect a continuation of the policy. Khrushchev seems to have relied on such an expectation to camouflage his change in policy. Put differently, originally it was Moscow's policy toward the deployment of strategic missiles that made Washington experience a low sense of vulnerability with respect to the potential installation of Soviet missiles in Cuba. Subsequently, it was Washington's low sense of vulnerability that convinced Moscow that it could alter its course dramatically at a relatively low risk.

If the shortest and most successful path to surprise is to do the unexpected, the simplest way of failing is to assume that surprise can be achieved without concealing that the expected has been replaced by the unexpected, especially when the implementation of the new policy is likely to require a considerable period of time. Moscow, aware that it would have to overcome numerous obstacles before it could claim victory, took various steps to keep Washington's sense of vulnerability at a low level.

Moscow's first step was to try to fuse the deployment of the offensive missiles with the shipment of conventional weapons. The first load of Soviet conventional weapons arrived in Cuba during the summer of 1960. The Kennedy administration estimated that by the summer of 1962 Cuba had received jet fighters, military boats, and approximately 100,000 tons of ground weapons and equipment.

During the first half of 1962 there was a noticeable reduction in the shipment of Soviet war materiel to Cuba. The reduction lasted until July of that same year.[42] Moreover, both the Cubans and the Soviets publicly acknowledged, for the first time, that the Soviet Union had been helping Cuba to strengthen its defensive capabilities. On January 10, 1962, Fidel Castro, while being interviewed by *Izvestia* and *Pravda,* boasted that the revolution had "created a powerful revolutionary armed forces that guarantees the defense of the conquests of the revolution against any imperialist efforts."[43] Castro ended the interview by acknowledging that the rebuilding of Cuba's armed forces would not have been possible without the extensive help of the Soviet Union. Some months later, near the end of May, Khrushchev publicly stated for the first time that Moscow had been supplying Cuba with arms to rebuild its defenses. He repeated the message at the beginning of June.[44]

The shipment of Soviet war equipment increased dramatically in late July 1962. The original Soviet expectation seems to have been that, although there had been a lull of approximately seven months in the shipment of arms, the United States would continue to infer that only defensive weapons were being delivered to Cuba. Past public statements by Castro and Khrushchev give a certain degree of credence to this view.

Washington, in the meantime, had been keeping a close watch on the increase in Soviet ships docking in Cuba. On August 24, the director of intelligence of the State Department, Roger Hilsman, announced during a background briefing that the Soviets had resumed large-scale deliveries of weapons to Cuba. The cargoes included large quantities of transportation, electronic, and construction equipment such as communication vans, radar vans, trucks, and mobile-generator units. Hilsman added that some crates might also include surface-to-air missiles (SAMs). He concluded by noting that three to five thousand Soviet military technicians had disembarked in Cuba.[45]

American reaction to the news was one of concern. Public displeasure over the way in which the Kennedy Administration had been handling the earlier deployment of Soviet weapons into Cuba had already become an issue that the Republican Party was ready to exploit during the 1962 congressional elections. The fresh news of Soviet military shipments to Cuba acted as the catalyst to the surge of Republican demands for immediate action. Calls for invasion of Cuba and/or the creation of an inter-American "peace fleet" to prevent further shipments of Soviet military supplies were made by several ranking Republican senators.

In response to Republican indictments, President Kennedy stated at his press conference on August 29 that there was no evidence of Soviet troops in Cuba, only of an "expanded advisory and technical mission."[46] He further emphasized that his government was watching the Cuban situation "with the closest attention."[47] The Kennedy Administration maintained its promise; within a week after the August 29 press conference, the American public was informed that the presence of anti-aircraft SAMs in Cuba had been confirmed and that the Soviets had also deployed MIG-21 fighter aircraft.[48]

Moscow, in the meantime, began to realize that it had to do something to persuade Washington that none of the new weapons being delivered to Cuba would pose a threat to the United States. Moscow chose two means to allay Washington's growing concern—one public, the other private. In a communique issued September 2 concerning the visit to Moscow by Cuba's Minister of Industries Ernesto Guevara, the Kremlin announced that it was helping Cuba with armaments to ensure its sovereignty and independence. Such action, the communique added, posed a threat to nobody, because the weapons being deployed were solely for defensive purposes. To ensure that President Kennedy and his associates would not overlook the last and possibly most crucial aspect of the message, the Soviet ambassador in Washington, Anatoly Dobrynin, met on September 4 with Attorney General Robert Kennedy. At the meeting, Ambassador Dobrynin reassured Kennedy that no ground-to-ground missiles or other major offensive weapons were being brought into Cuba.[49] A week later, on September 11, Moscow once again disclaimed any hostile intent toward the United States. It stated that the "armaments and military equipment sent to Cuba are designed exclusively for defensive purposes." It added:

> Our nuclear weapons are so powerful in their explosive force and the Soviet Union has so powerful rockets to carry these nuclear warheads, that there is no need to search for sites for them beyond the boundaries of the Soviet Union.[50]

President Kennedy was not appeased by Moscow's disclaimer. Two days later, at a press conference, he acknowledged that the new shipment of weapons did not constitute a threat to the United States. But, warned the president, if Cuba were to become at any time an offensive military base for the Soviet Union, the United States would take whatever measures were necessary to protect its own security and that of its allies.[51] To ensure that Moscow did not take his threat lightly, President Kennedy asked Congress to grant him standby authority to call up the reserves and quietly ordered that the frequency of the U-2 overflights of Cuba be doubled.

Moscow's attempt to control Washington's concern over Cuba via diplomatic means continued well into the month of October. In early October, Khrushchev's son-in-law, Aleksei Adzhubei, flew to Washington to interview President Kennedy. He informed the president that Moscow was sending only defensive weapons to Cuba and that none of the antiaircraft missiles being deployed could reach the United States. On October 13, Ambassador Dobrynin assured Chester Bowles, a long-time aide to President Kennedy, that Moscow had no intention of placing offensive missiles in Cuba. The same message was delivered by Khrushchev to the American ambassador to the Soviet Union, Foy D. Kohler.

The Soviets used diplomacy as a means of deception as long as they could. On October 16, just a few hours after President Kennedy had been informed that Moscow had been deploying strategic missiles in Cuba, the Soviet foreign minister, Andrei Gromyko, unaware that his sincerity was being tested, assured Kennedy that none of the weapons being installed in Cuba could be used offensively.[52]

In an attempt to conceal the inconsistency of its words and its actions, Moscow relied on secrecy. To avert disclosure of the cargo, everything was unloaded at night, mainly by Russians. In addition, very few Cuban ports were used, and most of those were guarded by Soviet soldiers. Finally, the equipment, immediately after being unloaded, was transported by road in night convoys to remote areas screened by hills and woods.[53]

Moscow, however, still faced one major problem: how to install the missiles without exposing their presence. The weather seems to have played an important role.

According to Graham Allison, careful examination of Soviet moves during the deployment of the missiles raises several questions.[54] His first question deals with the Soviet failure to coordinate the installation of the SAMs and the MRBMs. Common sense and past experience, contends Allison, should have convinced the Soviets that, in order to protect the MRBMs from detection by American U-2s, they should have made the SAMs operational before beginning to construct the sites of the strategic offensive missiles. But the SAM network did not become operational until about October 27, after most of the MRBMs had achieved operational readiness.[55] The Soviets seem to have committed the same mistake with respect to the installation of radar.

By failing to complete the radar system prior to the introduction of MRBMs, notes Allison, the Soviets denied themselves a way of monitoring the U-2 flights.

Third, the Soviets proceeded with the construction of the MRBM and IRBM sites without any attempt to camouflage them. In addition, Allison points out, the Soviets could have restricted construction activity to hours of darkness to minimize detection from the U-2s. Finally, the SAM, MRBM, and IRBM sites in Cuba were built to look exactly like the SAM, MRBM, and IRBM sites in the Soviet Union.

Most of these mistakes, contends Allison, can be explained if the implementation of the policy is viewed from an organizational perspective.[56] Until 1962, Moscow had adhered strictly to the policy of not deploying strategic missiles outside Soviet territory. This policy enabled organizations to develop sets of standard operating procedures to be followed during the placement of strategic missiles. When faced with the task of deploying missiles in Cuba, the organizations responsible for implementing different aspects of the plan relied on the same rules they had used in the past without considering that there might be a pronounced incongruity between the objectives that the old rules had helped fulfill and the objectives that the installation of missiles in Cuba were designed to fulfill.

If Allison is right in arguing that the Soviet organizations proceeded with their respective tasks as if the nature of the problem were no different from those of the past, then one must conclude that there was a major flaw in Moscow's overall strategy of surprise. In other words, after taking so many diplomatic steps to persuade the Americans that Moscow had no intention of introducing offensive weapons in Cuba and after unloading the weapons under a cloud of secrecy, the Soviets failed to provide Washington with the data it needed in order to accept Moscow's contention.

Allison's explanation does not take into consideration the possibility that something about the conditions under which the missiles were going to be deployed had persuaded the Soviets that it would be feasible to rely on the same old standard operating procedures. Analysts of the Cuban Missile Crisis acknowledge that bad weather hindered American attempts to ascertain the type of weapons the Soviets were placing in Cuba. But with the exception of one individual, Arthur Schlesinger,[57] they seem to assume that it was purely coincidental that Moscow chose to install strategic missiles at the peak of the rain and hurricane seasons in Cuba. We do not share this assumption.

In order to forward an alternative explanation, two types of information must be taken into account. Throughout history, military strategists have relied on the weather to conceal the movements of their armies. The most common problem they have faced has been the failure of the weather to provide a reliable cover. When viewed from a world comparative perspective, however, the weather pattern in the Caribbean is one of the most consistent.[58] It is quite easy to predict when the rain and hurricane seasons will begin, how long they will last, and how intense they will be. In Cuba, the rainy season has two peaks. The first begins and ends in June; the second begins in August and lasts until the end of October. Furthermore, the second rain peak coincides with the tropical storm season.[59]

The second type of information that must be taken into account is the extent to which the United States was dependent on the U-2 to gather intelligence on Cuba. The type of weather under which such aircraft could fly and perform effectively is also important.

To find out what was going in Cuba, the United States relied on four sources of intelligence. The four sources were: (1) routine shipping intelligence, (2) reports from refugees, (3) reports of intelligence agents in Cuba, and (4) photographs supplied by U-2 overflights.[60]

The first three sources of intelligence rarely provided American policy makers with the hard and fresh evidence they needed to formulate policies. The first source, shipping intelligence, could not reveal the contents of the ships. Refugee reports ranged from sober observations to the wildest rumors. Reports from intelligence agents, although of higher quality than refugee reports, took from ten days to two weeks to arrive in Washington. The fastest and most accurate intelligence came from the U-2 photography.[61]

The U-2 can fly up to 4,000 miles at altitudes of fourteen miles or better. Its cameras, aimed through seven portholes in the belly, can photograph a strip of earth 125 miles wide and 3,000 miles long.[62] Its major drawback is that it loses effectiveness when the sky is 25 percent or more overcast.[63] Because of this limitation and possibly because of costs, it was established that the predicted weather, not the actual weather, would determine whether a flight would take place. If more than a 50 percent cloud cover was predicted, then the flight was usually delayed.[64]

There seems to be little doubt that the Soviets knew about the semi-monthly flights over Cuba by U-2s.[65] In addition, it is reasonable to assume that, having captured the U-2 in which Gary Powers was downed over the Soviet Union, the Soviets had learned not only about its capabilities, but also about its limitations—that is, the fact that it lost effectiveness when the sky was overcast. With these assumptions in mind, we will contend that the Soviets could have calculated that the rain and hurricane seasons would hinder the ability of the United States to discover their true intention, at least until some of their MRBMs were operational and they could exercise their own counterdeterrence.

According to United States intelligence estimates, the SAMs did not arrive in Cuba until the end of August. In addition, it has been estimated that

the first MRBMs were unloaded in Cuba around September 8.[66] Faced with
the task of màking the SAMs and the MRBMs operational, the Soviets could
have delayed the construction of the MRBMs until they had completed the
installation of the SAMs. The need to do so, however, would not have seemed
a compelling one if it had been estimated that bad weather was going to
hinder the ability of the U-2s to photograph the missiles. In other words,
why would the Soviets want to concentrate on the construction of the SAM
network when they had calculated that the wet season would make it un-
important whether they denied the U-2s free airspace over Cuba? Indeed,
the SAMs seem to have been made operational just before the end of the
rainy season, on October 27.[67]

It could be argued, of course, that it is not very safe to rely on bad
weather to cover one's actions, regardless of how accurate past weather
predictions may have been. Moreover, had the Soviets installed the SAM
network first, they could have used it to scare the Americans away during
the days that the weather was clear.

One major problem arises with this argument. Regardless of how fast
the Soviet technicians could have made the MRBMs operational after having
installed the SAMs—and it is clear that they possessed the technology to
install them in a very short period of time[68]—the Soviets would have had to
use their antiaircraft missiles to protect the nature of their activities. However, it is unrealistic to assume that Washington would have been totally
deterred from finding out what was going on in Cuba after having one of
its U-2s shot down. In fact, had a U-2 been shot down flying over Cuba
prior to the discovery of the missiles, the Kennedy Administration would
have been compelled to find out by whatever means it had available why
Moscow was so determined to deny the U-2s free air space over Cuba and
to take retaliatory measures to signal to Moscow that Washington would
not be pushed around. Washington could accept the downing of a U-2 flying
over the Soviet Union, but a U-2 over Cuba was a totally different matter.
To be cowed by the threat of losing some U-2s over Cuba would have meant
that Washington could be bullied in other regions of the Caribbean and Latin
America. It is doubtful that Moscow believed that Washington's fighting
spirit had reached such a low state.

The Soviet decision not to complete the radar system prior to the introduction of the MRBMs is closely linked to the decision to delay the construction of the SAM network. It can be argued that, since the SAMs were
not being installed, there was very little reason to set up the radar. On the
other hand, with a radar system, the Soviets would have been able to monitor U-2 activity and would have been in a better position to estimate whether
the Americans had uncovered the true nature of their activities. It is not fully
evident, however, that such information would have been of much help to
Moscow. After all, if Washington discovered that missiles were being in-

stalled in Cuba, the only thing the Soviets could do would be to continue with their efforts. Furthermore, the fact that the radar could have monitored U-2 activity does not mean that it could have ascertained whether the aircraft had spotted the missiles. The general assumption, or hope, among the Soviets seems to have been that it would be unnecessary to monitor the U-2 because the bad weather conditions would make any attempt to gain information via photographs unproductive.

Finally, since the Soviets had no intention of concealing the presence of MRBMs and IRBMs in Cuba after they had become operational, the only reason for camouflaging them and constructing site patterns different from those in the Soviet Union would have been to disguise their presence during installation. But since weather conditions would have made it difficult for the American U-2s to spot the strategic missiles, the Soviets seem to have concluded that there was no need to waste precious time—in view of the shortness of the rainy season—camouflaging the missile sites and altering their patterns.

In sum, the Kremlin sought to achieve surprise with respect to its intention, rationale, military doctrine, and capability. Moscow's intention was to deploy strategic missiles in Cuba. Its rationale for deploying the missiles was primarily to narrow the nuclear advantage held by the United States. To fulfill this objective, Moscow also had to achieve surprise with respect to its decision to change the doctrine of deploying strategic nuclear missiles solely in Soviet territory, and with respect to the true nature of its military capability in Cuba.

The Soviets relied on five measures to implement their strategy of surprise. Moscow's first step was to try to fuse, and thereby to conceal, the deployment of offensive missiles with the shipment of conventional weapons. As the sea traffic between the Soviet Union and Cuba began to intensify, Moscow tried to persuade Washington through diplomatic channels that none of the weapons being delivered could threaten the security of the United States.

Negotiation was also used to divert Washington's attention away from developments in Cuba. On September 4 and September 6, Soviet Ambassador Dobrynin tried to persuade Attorney General Robert Kennedy and Theodore Sorensen, President Kennedy's special adviser, that Moscow would not complicate or aggravate the international situation before the American congressional elections.[69] Moscow's message came as a response to an earlier warning made by Sorensen to Dobrynin. During a meeting held on August 23 at the Soviet Embassy, Sorensen warned Dobrynin that the Soviets should not assume that the upcoming congressional campaign would inhibit President Kennedy's response to any pressure in Berlin.[70] Washington's behavior may have triggered the impression in the Kremlin that a series of Russian assurances would convince the Kennedy Administration that it was safe to concentrate on the upcoming elections.[71]

Finally, to guard itself against the possibility that one of Washington's intelligence sources might monitor the presence of aggressive weapons as they were being deployed, the unloading process was carried out at night and was limited to a few heavily guarded ports. Moreover, aware that Washington might not rest until it was convinced that the weapons being installed in Cuba would not pose a threat to its national security, the Soviets relied on Cuba's summer rains and tropical storms to hide the erection of MRBM sites from the U-2s.

Intention Strategy of Surprise

The two cases just considered indicate quite clearly that the conditions that determine an actor's choice of strategy of surprise vary significantly between those that place the emphasis on achieving surprise with respect to their intentions and those that concentrate on either the target or time dimension.

Several factors seem to have prevented Germany from attempting to achieve surprise with respect to the time and target of the attack. After the decision to attack the Soviet Union was made, Germany began to deploy its troops along its eastern borders. For a brief period of time, Hitler and his associates tried to persuade the Soviets that Britain, not the Soviet Union, would be Germany's next target. But as time went by and the number of troops along Germany's eastern borders continued to multiply, it became increasingly difficult to adhere to this story. The geographical closeness of the Soviet Union to Germany's military forces was bound to worsen Moscow's suspicion.

The German leaders estimated that to avert a two-front war they would have to defeat the Soviets within five to six months. To achieve a swift, decisive military victory, German troops had to avoid being drawn deeply into Russia's hinterland. Germany's strategy required that: (1) the Soviets deploy the core of their army along the western and southern borders of the Soviet Union, (2) the Soviet Army not be placed on a state of full alert, and (3) the Soviet Army be taken by surprise.

To induce the Soviets to deploy the core of their troops along the western and southern borders of the Soviet Union, Hitler had to convey a credible threat of violence and a possible time of attack. Hitler calculated that, if he deployed large forces along Germany's eastern borders, the Soviets would have to reciprocate and deploy their own troops.

Hitler wished to minimize the chances that the Soviets would place their deployed troops on a state of full alert, thereby exacting heavy losses for invading German troops and/or permitting an orderly withdrawal of large Soviet forces into the hinterland. Therefore, he did nothing to discredit Stalin's expectation that, although Germany would resort to war if necessary, Hitler would attempt negotiation first.

It is unlikely that Hitler could have opted for this strategy of surprise had it not been for Stalin's conviction that Germany would not attack so long as Britain remained a viable threat to it. Stalin justified his belief by arguing that Germany lacked the strength to fight against two powerful adversaries and besides was dependent on continuing to receive natural resources from the Soviet Union to stay in the war against Britain. These assumptions were of great benefit to Hitler in his attempts to control Stalin's sense of vulnerability.

Moscow's predicament in 1962 was quite different from the one Hitler faced some twenty years earlier. Moscow's choice of strategy was constrained by the relationships that had evolved among Cuba, the United States, and the Soviet Union and by Cuba's geographical proximity to the United States. Following the overthrow in 1959 of Cuba's president, Fulgencio Batista, the relationship between Cuba and the United States deteriorated rapidly. In contrast, Cuba and the Soviet Union steadily created new bonds. One of the most noticeable indications of the latter development was the supply of Soviet weapons to Cuba.

In view of Cuba's potential capability to destabilize the existing status quo in the Caribbean Basin and in Latin America, the United States monitored the deployment of Soviet weapons with great concern. The Kennedy Administration made it clear that it would not tolerate the presence of weapons in Cuba that could pose a threat to the general region.

Washington's warning must have been heard by the Soviets. They must have realized that disclosure of their intention to deploy strategic nuclear missiles outside Soviet territory would have posed some form of threat to the United States and would have led Washington to tighten surveillance of Cuba. In other words, it would have been unrealistic for Moscow to assume that it could disclose its intention without triggering Washington's sense of vulnerability or that it could disclose its intention and be able, at the same time, to conceal its target.

Another factor that could have influenced Moscow's decision to opt for an intention type of surprise was Washington's assumption that the Soviets would continue their policy of not deploying nuclear missiles outside Soviet territory. Knowledge of this belief could have led Moscow to conclude that Washington's sense of vulnerability with respect to the question of whether Soviet nuclear missiles would be deployed in Cuba was relatively low and would remain at that level so long as the change in intention was not divulged.

In sum, Moscow seems to have calculated that the only way it could succeed in its attempt to deploy some of its nuclear missiles in Cuba was by not increasing Washington's sense of vulnerability. Thinking that Washington's level of tension and mistrust would not increase so long as it continued to believe that the Soviet Union would not dare to install nuclear missiles in Cuba, Moscow must have decided that it could not disclose its intention to begin deploying missiles outside Soviet territory. Washington's bellicose relationship with Havana, on the one hand, and Havana's harmonious relationship with Moscow, on the other hand, prevented Moscow from taking this step. Finally, by not disclosing its intention, Moscow theoretically would have had little reason to worry about the target and time dimensions. These two dimensions were relevant only in relation to the intention dimension.

Hitler in 1941, like Khrushchev in 1962, attempted to achieve surprise with respect to his capabilities and/or military doctrine. In the case of Germany, emphasis was placed on achieving surprise with respect to the military doctrine that would guide the attack. One of Hitler's primary concerns, as noted earlier, had been that the Soviets would attempt to retreat into Russia's hinterland once they realized they could not withstand the German attack. It is evident, therefore, that to minimize the initial Soviet resistance and create disorganization within the Red Army it was imperative to attack by surprise.

The circumstances in 1962 were quite different. For Moscow, failure to conceal the deployment of its missiles in Cuba would at once have meant failure to achieve surprise with respect to its intentions, even though the exact objectives it hoped to pursue once the missiles were operational might still be unclear to Washington. A similar argument applies with respect to Moscow's military doctrine. Until 1962, one of Moscow's military policies had been never to deploy nuclear missiles outside Soviet territory. Had Moscow, in 1962, revealed the adoption of a new nuclear doctrine, it would have, in fact, disclosed its new intention.

The last factor of surprise that needs to be examined for Germany and the Soviet Union is the rationale dimension. This dimension played a critical role in the strategies of both actors.

Aware that Moscow had been revitalizing its armed forces and that Britain was still too weak to mount a major attack on the European continent, Hitler reasoned that it would be wise to strike the Soviet Union in 1941, thus removing the danger of having to confront both countries at the same time. Disclosure of this rationale would have been extremely costly to Germany. One of the reasons that Hitler opted for an intention-type strategy of surprise was that he assumed that Stalin believed Germany would not attack the Soviet Union until it defeated Britain. By concealing his own rationale for attacking, Hitler was trying to reaffirm Stalin's rationale for the reason that Germany would not attack.

Moscow in 1962 could not have sought an intention-type strategy of surprise without concealing its rationale. The two dimensions were inextricably intertwined. Moscow could not have disclosed that its principal rationale for deploying nuclear missiles outside Soviet territory was to narrow the missile gap without revealing that its intention was to deploy the missiles, possibly in Cuba.

It is of some significance that, of the three cases in which the would-be surprisers were not able to opt for a target-type strategy of surprise, the two who chose an intention-type surprise were the two whose power most closely approximated the power of their victims. Thus, it could be proposed that an actor will be less inclined to want to achieve surprise with respect to the target of its action when his power approximates that of his victim and when he cannot control his victim's concern over the geographical area where he plans to stage the surprise.

This hypothesis could lead to the argument that an actor's decision to opt for an intention-type surprise is a function only of relative capabilities and geographical distances. This conclusion, however, would be somewhat premature without an additional factor. In the analysis of the two earlier cases, it was argued that when the relationship between two actors has been characteristically conflictual, the would-be surpriser will be reluctant to place his hopes on an intention-type strategy of surprise. Adding credibility to the argument is the fact that Germany in 1941 and the Soviet Union in 1962 opted for this particular strategy against opponents with whom they had a limited adversarial relationship not marked by acute hostility.

In order to substantiate the hypothesis that will be proposed next, it would have been helpful to have considered cases in which the aggressors were significantly stronger than their victims. However, these actors are unlikely to resort to an intention-type strategy of surprise. Making threats of war to gain their diplomatic objectives against weaker opponents, thereby disclosing their contingent intentions to attack, would be much less costly.[72] Thus, provided this argument holds true, it can be proposed that an international actor is likely to resort to an intention-type strategy when he is approximately as strong as his victim, cannot control his victim's concern regarding the areas where he plans to stage the surprise, but believes he can control the level of tension and mistrust his victim feels.

Notes

1. Churchill, 1949, pp. 135–136.
2. *The New York Times,* December 13, 1941.
3. Salisbury, 1969, p. 69.
4. Quoted in Salisbury, 1969, p. 69.

5. See McSherry, Vol. 2, 1970, p. 141.

6. *Trial of the Major War Criminals Before the International Military Tribunal,* Vol. 26, 1947, p. 331.

7. *Fuehrer Conferences on Matters Dealing with the German Navy,* Vol. 2, 1947, pp. 70–71.

8. Gafencu, 1945, p. 207. As acknowledged by Jervis, Hitler was a master of manipulating indices of personal characteristics in the pursuit of his objectives. See Jervis, 1970, p. 45.

9. Whaley, 1973, p. 173.

10. Ibid., p. 173.

11. Ibid., p. 173.

12. Leach, 1973, Appendix IV, p. 270.

13. Whaley, 1973a, p. 173.

14. Hinsley, Vol. 1, 1979, p. 445; McSherry, Vol. 2, 1970, p. 219.

15. Irving, 1977, p. 189.

16. Quoted in Leach, 1973, p. 112.

17. *Documents on German Foreign Policy, DGFP, 1918–1945,* Vol. 11, pp. 712–715, 726, 772.

18. McSherry, Vol. 2, 1970, p. 199.

19. Ibid., p. 197.

20. Ibid., p. 192. Hitler's initial behavior vis-a-vis the Soviets also conforms with Jervis' contention that an actor who wants to convince others of his moderation and reasonableness may be willing to forego significant temporary gains. See Jervis, 1970, p. 47.

21. *Documents on German Foreign Policy, DGFP, 1918–1945,* Vol. 12, pp. 474–475.

22. Salisbury, 1969, p. 17.

23. McSherry, Vol. 2, 1970, pp. 120–124.

24. Ibid., p. 163.

25. Hinsley, 1951, p. 153.

26. McSherry, Vol. 2, 1970, p. 198.

27. Hinsley, 1951, p. 153.

28. McSherry, Vol. 2, 1970, pp. 206–212.

29. Ibid., pp. 212–213; Salisbury, 1969, p. 63.

30. Hinsley, Vol. I, 1979, p. 457.

31. Leach, 1973, p. 51.

32. Salisbury, 1969, p. 44.

33. Gafencu, 1945, pp. 190–191.

34. McSherry, Vol. 2, 1970, p. 222.

35. Ibid., pp. 222–223.

36. Gafencu, 1945, pp. 207–208.

37. Barton Whaley completely misinterprets the manner in which Hitler used negotiation to deceive the Soviets. He assumes that Hitler attempted to lull Russian suspicions via the maintenance of normal economic and diplomatic ties. To be sure, economic and diplomatic ties were maintained until the very last days, but, as we

have shown, they were far from being normal following Molotov's visit to Berlin in November 1940. See Whaley, 1973a, p. 176.

38. According to Whaley, one of the reasons that Hitler might have decided to surprise the Soviets was to avert a pre-emptive attack from them as his troops were preparing for the attack. We disagree with this interpretation. It is clear that, had Hitler been concerned about drawing a pre-emptive attack from the Soviets, he never would have threatened them to the extent that he did. The only occasion during which Hitler became concerned about a pre-emptive attack on the part of the Soviets was during Germany's campaign in the Balkans. And even then, Hitler was not worried about Stalin's ordering an attack on Germany; his main fear was that Stalin would order the occupation of some of Rumania's oil fields. See Whaley, 1973a, p. 170.

39. Abel, 1966, p. 23. See also Sorensen, 1965, pp. 670–671; Schlesinger, 1965, p. 795; Hilsman, 1967, p. 173.

40. Hilsman, 1967, p. 172.

41. Abel, 1966, p. 34; Schlesinger, 1965, p. 798.

42. For an in-depth analysis of what may have caused the lull, see Dinerstein, 1976, chapters 3–5.

43. Quoted in Dinerstein, 1976, p. 161.

44. Tatu, 1969, p. 234.

45. Hilsman, 1967, p. 170; Abel, 1966, p. 17.

46. *The New York Times,* August 30, 1962, p. 10.

47. *Washington Post,* August 30, 1962.

48. Sorensen, 1965, p. 670.

49. Abel, 1966, p. 19; Schlesinger, 1965, p. 798; George and Smoke, 1974, p. 469.

50. Quoted in Schlesinger, 1965, p. 799.

51. Ibid., p. 799.

52. Hilsman, 1967, p. 166.

53. Ibid., p. 165.

54. Allison, 1971, pp. 106–108.

55. Hilsman, 1967, p. 183.

56. Allison, 1971, pp. 110–113.

57. Schlesinger, 1965, p. 800.

58. Jackson, 1977, pp. 41 and 56.

59. Ibid.

60. Hilsman, 1967, p. 167.

61. Ibid., p. 168.

62. Abel, 1966, p. 21.

63. Ibid., p. 26.

64. Hilsman, 1967, p. 181, note 4.

65. Allison, 1971, p. 56.

66. Ibid., p. 103.

67. Another possible reason for the Soviets' not completing their SAMs before deploying MRBMs could have been the time delay of doing it sequentially and the expectation that introduction of SAMs would alert U.S. intelligence to look hard for

indications of MRBMs coming in. Hence, there would have been a greater likelihood of the United States' detecting the MRBMs if they had been deployed only after the SAMs had become operational. This argument reinforces our "weather" explanation.

68. Wohlstetter, July 1965, p. 698.

69. Schlesinger, 1965, p. 798; Sorensen, 1965, p. 667.

70. Sorensen, 1965, p. 667.

71. An alternative interpretation has been that Moscow hoped that, if the Kennedy Administration discovered the missiles, it would be unwilling to expose their presence on the eve of the national elections for fear that, if the American public learned that no demand had been made to withdraw the missiles, it would vote against the Democratic Party. See Horelick and Rush, 1966, p. 148; Ulam, 1974, p. 691. We do not think that this interpretation makes much sense. It is based, once again, on the unsupported assumption that Moscow expected a very weak reaction from Washington. If such an assumption were correct, then why would the Soviets take so many deceptive measures to conceal their intentions? To be sure, the Soviets assumed that Washington would give in if the missiles were discovered *after* they had become operational, but it is quite doubtful that they believed that Washington would back down if it discovered the missiles *while* they were being installed. In fact, the upcoming elections may have hardened President Kennedy's resolve to have the missiles removed from Cuba.

72. In 1954 and 1961, the United States prepared and financed the invasion of two weaker states, Guatemala and Cuba. In both instances the United States took very few measures to conceal its *intention;* in fact, it hoped that the leaders of both countries would learn that an invasion was forthcoming and would then surrender the reins of government to domestic chaos. See Hybel, 1985; Immerman, 1982; Matthews, 1975.

6
Why Were the Soviets but not the Americans Surprised in 1941 and 1962, Respectively?

Why Was Stalin Surprised by Hitler's Actions in 1941?

Of the cases analyzed in this study, the most interesting one is Germany's surprise attack on the Soviet Union in 1941. This case is different in that the would-be surpriser, Germany, never really tried to keep the sense of vulnerability of its victim, the Soviet Union, low by concealing the deployment of its troops or their actual strength. Instead, Germany sought to *increase* Stalin's sense of vulnerability by disclosing that preparations for a possible attack were under way, while at the same time encouraging Stalin's expectation that the Soviets could avert an attack by extending certain attractive concessions to Germany.

There is no question that Hitler's strategy of surprise was clever. However, it would be unjustifiable to contend that the Soviet Union was surprised because of Hitler's cunning behavior. Stalin failed to avert surprise mainly because he felt less vulnerable than was warranted by a careful assessment of the German build-up and because he was unwilling to assess alternative interpretations of Hitler's intentions.

To prepare the Soviet Union against a possible German attack, Stalin would at minimum have had to deploy the Red Army to the western and southwestern borders, place it on full alert, order the immediate shift-over of Soviet industry to war production, and propose to the British the creation of an anti-German coalition. Of these four steps, Stalin took only one—he deployed the Red Army. He did not place the Red Army on full alert; rather, it was scattered in the frontier areas over wide spaces, away from any defensive position, and engaged in routine duties. Stalin did not order the shift-over of Soviet industry to war production; the plan for doing so was not approved by him until June 6, 1941, and was not to be completed until the end of 1942. Finally, it is evident that the Soviets had no intention of proposing to the British the creation of an anti-German coalition. On April 18, 1941, Britain's ambassador to Moscow, Sir Stafford Cripps, was informed that for political reasons the Soviet premier, Molotov, would no longer hold meetings with him.[1]

Stalin did not undertake preparations to offset a German attack because to have done so would have meant negating the conciliatory steps that he had taken since March 1941 to express both his nonhostile intention and his willingness to accommodate reasonable German demands. In other words, Stalin estimated that, if he followed both paths simultaneously, Hitler would have received contradictory signals and thus would have gained exactly what Stalin was hoping to deny him—a justification to attack.

Stalin did believe that one day his country and Germany would engage in war against each other.[2] It was his hope, however, that he could avert the fight until the Red Army had gained enough power to defeat the German Army without accruing heavy losses. This meant, according to Stalin's estimations, that the Soviet Union would have to wait until at least mid-1942.[3] Thus, confronted with a powerful adversary who seemed to have hostile intentions, but who had not made it fully clear whether he planned to implement them, Stalin concluded that his only choice was to adopt a conciliatory stand. Stated differently, Stalin seems to have deduced that he could not risk incurring Hitler's wrath by deploying the Red Army and placing it on full alert, by ordering the immediate shift-over of Soviet industry to war production, and by joining the British in an anti-German coalition so long as the Soviet Union was not prepared for war and Hitler was leaving open the possibility of an attack on Great Britain and/or a compromise with Russia.[4]

Analysts who have been critical of the Soviets for failing to predict the German attack often point out how successful Winston Churchill was in predicting such an occurrence. Those who take this stand tend to forget that the British had almost as much difficulty as their Soviet counterparts in deciding what Hitler had in mind. Hitler was successful in confusing all the British leaders as to his real intentions until almost the end of March 1941. There are numerous indications that several of Britain's leaders speculated that Hitler would turn east if he failed to defeat England as early as the middle of 1940. Both Winston Churchill and his ambassador to Moscow, Sir Stafford Cripps, expressed such views privately sometime in June 1940.[5] But, until the end of March 1941, only a few items of information indicated that Hitler was no longer planning to invade Britain and was instead getting ready to march eastward. Churchill later described the situation as follows:

> Up till the end of March I was not convinced Hitler was resolved on mortal war with Russia, nor how near it was . . . There was no sign of lessening German strength opposite us across the Channel. The German air raids on Britain continued with intensity . . . all made it seem more likely that Hitler and Stalin would make a bargain at our expenses rather than a war upon each other.[6]

British estimation of Hitler's intention underwent a substantial change on March 27. On the previous day, British intelligence noted that three armored divisions and other elements in the German Army had been ordered to redeploy from the Balkans to Poland. Part of the transfer, however, was cancelled on March 27, the day of the coup d'etat in Yugoslavia. The conclusion derived from such events by the chief of the German section of British Air Section read as follows:

> It is significant that the day after Yugoslavia signed the Tripartite Pact orders were issued for the transfer of a large proportion of the German "Balkan" forces to the Russian front. This, together with . . . leads me to believe that Germany's intention is to move in the Ukraine in the near future. A Balkan conflagration would necessarily postpone it.[7]

Prime Minister Churchill recalled having reached the same conclusion when he noted that:

> The sudden movement to Cracow . . . would only mean Hitler's intention to invade Russia in May. . . . The fact that the Belgrade revolution had required their return to Rumania involved perhaps a delay from May to June.[8]

Other members of British intelligence, however, were not certain that Germany was planning to attack the Soviet Union. On April 1, for instance, military intelligence insisted that there was no reason to believe the numerous reports that Germany intended to attack Russia in the near future. Military intelligence estimated that Germany's main objective was to exert pressure on the Soviets to prevent them from interfering with Germany's Balkan plans.[9] Another view, issued at approximately the same time by the Joint Intelligence Subcommittee of the Chiefs of Staff, stated that Germany's main objective continued to be the defeat of Britain during 1941, by blockade and air attack if possible, by invasion if necessary.[10] The Joint Intelligence Subcommittee reasoned that an operation against Russia would be very unlikely because it would rule out an invasion of the United Kingdom, which, in turn, would open new possibilities for British operations against Germany.[11]

During the month of May, both military intelligence and the Joint Intelligence Subcommittee finally began to acknowledge that Germany's principal target was no longer Britain but the Soviet Union. Both groups, however, believed that Hitler was still trying to decide whether to use persuasion or force against the Soviets. It was not until the very last days before the German attack of the Soviet Union that all the British intelligence groups agreed that Germany would invade its adversary to the east.[12]

A final comment about British estimation of Hitler's strategy and German capabilities: earlier it was postulated that Hitler emphasized the needs to overcome Soviet resistance rapidly in order to rob the British of the opportunity to get a foothold on the European continent and to take advantage of the victory against the Soviets to pressure the British to negotiate an agreement with Germany. Three days after Germany attacked the Soviet Union, the British chiefs of staff, urged by Churchill, ordered that Britain be kept on alert and that the anti-invasion forces be brought to their highest state of efficiency by September 1, 1941. The order was issued because British leaders were certain that the Soviet Union would not survive for long the German attack.[13]

This estimate by Britain's policy makers has several interesting implications. It shows that, although Hitler failed in his campaign against the Soviet Union, such an outcome could not have been predicted as easily as many scholars have claimed with the help of hindsight.[14] Second, it indicates that Hitler's original expectation of a quick victory over the Soviets was not wholly unreasonable. The German leader sought to surprise the Soviets in part to avert fighting a protracted war. His main fear was that the British would exploit Germany's involvement in the east to get a firm foothold on the European continent. Surprise enabled Germany to achieve some major victories against the Soviets, which, in turn, helped convince the British that it would be in their best interest not to initiate any immediate offensive action against Germany.

In the final analysis, however, Hitler's strategy of surprise succeeded because the Soviet leader was unwilling to listen to the warnings being forwarded by some of his lower-ranked military officials and took an unreasonable risk. The warnings of a possible German attack came from several Soviet quarters. Marshal A.M. Vasilevsky, who had been a member of the Soviet group that visited Berlin in November 1940, was one of the first individuals to conclude that Germany would attack the Soviet Union.[15] Seven months after the visit to Berlin, and just a week before the attack took place, Marshal Vasilevsky, who at that time was a member of the Operations Office of the General Staff, had the opportunity to express his views to General of the Army M.I. Kazakov. According to Vasilevsky, Finland's mobilization of its armed forces and Germany's concentration of troops at its eastern frontier clearly indicated that the Soviet Union would be attacked sometime within the next fifteen to twenty days.[16]

Vasilevsky was not alone in his belief that war with Germany would break out soon. The Soviet Defense Commissariat had, by the end of January 1941, become so suspicious of Germany's actions vis-a-vis the Soviet Union that it began to draft a general directive to the border commands and the fleets. The directive, for the first time, named Germany as the most likely opponent in a future war. It was issued on February 23, and instructed the frontier regions to make appropriate preparations to retaliate against a German attack.[17] Very little came of this directive, principally because Marshal

Kirill A. Miretskov was replaced as chief of staff of the Soviet Defense Commissariat by an individual who shared Stalin's view that Germany would not attack, Marshal Georgi K. Zhukov.

The only military branch that seems to have succeeded in maintaining a consistent policy of alert through the months immediately preceding the attack was the Soviet Navy, under the leadership of Admiral Nilolai G. Kuztnetsov. According to Kuznetsov, the navy began to suspect early in 1941 that Hitler was planning to break the nonaggression pact with the Soviet Union.[18] Most of Kuztnetsov's information was coming from his commander in chief of the Baltic Fleet, Vice Admiral Vladimir Tributs. Admiral Tributs, who was responsible for the defense of Leningrad's sea approaches, was in an excellent position to be apprised of the activities of German planes, submarines, and transports. As early as March 1941, he began to report the arrival of troops at Memel, just across the new Soviet Baltic border, and daily German flights over most Baltic bases. By June 1941, Admiral Tributs informed Admiral Kuztnetsov that at least four hundred German tanks had been concentrated just a few miles from the Soviet Baltic border. When he passed this information to his superior he added that "an attack by Germany is possible at any moment."[19]

Based on the information he was receiving from Tributs and his fleet commander in Sevastopol, Kuznetsov concluded that Hitler was not concentrating his forces on the eastern borders to augment Germany's bargaining stand, as Stalin and other members of his entourage argued. Three factors convinced Kuztnetsov that Germany intended to attack. To begin with, he was not fully persuaded by the argument that Germany, by attacking the Soviet Union, would be fighting a two-front war. The war in the West in 1941 had, for all practical purposes, drawn to a standstill. Secondly, if Germany were building up its armed forces only as a precautionary measure, then it did not need to move them into Rumania and Finland. And finally, why would the Germans, if they did not intend to attack, fly reconnaissance planes over areas that presented no threat to them, such as Hango, a peninsula jutting into the Baltic Sea at the entrance of the Gulf of Finland, which was leased to the Soviet Union, and Poliarnyi, the main naval base of the Soviet Northern Fleet in the Arctic Circle?[20]

Stalin, like his subordinates, recognized that Hitler's forces were posing a major threat to the Soviet Union.[21] What distinguished Stalin from many other Soviet officials was his belief that it was in the interest of Germany not to attack the Soviet Union. His argument was based on the assumption that Germany did not have the power to engage in a two-front war. Moreover, the Soviet leader reasoned that Hitler had no need to attack the Soviet Union and would recognize that fact if he could be convinced that the Soviets would not attack Germany and were willing to acquiesce to some reasonable German demands.

Stalin's reasoning was faulty on two accounts. First, as some of his subordinates were keenly aware, an attack on the Soviet Union by Germany need not have been construed, at least at the outset, as a two-front war. To be sure, Germany and Britain were at war with each other, but very few German forces were actually engaged in the war. And second, Stalin failed to realize that by demonstrating that he had no intention of attacking Germany he was also making it less costly for Germany to attack the Soviet Union.

It could be inferred, therefore, that, although Hitler's strategy of surprise may have been well designed for the occasion, the Soviet Union, under a different leader, might have been able to avert surprise. A different Soviet leader, on learning that the vast majority of Germany's armed forces were pointing east, might have placed his own forces on a full state of alert. For all practical purposes, geography noticeably hindered Hitler's ability to conceal his intention. Even the most skeptical British analysts had to acknowledge finally that Hitler's sole intention on June 22, 1941, was to attack the Soviet Union.

Stalin's behavior during the crisis of June 1941 is an excellent example of what Robert Jervis has referred to as "irrational" consistency. According to Jervis, the principle of consistency is useful in that it helps decision makers make sense of new information as it relates to their past experiences, formulated as a set of expectations and beliefs.[22] The pursuit of consistency, however, becomes irrational when decision makers close their minds to new information or different points of view.[23]

Stalin not only disregarded any information that questioned the wisdom of his assumptions in regard to German intentions, but went so far as to punish some of the bearers.[24] Moreover, the Soviet leader was so convinced that Hitler would not attack that he persuaded himself that he could meet most of the German demands.[25]

How the Americans Averted Being Surprised by the Soviets in 1962

The scholarly literature has presented three views regarding the question of whether the Americans were surprised by the Soviet attempt to place nuclear missiles in Cuba in 1962. Roberta Wohlstetter, the noted analyst of the 1941 Pearl Harbor incident, takes the position that, although at one level the Cuban Missile Crisis seems an outstanding triumph for the United States, at another level it was a significant defeat in that the American intelligence community and decision makers failed to anticipate the crisis.[26] According to Wohlstetter, three major barriers limited the ability of the United States to conduct an objective evaluation of Soviet actions in Cuba.

To begin with, notes Wohlstetter, there was the cry-wolf phenomenon.[27] On September 9, the Central Intelligence Agency received a report from Cuban refugees that medium-range missiles had been spotted being moved into the San Cristobal area. The CIA was reluctant to accept this information because for the previous year and a half it had received many similar reports, none of which proved to be accurate.

Second, the Kennedy Administration wanted to avoid further friction with the Soviet Union.[28] For some time, Kennedy had been trying to relax tensions, hoping that improved relations would eventually lead to the signing of a test-ban agreement between Moscow and Washington. Because of this hope, American intelligence analysts ignored small clues, and Kennedy made very little allowance for the possibility of deception on the part of the Soviets.[29] For instance, American intelligence never became suspicious of the fact that many of the Soviet ships had especially large covered hatches and had been noted to be riding high in the water. Had the Americans been more suspicious, they might have surmised before October 14 that the Soviet ships could be carrying large-volume, low-density cargoes such as MRBMs.

Finally, there was a predisposition within the intelligence community to believe that it would be incompatible with Soviet policy to introduce strategic missiles into Cuba.[30] It was reasoned that, since the Soviets had never placed medium- or long-range missiles in any of their satellite countries, it was unlikely that they would place them 90 miles away from the United States, where they were bound to provoke a sharp American response.

A second valuable interpretation has been presented by Alexander George and Richard Smoke.[31] According to George and Smoke, the Cuban Missile Crisis can be classified as a near failure of American intelligence.[32] One of their basic concerns is explaining why the United States, aware that the Soviets had been supplying Cuba with very sophisticated weapons, would be willing to limit the photographic sweeps of U-2s to the portion of Cuba lying east of Havana.[33] Their response is that the Kennedy Administration was greatly concerned about the possibility of having one of its U-2s shot down while flying over Cuba—especially over its western side where SAM installations had been spotted—and the political repercussions such an event might cause throughout the world. But more importantly, note George and Smoke, the caution displayed by high-level officials in curtailing the U-2 flights was rationalized by their shared belief that the Soviets would not deploy offensive missiles in Cuba.[34] Underlying this assumption of Soviet restraint was the Kennedy Administration's belief that the Soviet leaders would regard a missile deployment as a high-risk strategy.[35]

Roger Hilsman, a high-ranking American official during the Cuban Missile Crisis, presents the third evaluation of the American intelligence effort. For Hilsman, the Cuban incident in 1962 must be marked as a victory for American intelligence.[36] Hilsman acknowledges, however, that there was one piece of information that should have alerted the American intelligence community to the need for gathering more concrete knowledge about developments in Cuba. On September 21, a CIA agent reported to Washington that nine days earlier he had spotted a truck convoy proceeding in a westerly direction from one of the secure port areas near Havana. What was distinctive about the convoy was that it included trailers sixty feet long whose contents were concealed by canvas.[37] On receiving this information, CIA headquarters concluded that the agent had probably seen trailers carrying SAMs, which are thirty feet long.[38] Had the CIA refrained from adding this comment, and had the intelligence community given more emphasis to the report, American attention might have turned to the western end of the island some ten days to two weeks sooner than it did.[39] This possibility does not imply, however, that an American U-2 could have discovered the MRBM sites much earlier than October 14, when they were actually identified. As Hilsman put it, "The earliest an MRBM site for launching the thousand-mile missile could have been identified from the air was October 8."[40]

The thrust of these three arguments is that, although Moscow failed with its strategy of surprise, Washington could not claim an across-the-board victory, because the missiles could have been identified earlier than October 14. In order to assess both conclusions, the first question that must be posed is: What went wrong with Moscow's strategy of surprise?

Earlier in this section it was proposed that Moscow's long-standing policy of not installing strategic nuclear weapons outside Soviet territory prejudiced Washington to expect a continuation of the policy and that Khrushchev relied on this expectation to camouflage his change in policy. Moscow realized that it had to keep Washington's sense of vulnerability low while it deployed its missiles in Cuba.

Cuba had been receiving military equipment from the Soviet Union since the summer of 1960. The flow of arms continued at a steady pace all through 1961. Beginning in 1962, however, the shipment of Soviet materiel to Cuba was slowed noticeably. The lull lasted until late July 1962. At this time, Moscow seems to have decided that, although there had been a lull of almost seven months in the shipment of weapons, it would be possible to persuade Washington that the new flow of arms was no more than a continuation of the same policy that had been in effect since the summer of 1960. This assumption was erroneous. Moscow failed to realize that Washington's sense of vulnerability in regard to Cuba did not depend solely on whether Soviet strategic nuclear weapons were deployed in the island. A detailed narration of the steps taken by Washington from the moment the flow of Soviet weapons to Cuba intensified until the missiles were discovered should illustrate this point.

On August 24, approximately a month after the new shipment of Soviet arms to Cuba had started, the Kennedy Administration decided that it was time to go public with its information. During a press conference it was disclosed that Moscow might be providing Cuba with SAMs. The possibility that the Soviets might be installing SAMs and other types of sophisticated defensive weapons in Cuba elicited a new set of attitudes among American high officials.

Initially, it led John McCone, the head of the CIA, to wonder why the Soviets would want to place antiaircraft missiles in Cuba. He reasoned that Moscow was not so naive as to believe that antiaircraft missiles would guarantee protection against a serious invasion attempt by the United States.[41] Having rejected this thought, on August 22 he told President Kennedy that he suspected that the SAMs were being installed to protect Soviet offensive missiles. McCone had no hard evidence to prove his point; he had arrived at it via deductive reasoning. Few American officials sided with his view.

It should not be inferred, however, that Washington proceeded to lose interest in what was going on in Cuba. On August 29, a U-2 covered most of the island.[42] Photographs from the flight revealed what Washington had been suspecting for some time—that the Soviets were getting ready to install SAMs in Cuba.

The August 29 flight proved to be of great significance. Until then, the U-2 overflight schedule had been limited to two flights a month. With the discovery of the SAMs, the schedule was stepped up. Between August 29 and October 7, there were seven U-2 flights over the island.[43] This action clearly indicated that Washington was becoming quite concerned about Moscow's behavior in Cuba. In fact, the Kennedy Administration was becoming sensitive to the point of nervousness.[44]

President Kennedy's public statements reflected his Administration's concern. At an August 29 press conference, President Kennedy assured the public that there was no evidence of Soviet troops in Cuba and added that his government was following developments on the island very closely. President Kennedy's tone on August 29 was very restrained. His main objective had been to head off the mounting Republican criticism of his Cuban policy and to reassure the American public. But equally pertinent was the fact that his Administration still did not have hard evidence that would indicate that the Soviets were installing antiaircraft missiles on Cuban territory.

President Kennedy's tone changed significantly after he was assured that Soviet SAMs were being erected in Cuba. On September 4, the president issued a statement once again trying to reassure the American public that no evidence existed of organized Soviet combat forces in Cuba, of offensive ground-to-ground missiles, or any other significant offensive capability. But then the president warned, "Were it to be otherwise the gravest issues would arise."[45]

Kennedy's statements obviously reflected a desire to calm the American public. However, the president's public behavior was not in tune with his Administration's continued concern over Cuba.

On September 5, another U-2 flew over Cuba. The photographs from this flight and from the August 29 mission enabled United States intelligence to determine that SAMs were being erected around the perimeter of the island in the *western* and *central* portions.[46] The photographs from both missions also showed a ramp fitted with what seemed to be a robot airplane with swept-back, stubby wings being installed at the harbor town of Barnes on the northeastern side of Cuba.[47] Because the August 29 and September 5 missions gave only a spotty coverage of the eastern portion of the island, a new flight was ordered. The flight was delayed by bad weather until September 17.[48] Photographs from that flight confirmed what the previous shots had revealed and showed that the installation at Barnes was a launching platform for a shore-to-ship missile.

In the meantime, Washington's concern continued to intensify. On September 7, three days after receiving assurances from Ambassador Dobrynin that Moscow had no intention of placing nuclear weapons in Cuba, President Kennedy requested from Congress standby authority to call up reserve troops. In addition, on September 13, two days after Moscow had claimed that it had no need to place nuclear weapons outside the boundaries of the Soviet Union, President Kennedy issued a new statement. This time he warned that—if the Soviet build-up in Cuba endangered in any way the American base at Guantanamo, the Panama Canal, space activities at Cape Canaveral, or the lives of American citizens in the United States, or if Cuba were to become an offensive military base for the Soviet Union—the United States would resort to whatever means it deemed necessary to protect its own security and that of its allies.[49]

Chance often disrupts even the best-laid plans. On September 9, a U-2 belonging to the Chinese Nationalists was destroyed in the air over the Chinese mainland. On the following day, the Committee of Overhead Reconnaissance (COMOR) met in McGeorge Bundy's office at the White House.[50] The participating members concluded that the U-2 flights over Cuba had to continue. But, in order to diminish the risks of having a U-2 shot down, it was suggested that instead of covering the whole island in a single flight, the flights should be shorter and more frequent, "dipping into Cuban airspace." Moreover, it was decided that flights should concentrate on the eastern half of Cuba rather than on the western tip, where SAMs were known to be approaching operational readiness.[51]

On September 19, nine days after the COMOR met and two days after a U-2 had flown over the northeastern section of Cuba, the United States

Intelligence Board met to reassess the Soviet arms build-up in Cuba. By then, the United States knew that (1) SAM sites were being constructed around the perimeter of Cuba's western and central portions, (2) additional MIG fighters had been deployed at various airfields, and (3) Cuba's ground forces and patrol boats had been reinforced. Most of this information came as a result of missions flown over Cuba on August 29, September 5, and September 17.

On reviewing the estimate, the Intelligence Board agreed with the assessment that the Soviets would not introduce offensive missiles in Cuba. The estimate noted, however, that the placement of medium- and intermediate-range missiles in Cuba would alter dramatically the strategic balance of power between East and West. It urged the intelligence community to remain alert.[52]

Two more U-2 missions were flown during the month of September. On September 26, after being delayed for several days by persistent cloud coverage, a U-2 flew over the eastern side of Cuba. The objective of this flight was to photograph areas on the eastern side that the September 17 flight had failed to cover because of cloudy skies. Three days later, a U-2 flew over the Isle of Pines, southwest of Cuba, and over the Bay of Pigs. Both flights revealed the installation of more SAMs. By this time, the White House was really alarmed. And yet, it still saw no reason to believe that Moscow planned to introduce strategic nuclear missiles in Cuba; in fact, the White House staff felt that the military build-up in Cuba did not pose much of a military threat to the United States. The threat, it was agreed, was of a political nature, and it pointed to Latin America.[53]

During the first days of October, the Kennedy Administration saw itself facing a major problem—how to respond to the Soviet military build-up. On the one hand, it faced mounting Republican criticism and demands that it adopt a more forceful policy against Cuba. On the other hand, the European and Latin American communities, fearful that the United States might opt for a military solution to the Cuban problem, urged the Kennedy Administration to be prudent.

The dilemma faced by the Kennedy Administration was resolved, to a large extent, by two individuals—Colonel John Ralph Wright, Jr., of the Defense Intelligence Agency (DIA), and John McCone, the CIA director. By the end of September, Colonel Wright, who had been studying closely the results of the September 5 overflight, discovered that the trapezoidal pattern of SAM installations in the San Cristobal area in the western section of Cuba resembled the patterns in the Soviet Union.[54] Colonel Wright suggested to his boss, General Joseph Carroll, that the San Cristobal area be photographed.[55]

On October 4, after receiving more reports about unusual activities in Pinar del Rio at the western end of Cuba, members of COMOR were assembled to consider flights over the western end of the island. At the meeting, John McCone showed a rhomboid-shaped area covering San Cristobal and Guanajay, which had not been covered by U-2 flights since September 5. McCone seems to have emphasized the need to cover the area with U-2 overflights because it was there where the SAMs were most likely to be in or near operational condition.[56]

According to Hilsman, the decision to cover the western section of Cuba was reached without consideration of the possibility of missiles in the area.[57] But according to Allison, the DIA and CIA had already concluded that the Soviets were placing strategic missiles in the San Cristobal area.[58]

From then on, confirmation of strategic missiles was just a matter of time. On October 9, President Kennedy approved new U-2 flights over western Cuba. On October 14, after a brief delay caused by bad weather and the training of new Air Force pilots, two U-2s were dispatched to fly over the western side of Cuba. By Monday evening, October 15, intelligence analysts were quite certain that the Soviets were beginning to install strategic missiles. When informed about the findings, President Kennedy "took the news calmly but with an expression of surprise."[59]

From a purely technical point of view, President Kennedy and his closest advisors, including State Department officials, were surprised by Moscow's actions. These individuals had never suspected that Moscow had decided to place strategic missiles in Cuba. In other words, the White House was surprised with respect to Moscow's intention.

President Kennedy and his closest advisors failed to predict Moscow's intention mainly because they could not envision the Soviets taking the risks that such a venture would generate. They had estimated that, if the Soviets succeeded in placing a substantial number of medium- or intermediate-range missiles in Cuba, the strategic balance of power between East and West would be altered significantly. The White House did not think that the Soviets would take such a step, because never in the past had they placed offensive missiles outside the Soviet Union. Rather, they had always acted cautiously. So the White House was surprised with respect to Moscow's nuclear doctrine and rationale.

Having failed to estimate Moscow's intention, rationale, and nuclear doctrine, the White House was bound to be surprised by the presence of nuclear missiles in Cuba. Thus, Moscow also succeeded in surprising the White House with respect to its capabilities in Cuba.

To argue that President Kennedy and his closest advisors were surprised by Moscow's behavior does not mean that other members of the United States government involved in assessing the developments during the period preceding October 14 were similarly surprised. The evidence clearly indicates that by the end of September a number of intelligence analysts within the CIA and DIA had concluded that there was a very high probability that the

Soviet Union was placing offensive missiles in the San Cristobal area.[59] Although the reasoning that went on within the intelligence community is still highly guarded, enough of the story is known to enable us to consider why some individuals were more inclined than others to assume that the Soviets would place offensive missiles in Cuba.

Everybody agreed that the presence of Soviet offensive missiles in Cuba would affect the balance of power between East and West. President Kennedy and his closest advisors, however, seem to have sided with the view that such a venture would be very risky. And, since the Soviets were very cautious when it came to nuclear matters, it was considered unlikely that they would attempt to alter the balance of power by placing missiles in Cuba.

CIA Director McCone and Colonel Wright seem to have concentrated less on the risks involved in such a venture. Instead, they both placed a great deal of weight on the fact that SAMs were being installed throughout Cuba. McCone argued that it made very little sense for Moscow to try to protect Cuba with SAMs when it knew that their presence would not deter a serious American invasion attempt. Wright, on the other hand, found it particularly intriguing that the SAMs in Cuba were being deployed in a pattern similar to that used in the Soviet Union to protect offensive missiles.[61]

One conclusion can be reached at this point. An international actor who hopes to achieve surprise with respect to his intention vis-a-vis an adversary whose strength is not much greater than his own must be extremely careful to conceal any changes in his capabilities that could alter his adversary's sense of vulnerability. Moscow's mistake was to reveal exactly that which it had assumed was safe to disclose—the presence of SAMs. It can be argued, therefore, that CIA Director McCone and Colonel Wright were not surprised by the presence of offensive missiles because the SAMs had heightened their sense of vulnerability.

Initially, it was stated that from a purely technical point of view, President Kennedy and his closest advisors were surprised. That they did not have to pay a very high price for their error can be credited partly to those individuals whose sense of vulnerability had been heightened by Moscow's activities in Cuba. And yet, it would be wrong to assume that President Kennedy's sense of vulnerability and that of his closest advisors had remained unaltered.

Moscow's activities, as nearly as Kennedy and his advisors could gather, were not posing a direct military threat to the United States. The White House, however, was not ready to relax its guard. Three potential dangers seem to have convinced the White House that vigilance was imperative. Although it was believed that Moscow would refrain from introducing offensive missiles in Cuba, nobody in Washington had discarded the possibility that the Soviet Union might try to turn Cuba into a major military base. Second, as Soviet activities in Cuba became more obvious, the Republican

Party began to pressure the Kennedy Administration to pursue a more aggressive policy. And finally, there was a persistent fear among many White House and State Department officials that if the United States failed to put a stop to Cuba's militarization, Moscow might construe the inaction as a green light for future aggressive moves in Latin America. So it can be said that in many respects the sense of vulnerability of many of Kennedy's top officials was augmented by Moscow's activities in Cuba.

One question remains to be addressed. Would those who did not believe that the Soviets would install missiles in Cuba have requested that a U-2 be flown over the western side of Cuba had CIA Director McCone not proposed it? According to Graham Allison, when members of COMOR convened on October 4, it was McCone who brought up the issue of flying U-2s over the western side of Cuba. Allison implies that McCone argued that it was necessary to cover the western side of the island not only because the SAMs that had been spotted were the most likely to have reached their operational stage, but also because there was a significant probability that the Soviets were installing offensive missiles. After listening to McCone's presentation, representatives of the State Department were reluctant to agree with his proposal because they feared the consequences if a U-2 was lost over Cuba.[62]

At first glance, one may be inclined to conclude that those who had qualms about flying a U-2 over the western section of Cuba might have taken such a position partly because they did not believe that McCone's argument was sound. This conclusion overlooks a major point.

Near the end of September, Roger Hilsman, aware of the need to have reliable surveillance of the island and aware also of the danger to the U-2 posed by the SAMs, suggested an alternative means of gathering information.[63] His concern about the possibility of losing a U-2 was real. As Allison put it, "American overflight of the western end of Cuba was a matter of *real* concern. There was a significant probability that a U-2 would be downed."[64]

The disagreement between those who favored flying a U-2 over the western end of Cuba and those who had qualms reflected a discrepancy in priorities. The White House and the State Department, although aware that there was a real need to have the best possible up-to-date intelligence, were also very concerned about the negative worldwide political effects that the downing of a U-2 over Cuba would generate. The CIA and DIA, on the other hand, showed less concern about the immediate political consequences and greater interest in knowing Moscow's exact military status in Cuba. The discrepancy in priorities reflects the different organizational roles. However, even the parties that had qualms about sending a U-2 eventually concluded that the circumstances warranted the risk. The sense of vulnerability of the parties involved in the decision-making process had been heightened sufficiently that they could all agree on a decision.

In sum, when the question of whether Moscow surprised Washington is posed, two answers—yes and no—can be advanced. Which of the two an-swers is chosen depends on whom one considers to have been the target in Washington.

An argument could be made that, since Kennedy and his closest advisers were the central policy makers and since they continued to believe that the Kremlin would not deploy strategic missiles outside the Soviet Union until the moment the missiles were uncovered, Moscow succeeded in surprising the United States. On the other hand, it could be noted that the United States flew two U-2s over Cuba on October 14 mainly because certain members of the governmental bureaucracy feared that Moscow was planning to in-troduce offensive missiles. From this perspective, then, the first conclusion—that the Soviets achieved surprise—would have to be rejected.

For two reasons, the second conclusion is preferable to the first. On October 9, President Kennedy authorized the flight of two U-2s over the western end of Cuba. This fact does not prove that Kennedy believed that the Soviets were installing strategic missiles in Cuba. It demonstrates, how-ever, that he did not totally discard the possibility.

To be sure, President Kennedy may have experienced so much bureau-cratic pressure that he had no choice but to agree to the overflights. If such was the case, then the organizations exerting the pressure were in fact per-forming their proper institutional functions. In sum, it is fair to conclude that the United States was not surprised in any of the facets of surprise sought by Moscow because some of the organizations in the United States government performed their intelligence functions properly.

Viewed from a different perspective, Moscow's failure can be attributed to the Soviets' inability to keep Washington's sense of vulnerability low. Moscow's first miscalculation was assuming that it could persuade Wash-ington that the weapons being shipped to Cuba—after a lull of seven months—posed no threat to American security. Moscow failed to under-stand that it was not enough simply to extend such reassurance to Wash-ington. Since Castro had become one of Moscow's junior partners, Cuba's strategic and political importance had greatly increased. The mere increase in the flow of Soviet military equipment to Cuba raised Washington's inter-est and concern.

Moscow's first miscalculation created a host of problems about which, given the lack of data, we can only conjecture. By assuming that Washington could be persuaded not to feel threatened, Moscow must also have assumed that the number of U-2 flights over Cuba would remain low. In addition, Moscow seems to have concluded that time was precious and that, the longer it took to install the missiles, the greater was the chance that America would uncover them before they became operational. This reasoning may have influenced Moscow to give up any attempt to camouflage or disguise the construction of the missile sites. Finally, the Kremlin seems to have calculated that any attempt to use the SAMs to discourage the flights of American U-2s over Cuba would have, in fact, augmented Washington's need and resolve to learn exactly what the Soviets were so set on concealing. These conclusions—that American flights over Cuba would remain at two per month, that any attempt to camouflage or disguise the construction of missile sites would consume precious time, and that the use of SAMs before the offensive missiles were made operational would increase Washington's curiosity—evidently persuaded the Soviets that Cuba's rain and hurricane seasons would provide their operations with enough cover for the necessary period.

Moscow's luck might have been different had it managed to control Washington's concern over Cuba via diplomatic channels. Had diplomacy worked, the Kennedy Administration would not have felt so threatened and might not have ordered an increase in the U-2 flights. In view of weather conditions, and with only two flights a month, Washington's chances of getting a clear picture of Soviet activities in Cuba would have been much smaller.

However, having failed to control Washington's sense of vulnerability, almost every step that Moscow took afterward was bound to expose a new dimension of its strategy. Threatened by the increase in Soviet activities in Cuba, Washington increased its vigilance over Cuba in an attempt to uncover the meaning of these activities. In spite of weather conditions, Washington began to draw a fairly accurate picture of what was transpiring militarily in Cuba. Washington's major obstacle was, for a period of time, its own belief that Moscow was too rational to deploy offensive missiles in Cuba. But the presence of SAMs and the manner in which they were deployed challenged the soundness of this belief. As soon as doubt began to spread through the intelligence community in Washington, it became only a matter of time before Moscow's hand was revealed.

To a large extent, Moscow's strategy of surprise was based on a miscalculated risk, that is, a calculated risk that went awry. The objective of the strategy had been to facilitate the introduction of nuclear missiles in Cuba in order to narrow the nuclear advantage held by the United States. What Moscow failed to take into account was that Washington could ill afford not to be tuned to developments in Cuba. Without even suspecting that the Soviets planned to introduce strategic missiles, Washington, cognizant of the balance of power that existed between the Soviet Union and the United States, sought to unveil any act that could have altered it.

In the final analysis, Washington's initially firm view that Moscow would not risk placing strategic missiles on foreign territory gave way as its sense of vulnerability was heightened by the Soviet military build-up in Cuba. Moscow's increasing involvement in Cuba posed a threat to the interests of the United States that could not be ignored or minimized, and in response

Washington increased its efforts to decipher the true nature and magnitude of the threat.

Conclusion

The two cases just discussed provide additional support to the contention that would-be surprisers design their strategies around the preconceptions of their respective victims. More importantly, however, we have been able to isolate some of the conditions that can hinder or enhance the ability of potential victims to avert surprise as they become exposed to critical information.

In 1941 and 1962, the Germans and the Soviets, respectively, sought to achieve surprise primarily with regard to intention. Although the Germans succeeded and the Soviets failed in their attempts, it is reasonable to argue that both strategies of surprise should have ended in failure. In view of the environmental constraints faced by Germany in 1941, Hitler designed an ingenious strategy. However, the Soviet leadership had enough information to infer that a German attack lay within the realm of the probable. The Soviets failed to avert surprise primarily because Stalin could not reconcile himself to the idea that Germany would attack the Soviet Union. He rejected any information that might challenge his preconceptions and placed unjustifiable weight on his belief that he could reach a reasonable agreement with Hitler.

The story regarding the events in 1962 was noticeably different. The Americans also based their estimates on a set of deep-rooted assumptions. But, as new information of Soviet activities was channeled into the different compartments of the American intelligence system, new questions were raised, and eventually it was realized that the Soviets were not acting as initially expected. In other words, a set of deep-seated beliefs did not prevent the search for additional information nor the communication of interpretations that were in direct contradiction with past estimates. Equally important, President Kennedy and his closest advisers were not so set in their opinions that they were unwilling to accept the possibility that they might be wrong. When it came time to decide whether to fly a U-2 over the western side of Cuba where SAM installations had been spotted, Kennedy seems to have concluded that the costs of not knowing what the Soviets had been doing in that part of the island could be greater than the costs of creating an international incident should one of the U-2s be shot down over Cuban territory. His decision was an indication not only that he was willing to consider the viability of an alternative interpretation of Soviet behavior, but also that the decision-making structure was open enough to permit the formulation and dissemination of assessments at variance with the prevailing view.

In sum, the German and Soviet cases have strengthened the earlier argument that the likelihood of an international actor's succeeding in his attempt to surprise another is dependent on the accuracy of his estimate of his victim's sense of vulnerability and the extent to which he can control it. That these two factors are closely interrelated is well demonstrated by the 1962 case. The Soviet strategy of surprise failed primarily because the Soviets assumed, incorrectly, that they could control the sense of vulnerability of the United States as they were deploying nuclear missiles.

Part of the credit for averting surprise must also go to some of the American intelligence analysts who did not accept at face value the preconceptions of their leaders and the picture the Soviets were trying to project. Thus, if one compares this case with the 1941 German surprise attack, it could also be argued that, in instances in which an international actor cannot fully conceal his intention, he may still be able to achieve surprise against an adversary who has a well-defined set of images of others and finds it very difficult to incorporate information that might challenge the existing images.

Finally, if one accepts the argument that Stalin's relatively low sense of vulnerability could not be justified from a fully rational perspective, it could be proposed that it is more difficult for an international actor who resorts to an intention-type strategy of surprise to control a victim's sense of vulnerability and thus to achieve surprise, than for one who opts for either a time- or target-type of strategy. This argument concurs with our previous contention that it is very difficult for an international actor to conceal his intention either to resort to war or to deploy new weapons to augment his own capabilities as he mobilizes his forces.

Notes

1. McSherry, Vol. 2, 1970, p. 223.
2. Whaley, 1973a, p. 200.
3. Salisbury, 1969, pp. 67–68.
4. This view concurs with A.M. Nekrich's accounts in his critical book, *June 22, 1941.* See Nekrich, 1968, pp. 182–195.
5. Whaley, 1973a, p. 229.
6. Churchill, Vol. 3, 1948–1953, p. 317.
7. Hinsley, Vol. 2, 1979, p. 451.
8. Churchill, Vol. 3, 1948–1953, p. 319.
9. Hinsley, Vol. 2, 1979, p. 455.
10. Ibid., p. 456.
11. Ibid., p. 457.
12. Ibid., pp. 469–480.
13. Ibid., p. 482.
14. See Dallin, 1957; Leach, 1973; Seaton, 1971.

15. Salisbury, 1969, p. 57.

16. Kazakov, 1969, p. 188.

17. Salisbury, 1969, p. 59.

18. Kuztnetsov, 1969, p. 189.

19. Salisbury, 1969, p. 17.

20. Kuztnetsov, 1969, p. 190.

21. Nekrich confirms this point when he writes: "All this information [of German activities], passing through service channels beginning at frontier posts went to the appropriate section of the Main Directorate of Border Troops (GUPV) which immediately informed the general staff of the People's Commissariat of Defense, and the government." See Nekrich, 1968, p. 165.

22. Jervis, 1976, pp. 17–42; Lebow, 1981, pp. 104–105.

23. Lebow, 1981, p. 104.

24. Ibid., p. 153, note 14.

25. As Jervis has noted, when there is disagreement with regard to a policy, those who favor it will invariably estimate its chance of success as higher than those who oppose it. Jervis, 1976, pp. 128–130.

26. Wohlstetter, July 1965, pp. 691–692.

27. Ibid., p. 699.

28. Ibid., pp. 699, 702.

29. Ibid., p. 702.

30. Ibid., p. 701.

31. George and Smoke, 1974.

32. Ibid., p. 473.

33. Ibid., p. 475.

34. Ibid., p. 477.

35. Ibid., pp. 478–479.

36. Hilsman, 1967, p. 191.

37. Ibid., p. 174.

38. Ibid., p. 175.

39. Ibid., p. 189.

40. Ibid., p. 185.

41. Abel, 1966, p. 18.

42. Hilsman, 1967, p. 171.

43. Abel, 1966, p. 22. Weather conditions had by then deteriorated pronouncedly.

44. Hilsman, 1967, p. 189.

45. *The New York Times*, September 5, 1962, p. 2.

46. Hilsman, 1967, pp. 171–172.

47. Ibid., p. 171.

48. Ibid., p. 171.

49. Ibid., p. 171.

50. Abel, 1966, p. 25.

51. Abel, 1966, p. 25; Allison, 1971, p. 121.

52. Hilsman, 1967, p. 172.

53. Schlesinger, 1965, p. 799.

54. Allison, 1971, p. 122.

55. Abel, 1966, p. 26.

56. Ibid., p. 26; Hilsman, 1967, p. 175.

57. Hilsman, 1967, pp. 175–176.

58. Allison, 1971, p. 122.

59. Sorensen, 1965, p. 673.

60. Allison, 1971, pp. 122 and 192.

61. Ibid., p. 122.

62. Ibid., pp. 122 and 192.

63. Hilsman, 1967, p. 176. Hilsman's proposal was turned down because it would have meant a delay.

64. Allison, 1971, p. 192.

The Logic of Surprise and Surprise Avoidance

Accrding to Janice Gross Stein, attempts to deceive almost always lead to surprise because the requirements of a successful strategy of deception are not overly demanding.[1] If Stein were right, then it would be a futile endeavor to address the problem of surprise avoidance. However, as we hope to have demonstrated, the requirements for the successful implementation of a strategy of deception are quite demanding. In order to achieve surprise, an international actor must have an acute understanding of the obstacles he must surmount and of the means of deception he can rely on to overcome them. Therefore, it can be proposed that surprise avoidance depends mainly on the ability of a potential victim to understand the logic of surprise and to translate this understanding to the circumstances confronting his adversary.

From the outset it can be acknowledged that it will be nearly impossible for an actor to prevent being surprised by a rival who does not carefully consider his actions in advance and who carries them out without any major preparation. This study has concentrated solely on cases in which each would-be surpriser had a reason for acting as he did, assessed the pros and cons of surprising his victims, and took a variety of secret and deceptive steps to conceal the true nature of his own activities.

Why Would an International Actor Want to Achieve Surprise?

The first step any potential victim must take in order to avert surprise is to understand why an international actor might want to surprise him. He must keep in mind that the determination of an international actor to resort to surprise is likely to be a function of (1) how much he values the interests threatened by his adversary, (2) how much stronger or weaker he is than his adversary, (3) how well informed he is regarding his adversary's capabilities, including how fast his adversary can recover from a surprise attack, and (4) how much of a risk taker he is.

These factors do not function independently of one another. The interrelationship between the first two factors and an international actor's propensity to resort to surprise was fully established by the cases considered in this study and can be expressed as follows:

> *Proposition 1:* An international actor's disposition to resort to surprise will be higher when his most valued interests are threatened by an adversary who is as strong or stronger than he is than when they are threatened by a much weaker adversary.

One of the important things we learned from the decision by Egypt and Syria to attack Israel by surprise is that an international actor does not always have the capability to pursue his most valued objectives, even with the aid of surprise. However, this case also taught us that such obstacles might not inhibit an actor's determination to resort to surprise if he is convinced that surprise will help him fulfill a more limited, but still very important, objective.

> *Proposition 2:* An international actor's disposition to resort to surprise will remain high even in instances in which the achievement of surprise will not be sufficient to compensate for the discrepancy in capabilities, if he is convinced that it would help him accomplish a less important but still highly valued objective.

It has been argued that an international actor who underrates the strengths of his adversary, including his ability to recover from a surprise attack, will have, all other things being equal, a greater incentive to resort to surprise than if he had estimated his adversary's strengths accurately.[2] The surprise attack launched by Germany against the Soviet Union in 1941 substantiates this argument. Thus, for a potential victim facing an adversary as strong as he is or less strong, it is very important to keep in mind that:

> *Proposition 3:* An international actor's disposition to resort to surprise against an adversary who is as strong or stronger than he is will be higher when he underrates his opponent's capabilities than when he estimates them accurately.

Finally, we have also addressed the question of whether an international actor's propensity to take risks has an impact on his disposition to resort to surprise. At face value, it would seem reasonable to argue that these two variables are directly related. Hitler, Yamamoto, Khrushchev, and Sadat were leaders known for their predilection toward risk taking. But the fact that a leader who attempts surprise may be a risk taker is not, in and of itself, sufficient evidence to substantiate the argument that the decision to resort to surprise can be attributed to a predilection toward risk taking. As explained during the discussion in chapter 2 of the reasons Israel opted to pre-empt the Arabs with a surprise attack in 1967 but not in 1973, it is always imperative to define the conditions under which decision makers must make their choices. During both crises, Israel was led by leaders who had no great propensity to take risks. The relevant difference was that in 1967 Israeli decision makers questioned Israel's ability to overcome a pre-emptive, joint Arab attack. This doubt did not recur six years later. Moreover, in 1973 Israel was under intense pressure from the United States not to launch a pre-emptive attack.

The argument just presented does not invalidate the contention that an actor's propensity to take risks and his decision to resort to surprise are related. However, it gives us sufficient reason to pause and to ask under what conditions an actor's propensity to take risks would be a relevant factor. We know that the main supporters of surprise in the four major cases considered in this study were risk takers. In addition, it is clear that neither Hitler in 1941 nor Khrushchev in 1962 was so pressured by international and domestic factors that each could not have opted for other alternatives. On the other hand, the pressures faced by the Japanese and Arabs in 1941 and 1973, respectively, were so intense that their choices were severely bounded. These four cases suggest that:

> *Proposition 4:* The impact of an international actor's propensity to take risks on his disposition to resort to surprise will be greater when his freedom of choice is not severely constrained by domestic and international pressure than when it is markedly bounded.

The four propositions advanced thus far are summarized in Table 7–1.

Now that part of the stage is set, we can begin to explain how the understanding of the logic behind the decision to resort to surprise can help reduce the chances of surprise. The first order of business is to relate the propositions to the targets of surprise attempts.

Every potential victim must always keep in mind that, after estimating what it would cost an adversary to initiate a hostile act against him, he must carefully re-evaluate the extent to which the estimate would change if his adversary were to achieve surprise. If the re-evaluation is marked by a substantial increase in benefits, then it behooves the potential victim to try to consider why his adversary might want to surprise him. The analysis must proceed in a precise fashion. A potential victim must first assess his adversary's dissatisfaction with the situation at hand. In addition, he must estimate the extent to which he is being blamed for the problems faced by his adversary and whether the adversary has the power to extricate himself from those problems. Moscow and Washington in 1941, and Tel-Aviv in 1973, each asked some of these questions, but did not address them properly. Stalin never fully realized that Hitler was indirectly blaming him for his problems

Table 7–1
Factors that Motivate or Discourage International Actors to Opt for Surprise, by Case

Cases	Relative Value of Interests at Stake as Perceived by Potential Aggressor	Relative Strength of Adversary as Perceived by Potential Aggressor	Was Power of Adversary Underestimated by Potential Aggressor?	Was Most Important Objective Replaced by Highly Valued, Lower Ranked Objective?	Was Potential Aggressor a Risk Taker?	Was Surprise Attempted?
Japan USA, 1941	Higher	Stronger	Yes	No	Yes	Yes
Egypt–Syria Israel, 1973	Higher	Stronger	No	Yes	Yes	Yes
Germany USSR, 1941	Higher	Roughly equal	Yes	No	Yes	Yes
USSR USA, 1962	Higher	Roughly equal	No	No	Yes	Yes
Israel Egypt, 1967	Higher	Roughly equal*	No	No	No	Yes
Israel Egypt–Syria, 1973	Lower	Weaker	Yes	No	No	No
USA USSR, 1962	Lower	Weaker	No	No	No	No

*Israel's military strength was superior to that of Egypt. Israel, however, became quite concerned about having to face Egypt and its Arab allies.

with Britain. Moreover, the Soviet leader was fully convinced that Germany would not attack the Soviet Union because it lacked the power to fight a new war while still fighting Britain. His mistake was to project the costs and benefits Germany would incur by attacking the Soviet Union without ever considering how these values could be modified by a surprise attack on the Soviets. Had Stalin supplemented the first projection with the second one, he would have realized that Germany would *not* be fighting a two-front war if the Soviet Union were defeated rapidly, and that a surprise attack might make a rapid defeat more likely.

The problem with this kind of calculation is that the potential victim must also be able to measure correctly his adversary's own estimates. Stalin seems to have assumed that Hitler knew how powerful the Soviet Union was. However, partly because Stalin had made it so difficult for outsiders to gather reliable information on the Soviet Union, Hitler underestimated the power of the Soviet Union. Had Stalin considered this possibility, he could have inferred that with the correct information Hitler would find a surprise attack less attractive.

A potential victim can face a similar problem when trying to assess the goals his adversary is hoping to achieve. One of Israel's major mistakes in 1973 was to assume that an Egyptian–Syrian attack would be initiated only to inflict a resounding military defeat on Israel. Since the Arab states were not yet strong enough to fulfill this objective, Israeli policy makers inferred that the attack would not be immediately forthcoming. However, had Israel considered the possibility that the Arabs might opt for a more modest goal, it would have been in a better position to recognize that its adversaries did not need to augment their capabilities to the extent originally estimated and thus could launch the attack earlier. Moreover, had Israel taken into account the possibility that Egypt–Syria might try to achieve surprise during the attack, it would have also had to reconsider the possibility that the attack could come earlier than originally expected.

The problem faced by Washington in 1941 was significantly more complex. Its decision makers seem to have realized that, for Japan, becoming the dominant power in East and Southeast Asia was not only a matter of politics and economics, but also a matter of pride. Thus, Washington had no problem in concluding that Japan would go to war. But, in order to ascertain whether Japan would attempt to launch a surprise attack against Pearl Harbor, Washington should have asked itself how Japan's cost-benefit analysis of going to war would be affected by the knowledge that its capabilities had been underestimated and by the achievement of surprise. Had Washington considered the possibility that it was underestimating Japan's capabilities, the idea of a surprise attack on Pearl Harbor would have not seemed outlandish. Moreover, had this calculation been linked with an estimate of the benefit Japan would accrue from a successful attack on Pearl Harbor, Washington's reluctance to acknowledge the possibility of such an attack would have been further diminished.

An analysis of the reasons that an international actor resorts to surprise will rarely be exact. Unknown factors are bound to materialize. Thus, to minimize the chances of being surprised, the study of *why* must always proceed in conjunction with a careful analysis of (1) the types of surprise that might lie within the reach of his adversary, (2) the obstacles his adversary would have to surmount to achieve surprise, (3) the way his adversary acts, and (4) the degree of compatibility between his actions and the surprises that lie within his range.

Three Strategies of Surprise

The most striking characteristic of this study has been the predominance of the need to control the victim's sense of vulnerability. Japan's choice of a target-type strategy of surprise in 1941 depended on its policy makers' belief that they could control Washington's sense of vulnerability by concealing both the rate at which and the extent to which Japan was augmenting its capabilities. Similarly, Egypt–Syria might not have sought to achieve surprise with respect to the time of the attack had they not believed that they could control Israel's sense of vulnerability. In the case of Germany in 1941, the picture was more complex. Hitler seems to have wanted to increase Stalin's sense of vulnerability, but to keep it from rising too high. Finally, the Soviets in 1962 took numerous precautionary measures to disguise the deployment of their missiles in an attempt to keep Washington's sense of vulnerability at the same level that it had been since Moscow had begun to provide Cuba with defensive weapons.

In order to assess fully the importance of this variable, it would have been helpful to compare these four cases with instances in which those considering the possibility of resorting to surprise recognized that they could *not* control the sense of vulnerability of their respective victims. Thus, we can only tentatively suggest that:

> *Proposition 5:* An international actor's disposition to resort to surprise will be greater when he believes that he can control his victim's sense of vulnerability than when he believes that this task is beyond his reach.

The fact that an international actor believes that he can control his adversary's sense of vulnerability does not mean that he will be able to select randomly a strategy of surprise. Factors that will be of great concern to him are (1) the extent to which his power differs from that of his adversary, (2) his adversary's geographical location, and (3) the type of adversarial relationship he has had with his victim.

It was not simple coincidence that the actors who chose the intention-type strategy of surprise were the two whose powers most closely approximated the powers of their adversaries.[3] An international actor who discloses his intention to take aggressive measures to pursue his objectives knows that, if he and his victim are equally strong, his threats will be taken more seriously than if the victim is much stronger. It can be proposed that:

> *Proposition 6:* An international actor's disposition to choose an intention-type strategy of surprise will be greater when his power and that of his target are approximately the same than when the power of his target is noticeably greater than his own.

The implementation of an intention-type strategy of surprise is quite difficult. As argued in the Germany–Soviet Union case of 1941 and the Soviet Union–United States case of 1962, an international actor must be able to control the level of tension and mistrust his adversary feels toward him. To do so, he must rely not only on his skills as a negotiator, but also on his ability to control his adversary's sense of vulnerability. Therefore:

Proposition 7: To achieve surprise with respect to his intention, an international actor must control his adversary's level of tension and mistrust and his sense of vulnerability.

The fact that an international actor may be able to disclose his intention because he is much weaker than his adversary does not automatically free him to choose a strategy of surprise randomly. For instance, before he decides that he would like to achieve surprise with respect to his target, he must carefully evaluate whether his adversary will *believe* that the instruments of war will be used against other targets. As demonstrated by the surprise attacks on Pearl Harbor in 1941, and on Israel in 1973, the geographical locations of the targets may have been the principal reason that the attackers chose different strategies.

The Japanese leaders opted for a target-type strategy of surprise because they knew that the United States downgraded Japan's military capabilities, and because they believed that the vast distances separating their two targets—Southeast Asia and the Hawaiian Islands—would help them conceal their forces as they navigated toward Pearl Harbor. The relationship between these two factors was very important. Tokyo had to keep Washington's sense of vulnerability low to ensure that, as Japan's intention to attack Southeast Asia was disclosed, Washington would continue to assume that Japan lacked the capability to launch simultaneously two large and exceedingly complex attacks against targets thousands of miles apart and thus would not search for the Japanese armada that was moving toward Pearl Harbor.

Egypt and Syria, on the other hand, although known to be much weaker than Israel, did not have the geographical advantage possessed by Japan. The sharing of boundaries with Israel and the hostile atmosphere that had permeated their relationship prevented the Arab leaders from trying to convey the impression that they would direct their forces against other targets. Their only alternative was to achieve surprise regarding the *time* of the attack, by controlling Israel's sense of vulnerability. These two cases enable us to forward the following propositions:

Proposition 8: An international actor's disposition to choose either a target- or time-type strategy of surprise will be greater when his power is significantly inferior to that of his adversary than when it is similar.

Proposition 9: An international actor who is significantly less powerful than his adversary is unlikely to opt for a target-type strategy of surprise when his relationship with his adversary has been uncharacteristically conflictual and they share common borders.[4]

The ability of an international actor to implement a target-type strategy of surprise, as discovered during the analysis of the surprise attack on Pearl Harbor, can be described as follows:

Proposition 10: To achieve surprise with respect to his target, an international actor must control his adversary's concern with respect to the geographical areas where he intends to stage the surprise.

Proposition 11: To control his adversary's concern with respect to the geographical areas where he intends to stage the surprise, an international actor must control his adversary's sense of vulnerability and be located in an area from which he can pretend that his deployed forces will be used to attack not his adversary, but other targets.

From the study of the coordinated surprise attack on Israel in 1973 by Egypt and Syria, it can be proposed that:

Proposition 12: To achieve surprise with respect to the time of his action, an international actor must control his adversary's sense of vulnerability.

The four cases have shown quite clearly that, regardless of whether an international actor opts for a target-, time-, or an intention-type strategy of surprise, there are three other dimensions he must also attempt to conceal:

Proposition 13: To achieve surprise with respect to either intention, target, or time, an international actor must be able to conceal his rationale, military capabilities, and/or military doctrine.

The empirical analysis supports the general contention that it is easier for an international actor to control the sense of vulnerability of an adversary who is significantly more powerful than of one who is equally powerful. (It was easier for Japan and Egypt–Syria to control the sense of vulnerability of the United States and Israel, respectively, than it was for Germany and the Soviet Union to control the sense of vulnerability of the Soviet Union and the United States, respectively).[5] In the four instances in which surprise was attempted, the only actors who opted for an intention-type strategy of surprise were the two whose power differed the least from their respective adversaries, and, since one failed to achieve surprise and the other succeeded primarily because his adversary was unwilling to listen to his advisers, it can be proposed that:

> *Proposition 14:* An international actor who must achieve surprise with re-spect to his intention is less likely to succeed than one who must achieve surprise with respect to the target or time of his action.

All along, this study has emphasized that in order to achieve surprise an international actor must carefully assess the environmental constraints that could obstruct the proper implementation of his strategy. This reality not-withstanding, it is imperative to recognize the critical role played by the concept, *sense of vulnerability*. As inferred by the analysis of the Soviet attempt to surprise the United States in 1962, an international actor's ability to achieve surprise can be related to the sense of vulnerability in three dif-ferent ways. It can be related in terms of (1) how vulnerable the victim feels vis-a-vis the aggressor, (2) how precise is the aggressor's estimate of his vic-tim's sense of vulnerability, and (3) how well the aggressor can control his victim's sense of vulnerability. Expressed in propositional form:

> *Proposition 15:* An international actor's chance of achieving surprise is inversely related to his adversary's sense of vulnerability and directly related to his own ability to accurately estimate and control his adversary's sense of vulnerability.

Before moving into the final phase of this study, it is important to deal with one more factor that could have a significant impact on a would-be surpriser's ability to achieve surprise. In formulating a theory of surprise, one of the elements necessary to take into account is the amount of infor-mation that a potential victim would need to have as a prerequisite for responding to a potential attack.

According to Stein, one of the reasons Israel's policy makers in 1973 were unwilling to respond to the increase in threatening signals emanating from Egypt and Syria was that they were looking for certainty.[6] This con-clusion has been partially confirmed by our study. Israeli high officials not only were concerned about hows costly it had been in the past to respond to false alarms, but also were mindful of how difficult it was to control escalation. Moreover, Prime Minister Golda Meir did not dare launch a pre-emptive attack for fear that Israel would be castigated by world public opin-ion and would lose American support. Meir was convinced that it had to be clear beyond the shadow of a doubt who began hostilities.[7]

The American situation in 1941 does not support or challenge Stein's basic argument. Because of the strong opposition to war by the American public and Congress, Washington was very careful to avoid taking steps that could have been construed at home and abroad as being hostile in nature. However, this nonhostile stance had little bearing on Washington's decision not to prepare Pearl Harbor for a Japanese attack. President Roosevelt and his advisers had a very good idea of what Japan intended to do and when it intended to do it. But they had no information that would have justified an aggressive American reaction, for it was not known that Pearl Harbor would also be attacked. In other words, near certainty that a Japanese attack would ensue did not reduce the uncertainty as to whether Pearl Harbor would be a target.

Stalin's freedom to act in 1941 was severely bounded by his need for certainty that an attack would be forthcoming. So long as there was a ray of hope that Hitler might not attack, Stalin wanted to make sure that his actions would not provide the German leader with a justification to attack.

The Cuban Missile Crisis is a complex case. The Kennedy Administration had come into office hoping to bring about significant changes in the structure of the cold war. In 1962, however, the new administration came under intense domestic pressure to take major steps to stop the flow of Soviet weapons to Cuba. President Kennedy withstood the pressure and did not react in a forceful manner until the intelligence community had gathered sufficient information to demonstrate that the Soviets were installing offensive weapons, not just defensive weapons as they had been claiming. What must be taken into account when comparing this case with the other three is that with incomplete information it is simpler to infer that an adversary is installing nuclear weapons than to infer that he is going to use them to initiate a nuclear attack. Had the Kennedy Administration decided that it would act forcefully only if it could prove that the Soviets were actually going to use the missiles to attack the United States, discovery of the missiles per se would not have been enough to justify the blockade.

In sum, three of the four cases considered in this study support Stein's argument. It could be postulated, therefore, that:

Proposition 16: An international actor's chance of achieving surprise is directly related to the degree of certainty required by his adversary that an act of aggression will be initiated against him before he decides to begin his own acts of aggression: The greater the degree of certainty required, the greater is the likelihood that surprise will be achieved.

Some of the arguments presented since Table 1 are summarized and compared in Tables 7–2 through 7–4.

This study can now be brought to its natural conclusion by discussing the way in which the understanding of the logic behind the choice of a specific strategy of surprise can help a potential victim reduce the chances of being surprised. The first order of business for a potential victim, after

Table 7–2
Dimensions of Surprise Sought, by Case

Cases	Target	Time	Intention	Rationale	Military Capability	Military Doctrine
			Dimensions of Surprise Sought			
Japan USA, 1941	Yes	No	No	Yes	Yes	Yes
Egypt–Syria Israel, 1973	No	Yes	No	Yes	Yes	Yes
Germany USSR, 1941	No	No	Yes	Yes	No	Yes
USSR USA, 1962	No	No	Yes	Yes	Yes	Yes

having concluded that one of his adversaries may benefit from resorting to a strategy of surprise, is to ask himself (1) how vulnerable he feels vis-a-vis his adversary, and (2) how easily could his adversary control his sense of vulnerability. If the potential victim comes up with a negative answer to the first question and a positive answer to the second question, he would have good reason to conclude that his adversary might be seriously contemplating a strategy of surprise. At this stage, the potential victim will want to proceed with a careful analysis of (1) the types of surprises that lie within reach of his adversary, (2) the obstacles his adversary would have to surmount to achieve surprise, (3) the way his adversary acts, and (4) the compatibility of his actions with the surprises that lie within his range and the obstacles that he would have to surmount to achieve surprise.

Regarding the first concern, a potential victim will want to keep in mind that generally there are two factors that could undermine an actor's ability to implement an intention-type strategy of surprise. First, any international actor who resorts to such a dramatic step as attacking another actor will usually do it to remedy some major differences. In many instances the would-be victim will be aware of the problem and might even have concluded that his adversary would resort to violent means. The United States and Israel knew very well that their respective adversaries were dissatisfied with the status quo and were preparing to resort to war to alter it.

In some cases, however, when the displeased party does not fully disclose his dissatisfaction, the problem becomes more complex. Stalin was aware that Hitler was unhappy with the way the Soviet Union had been behaving toward Germany. But the Soviet leader had no way of knowing the intensity

Table 7–3
Dimensions of Surprise, Objectives of Deception Sought, and Means Used to Mislead Victims, by Cases

Cases	Strategies of Surprise	Objectives of Deception Sought	Means Used to Mislead Victim
Japan USA, 1941	Target, rationale, military capability and doctrine	Control USA's sense of vulnerability over Pearl Harbor	1. Conceal rate at which new military equipment was produced 2. Conceal adoption of new offensive naval strategy 3. Conceal attempts to perfect aerial torpedoes 4. Conceal attempts to improve cruising range of ships 5. Display intention to launch attacks in Southeast Asia 6. Conceal deployment of Pearl Harbor Task Force 7. Negotiate with USA
Egypt–Syria Israel, 1973	Time, rationale, military capability and doctrine	Control Israel's sense of vulnerability	1. Conceal rate at which new military equipment was acquired 2. Conceal adoption of new military doctrine 3. Conceal deployment of offensive forces 4. Conceal formation of war alliance between Egypt–Syria 5. Conceal alteration of ranking of goals 6. Create diversionary threat 7. Negotiate with USA
Germany USSR, 1941	Intention, rationale, military doctrine	Control Moscow's sense of vulnerability and its level of tension and mistrust	1. Display intention to launch attack against Britain (used for limited period) 2. Conceal adoption of new military strategy 3. Negotiate with USSR
USSR USA, 1962	Intention, rationale, military capability and doctrine	Control USA's sense of vulnerability and its level of tension and mistrust	1. Conceal deployment of nuclear missiles 2. Conceal change of policy with respect to deployment of nuclear missiles outside Soviet territory 3. Maintain contact with American leaders in attempt to persuade them that weapons being deployed to Cuba could not be used against USA

Table 7–4
Conditions and Actions that Aided or Prevented the Achievement of Surprise, by Case and Strategy

Cases and Strategies	Level of Vulnerability of Potential Victim	Was Level of Vulnerability Controlled?	Level of Tension and Mistrust Experienced by Potential Victim	Geographical Relationship Between Adversaries	Was Level of Tension and Mistrust Controlled?	Was Available Information Properly Assessed by Potential Victim?	Degree of Certainty Required by Potential Victim Regarding the Actions of his Adversary before Attempting to Counteract Them	Was Surprise Achieved?
Japan USA, 1941 (Target)	Low (+)	Yes (+)	High (0)	Separated by vast distance (+)	No (0)	Yes (0)	Was not an issue (0)	Yes
Egypt–Syria Israel, 1973 (Time)	Low (+)	Yes (+)	High (0)	Shared common borders (0)	No (0)	Yes (0)	High (+)	Yes
Germany USSR, 1941 (Intention)	Low (+)	Yes (+)	Moderate (+)	Shared common borders (0)	No (0)	No (+)	High (+)	Yes
USSR USA, 1962 (Intention)	Low (0)	No (−)	Moderate (0)	Separated by short distance* (0)	No (−)	Yes (−)	Moderate (−)	No

Symbols: (+) Indicates that the condition or action helped the would-be surpriser achieve surprise.

(0) Indicates that the condition or action had no impact on the would-be surpriser's ability to achieve surprise.

(−) Indicates that the condition or action had a negative impact on the would-be surpriser's ability to achieve surprise.

* Refers to Cuba's geographical proximity to the United States.

of that displeasure, for Hitler had been very careful to conceal it. Similarly, the Kennedy Administration must have realized that the disclosure of its knowledge that the balance of power was tilted heavily in favor of the United States had created a major predicament for Moscow. But Khrushchev's decision not to publicly acknowledge the degree of his concern made it very difficult for Kennedy and his advisers to fathom Moscow's attempt to place strategic nuclear missiles in Cuba.

This type of advantage for the would-be surpriser is unlikely to hold its attractiveness for a long period of time. It is nearly impossible for a would-be surpriser to attack or deploy missiles without taking some major preliminary steps. These steps are unlikely to reveal immediately what the would-be surpriser intends to do. However, they can alert the potential victim that it is time for him to consider carefully what these actions could signify. In particular, it is important to place the actions in their proper context, to consider whether they could reveal an attempt by their initiator to shape an inaccurate estimate of his intention, and to ask how much the initiator of the actions might benefit from an inaccurate estimate of his intentions.

A good illustration of the steps that can be taken is the way in which the Kennedy Administration sought to uncover Moscow's intention. Although Kennedy and his advisers were quite secure in their belief that Moscow would not dare to deploy strategic nuclear missiles in Cuba and had not been able to establish how badly Moscow had been hurt by the disclosure that the United States remained the most powerful international actor, they never accepted at face value the Soviet claim that Cuba was not being supplied with offensive weapons. Their desire to know exactly what was going on in Cuba was born both of the need to be fully informed as to the true nature of the threat that Cuba could pose, and of mistrust for what the Soviets were so persistently attempting to convey.

In contrast to Kennedy's actions was Stalin's immobility prior to the German attack. The Soviet leader, with no firm information as to what Hitler intended to do, seemed quite willing to give him the benefit of the doubt. His confidence in his belief that Hitler would not attack for fear of getting entangled in a two-front war prevented Stalin from considering that the opposite of what he was predicting could ensue and that his own actions would make such a development not only more likely, but also less costly to the Germans.

During the early stages of implementation of an intention-type strategy of surprise, a would-be victim is likely to know very little about his adversary's plan. His adversary's determination to conceal the nature and the extent of his dissatisfaction could be the principal factor contributing to his uncertainty. As the adversary begins to take more complex steps to carry out the strategy, the potential victim is bound to realize that not all is well and that he must begin to consider whether his adversary's past silence might have had a misleading purpose. Although it might not be feasible to come up with a definitive answer, the would-be victim must also reassess his original estimates of his adversary's capabilities and question whether by underestimating them he might have unintentionally prompted his adversary to exploit the misperception. Finally, a persistent effort by his adversary to persuade him that his intention is more accurately reflected by his words than by his actions ought to induce the would-be victim to estimate what the adversary might gain if the converse were to be true.

A potential victim may have few doubts that his adversary will follow a warlike path, but wonder whether he will be among the targets. He can reach a tentative answer by evaluating whether his adversary could disclose his intention to go to war and the identity of some of his targets via a series of conspicuous acts, while conveying the impression that he—the concerned target—will not be attacked. A potential victim in this kind of predicament must ask himself three questions. First, he will want to know whether his adversary can march his forces with little cover in one direction to signal that he intends to attack certain targets in a specific area, and at the same time deploy another element of his forces toward him under a cloud of secrecy. A positive answer to this question will not necessarily indicate that the potential victim will be attacked. It will merely point out that an attack is feasible and that he must ask himself a second question.

At this juncture, the would-be victim must carefully reconsider how well informed he and his adversary are about each other's capabilities. In particular, he will want to consider how his adversary's determination to attack him could be affected if both are unknowingly underestimating each other's actual and potential capabilities, but his adversary *knows* that his power is being underestimated. This step will be very similar to the one he took to establish the reason his adversary may want to resort to surprise. However, he will have to make a special effort to come up with a more accurate picture of his adversary's capabilities. Since it is not always feasible to gather the kind of information necessary to develop an accurate projection of his adversary's capabilities, it is very important that the potential victim pay close attention to the type of information his adversary discloses with respect to his own capabilities. Israel, for instance, seemed quite willing to accept false disclosures by Egypt–Syria that they were having problems adapting Soviet weapons to their own needs.

It should not be assumed that the potential victim will be able to infer automatically that he will be among the targets if he discovers that he and his adversary have underestimated each other's strengths. He could conclude that, although the two estimates were off, he is still so much stronger that his adversary would be blind not to notice the discrepancy.

To use this argument as justification for not having been prepared for an attack may be rational, provided rationality is viewed from a very narrow perspective. But a potential victim must always keep in mind that rational analysis is not bound by any one specific ranking of goals. Thus, a potential victim who is convinced that it would be impossible to overlook his superior strength must ask himself the following: (1) What kind of actor might be undeterred by this reality? (2) What could incite an actor to take such a potentially costly step? (3) What action could limit the costs of taking such a step?

There is little indication that the United States in 1941 took any of these steps. American foreign policy makers had considered the possibility that Japan might try to attack Pearl Harbor by surprise, but little weight was given to this possibility when it became evident that Japan would concentrate its military efforts in Southeast Asia. American policy makers from this point on could not envision the possibility that Japan with its limited military capability, might launch two major operations simultaneously.

This particular conclusion should have warned the Roosevelt Administration that it was time to sit back and reassess its estimates. Washington should have asked itself whether Japan might be tempted to attack Pearl Harbor if it had unknowingly underestimated the actual and potential strength of the United States and knew that Washington had underestimated Japan's power. Moreover, Washington should have been especially careful to assess (1) the factors that might incite Japan to disregard the superior power of the United States, and (2) the extent to which surprise could surmount some of Japan's weaknesses.

The steps a potential victim must take in order to reduce the chances of failing to predict *when* he will be attacked differ very little from those just discussed. If he suspects that he will be attacked, but does not know when, by asking the same set of questions he might be able to discover that his original projection could have facilitated his adversary's task of launching an attack unexpectedly at an earlier time.

Conclusion

Surprise is an art form created through deception and bounded by rationality and misperception. No two strategies of surprise are exactly alike, and yet all surprises are guided by the same principles.

The search for surprise is founded on the idea that an actor can induce another to derive a false rational assessment of the first actor's actions without knowing that the interpretations are the result of miscalculations. To discover that his rational analysis may not be an accurate assessment of the first actor's actions, the second actor must always keep in mind that reality is not always apparent, and that illusions are sometimes deliberately created.

There is no sure method for avoiding surprise. But it is feasible to minimize surprise by understanding the circumstances under which it might be sought, the variety of obstacles that must be surmounted in order to achieve different surprises, and the types of steps that must be taken to overcome such obstacles. Surprise, in its simplest form, is the creation of a false rational, near certainty assessment. The avoidance of surprise in its most complex form, is the discovery of where such falseness lies.

Notes

1. Stein, 1982, p. 95.
2. Handel, 1976, p. 21.
3. In relative terms the differences in power capabilities between Germany and the Soviet Union in 1941, and the Soviet Union and the United States in 1962, were significantly smaller than the differences in power capabilities between the countries involved in the other instances of surprise.
4. Because of the small number of cases considered in the study, it is not feasible to test whether an international actor would choose a target-type strategy of surprise over a time-type strategy of surprise, or vice versa, when he has the freedom to decide between the two.
5. An international actor who is significantly more powerful will feel less vulnerable and is likely to be less attentive to the actions of his adversary.
6. Stein, 1980, p. 167.
7. Brecher, 1980, pp. 177–178.

Bibliography

Abel, Elie. *The Missile Crisis*. Philadelphia: J. B. Lippincott, 1966.

Agranat Commission of Inquiry, Interim Report. Jerusalem: Government Printing Office, April 1974.

Allison, Graham T. *Essence of Decision*. Boston: Little, Brown & Co., 1971.

Aviation Week March 16, 1975.

Axelrod, Robert. "The Rational Timing of Surprise." *World Politics* January, 1979, Vol. 31, No. 2, pp. 228–246.

Baker, A. J. *The Yom Kippur War*. New York: Ballantine Books, 1974.

Bell, Coral. "The October Middle East War" *International Affairs* October 1974, Vol. 50, No. 4, pp. 531–553.

Ben-Zvi, Abraham. "Hindsight and Foresight: A Conceptual Framework for the Analysis of Surprise Attacks." *World Politics* April, 1976, Vol. 28, No. 3, pp. 381–395.

Betts, Richard K. "Analysis, War, and Decision: Why Intelligence Failures Are Inevitable." *World Politics* October, 1978, Vol. 31, No. 1, pp. 61–80.

Brecher, Michael. *Decisions in Crisis*. Berkeley: University of California Press, 1980.

Butow, Robert J. C. *Tojo and the Coming of the War*. Stanford, CA: Stanford University Press, 1961.

Central Intelligence Agency. "Glossary of Camouflage, Concealment, Deception and Security Terminology." Washington: Office of Research and Development, February 1981.

Churchill, Winston. *The Second World War*. Vol. 3. Boston: Houghton Mifflin Co., 1948–1953.

Clausewitz, Carl Von. *On War*. Vol. III. London: Kegan, Paul, Trench, Trubner, 1911.

Cohen, Bernard C., and Harris, S. A. "Foreign Policy." In *Handbook of Political Science*. Vol. 6. Edited by Fred Greenstein and Nelson Polsby. Reading, MA: Addison–Wesley, 1975.

Collier, Basil. *The War in the Far East, 1941–1945*. New York: William Morrow & Co., 1969.

Converse, Philip. "The Nature of Belief Systems in Mass Publics." In *Ideology and Discontent*. Edited by David Apter. New York: The Free Press, 1964.

Crowley, James B. *Japan's Quest for Autonomy*. Princeton: Princeton University Press, 1966.

Dallin, Alexander. *German Rule in Russia, 1941–1945*. New York: St. Martin's Press, 1957.

DeWeerd, H. A. "Strategic Surprise in the Korean War," *Orbis* 6, Fall 1962.

Dinerstein, Herbert. *The Making of a Missile Crisis: October 1962*. Baltimore: The Johns Hopkins University Press, 1976.

Documents on German Foreign Policy, DGFP, 1918–1945. Vols. 11 and 12. Washington, DC: U.S. Government Printing Office. (Undated).

Dupuy, Trevor N. *Elusive Victory—The Arab–Israeli Wars, 1947–1974*. New York: Harper & Row Publishers, 1978.

Eckstein, Harry. "Case Study and Theory in Political Science." In *Handbook of Political Science*. Vol. 7. Edited by Fred Greenstein and Nelson Polsby. Reading, MA: Addison–Wesley, 1975.

Etheredge, Lloyd S. "Personality Effects on American Foreign Policy, 1896–1968: A Test of Interpersonal Generalization Theory." *American Political Science Review* June, 1978, Vol. 72, No. 2, pp. 434–451.

Fuehrer Conferences on Matters Dealing with the German Navy. Vol. 2. Washington, DC: Office of Naval Intelligence, 1947.

Fugate, Bryan I. *Operation Barbarossa: Strategy and Tactics on the Eastern Front, 1941*. Novato, CA: Presidio Press, 1984.

Fukudome, Shigeru. "Hawaii Operation." In *The Japanese Navy in World War II*. Annapolis: U.S. Naval Institute, 1969.

Fulbright, J. William. "Some Reflections upon Recent Events and Continuing Problems." *The Congressional Record*, June 29, 1961.

Gafencu, Grigore. *Prelude to the Russian Campaign*. London: Muller, 1945.

George, Alexander L. *Presidential Decision Making in Foreign Policy: The Effective Use of Information and Advice*. Boulder, CO: Westview Press, 1980.

———. "Warning and Response: Theory and Practice." In *International Violence: Terrorism, Surprise and Control*. Edited by Yair Evron. Jerusalem: Hebrew University of Jerusalem, 1979.

———, and Smoke, Richard. *Deterrence and American Foreign Policy*. New York: Columbia University Press, 1974.

Gilpin, Robert. *War and Change in World Politics*. Cambridge: Cambridge University Press, 1981.

Halperin, Morton. *Bureaucratic Politics and Foreign Policy*. Washington, DC: Brookings Institution, 1974.

Handel, Michael. "Crisis and Surprise in Three Arab–Israeli Wars." In *Strategic Military Surprise*. Edited by Klaus Knorr and Patrick Morgan. New Brunswick, NJ: Transaction Books, 1983.

———. *The Diplomacy of Surprise: Hitler, Nixon, Sadat*. Cambridge: Harvard University Press, 1981.

———. "Perception, Deception and Surprise: The Case of the Yom Kippur War." *Jerusalem Papers on Peace Problems* 19. Jerusalem: Leonard Davis Institute of International Relations, Hebrew University of Jerusalem, 1976.

Hart, Liddell. *Strategy: The Indirect Approach*. New York: Praeger Publishers, 1954.

Hearings Before the Joint Committee of the Investigation of the Pearl Harbor Attack, Congress of the United States, Seventy-ninth Congress, Parts 2, 6, 14, 15, 22, 28, 33, and 39. Washington, D.C.: U.S. Government Printing Office, 1946.

Heikal, Mohamed. *The Road to Ramadan*. New York: Quadrangle, 1975.

Herzog, Chaim. *The War of Atonement*. Boston: Little, Brown & Co., 1975.

Hilsman, Roger. *To Move a Nation*. New York: Doubleday & Co., 1967.

Hinsley, F. H. *British Intelligence in the Second World War*. Vols. 1 and 2. London: Her Majesty's Stationery Office, 1979.

———. *Hitler's Strategy*. Cambridge: The University Press, 1951.

Horelick, A., and Rush, M. *Strategic Power and Soviet Foreign Policy*. Chicago: University of Chicago Press, 1965.

Hosoya, Chihiro. "Retrogression in Japan's Foreign Policy Decision Making Process." In *Dilemmas of Growth in Prewar Japan*. Edited by James W. Morley. Princeton: Princeton University Press, 1971.

Hybel, Alex R. "Analogies from the Past: Patterns of U.S. Intervention." Paper delivered at the annual meeting of the International Society of Political Psychology, Washington, DC: June 1985.

Ike, Nobutaka. *Japan's Decision for War, Records of the 1941 Policy Conferences*. Stanford, CA: Stanford University Press, 1967.

Immerman, Richard. *The CIA in Guatemala*. Austin: University of Texas Press, 1982.

Insight Team of The London Times. *The Yom Kippur War*. New York: Doubleday & Co., 1974.

Iriye, Akira. "The Failure of Military Expansionism." In *Dilemmas of Growth in Prewar Japan*. Edited by James W. Morley. Princeton: Princeton University Press, 1971.

Irving, David. *Hitler's War*. New York: The Viking Press, 1977.

Ishii, Kikujiro. "The Permanent Bases of Japanese Foreign Policy." *Foreign Affairs*, Vol. XI, No. 2, January 1930, pp. 220–229.

Jackson, I. J. *Climate, Water, and Agriculture in the Tropics*. London: Longman, 1977.

Janis, Irving L. *Groupthink*. Boston: Houghton Mifflin Co., 1982.

Jerusalem Post, August 11, 1973.

Jervis, Robert. *Perception and Misperception in International Politics*. Princeton: Princeton University Press, 1976.

———. *The Logic of Images in International Relations*. Princeton: Princeton University Press, 1970.

Kalb, Marvin, and Kalb, Bernard. *Kissinger*. Boston: Little, Brown & Co., 1974.

Kazakov, M. I. "At the General Staff." In *Stalin and His Generals*. Edited by Seweryn Bialer. New York: Western Publishing Co., 1969.

Khrushchev, Nikita. *Khrushchev Remembers*. Introduction and notes by Edward Crankshaw. Boston: Little, Brown & Co., 1970.

Kinhide, Mushakoji. "The Structure of Japanese–American Relations in the 1930s." In *Pearl Harbor as History*. Edited by Dorothy Borg and Shumpei Okamoto. New York: Columbia University Press, 1973.

Knorr, Klaus. "Strategic Surprise: The Incentive Structure." In *Strategic Military*

Surprise. Edited by Klaus Knorr and Patrick Morgan.New Brunswick, NJ: Transaction Books, 1983.

———. "Failures in National Intelligence Estimates: The Case of the Cuban Missiles." *World Politics* April 1964, Vol. 16, No. 1, pp. 462–463.

Knorr, Klaus, and Morgan, Patrick, eds. *Strategic Military Surprise.* New Brunswick, NJ: Transaction Books, 1983.

Kuztnetsov, N. G. "At Naval Headquarters." In *Stalin and His Generals.* Edited by Seweryn Bialer. New York: Western Publishing Co., 1969.

Langer, William, and Cleason, S. Everett. *The Undeclared War, 1940–1941.* New York: Harper & Brothers Publishers, 1953.

Leach, Barry. *German Strategy Against Russia, 1939–1941.* Oxford: Clarendon Press, 1973.

Lebow, Richard Ned. *Between Peace and War.* Baltimore: The Johns Hopkins University Press, 1981.

Lijphart, Arend. "The Comparable-Cases Strategy in Comparative Research." *Comparative Political Studies* July 1975, Vol. 8, No. 2, pp. 158–177.

———. "Comparative Politics and the Comparative Method." *American Political Science Review* September 1971, Vol. 65, No. 3, pp. 682–693.

Manchester, William. *American Caesar.* New York: Dell Publishing Co., 1979.

March, James. "Bounded Rationality, Ambiguity and the Engineering of Choice." Paper presented at Carnegie–Mellon University, October 1977.

Matthew, Herbert L. *Revolution in Cuba.* New York: Charles Scribner's Sons, 1975.

McSherry, James. *Stalin, Hitler and Europe.* Vol. 2. New York: The World Publishing Co., 1970.

Mefford, Dwain. "Formulating Foreign Policy on the Basis of Historical Analogies: An Application of Developments in Artificial Intelligence." Paper presented at the 25th annual convention of the International Studies Association, March 27–31, 1984.

Mill, John Stuart. *Philosophy of Scientific Method.* Edited by Ernest Nagel. New York: Hofner Publishing Co., 1950.

Morgenthau, Hans J. *Politics Among Nations.* New York: Alfred A. Knopf, 1966.

Morison, Samuel E. *The Rising Sun in the Pacific 1931–April 1942.* Vol. III. Boston: Little, Brown & Co., 1951.

Nekrich, A. M. *June 22, 1941.* Translated by Vladimir Petrov. Columbia, SC: University of South Carolina Press, 1968.

The New York Times December 13, 1941; August 30, 1962; September 5, 1962; September 29, 1973.

Newsweek, April 9, 1973.

"The Nuremberg Judgment—Victor's Verdict: Blunder Thrown Out of Court." In *The Outbreak of the Second World War.* Edited by John L. Snell. Lexington, MA: D. C. Heath & Co., 1962.

Palumbo, Dennis. "Organization Theory and Political Science." In *Handbook of Political Science.* Vol. 2. Edited by Fred Greenstein and Nelson Polsky. Reading, MA: Addison–Wesley, 1975.

Perlmutter, Amos. "Israel's Fourth War, October 1973: Political and Military Misperception." *Orbis* Summer 1975.

Prange, Gordon W. *At Dawn We Slept.* Middlesex, England: Penguin Books, 1981.

Rich, Norman. *Hitler's War Aims.* Vol. I. New York: W. W. Norton, 1973.

Riker, William H. "The Paradox of Voting and Congressional Rules for Voting on Amendments." In *American Political Science Review* June 1958, Vol. 52, No. 2, pp. 349–366.

Russett, Bruce. "Pearl Harbor: Deterrence Theory and Decision-Making Theory," *Journal of Peace Research* 1967, Vol. 4.

Salisbury, Harrison E. *The 900 Days—The Siege of Leningrad.* New York: Harper & Row, 1969.

Schlesinger, Arthur. *A Thousand Days.* Boston: Houghton Mifflin Co., 1965.

Seaton, Albert. *The Russo-German War, 1941–1945.* London: Arthur Baker, 1971.

Shimada, Koichi. "Air Operation in the Philippines." In *The Japanese Navy in World War II.* Annapolis: U.S. Naval Institute, 1969.

Shlaim, Avi. "Failures in National Intelligence Estimates: The Case of the Yom Kippur War." *World Politics* April 1976, Vol. 27, No. 3, pp. 348–380.

Simon, Herbert A. *Models of Man.* New York: John Wiley & Sons, 1957.

Snyder, Glenn, and Diesing, Paul. *Conflict Among Nations.* Princeton: Princeton University Press, 1977.

Snyder, R. C., Bruck, H. W., and Sapin, B. *Foreign Policy Decision-Making.* New York: The Free Press, 1962.

Sorensen, Theodore C. *Kennedy.* New York: Harper & Row, 1965.

Stech, Frank. *Political and Military Intention Estimation.* Bethesda: Mathtech, 1979.

Stein, Janice Gross, and Tanter, Raymond. *Rational Decision Making: Israel's Security Choices, 1967.* Columbus: Ohio State University Press, 1980.

———. "Military Deception, Strategic Surprise, and Conventional Deterrence: A Political Analysis of Egypt and Israel, 1971–73." *The Journal of Strategic Studies* March 1982, Vol. 5, No. 1, pp. 94–121.

———. " 'Intelligence' and 'Stupidity' Reconsidered: Estimation and Decision in Israel, 1973." *The Journal of Strategic Studies* September 1980, Vol. 3, No. 2.

Steinbruner, John. *The Cynbernetic Theory of Decision.* Princeton: Princeton University Press, 1974.

Tatu, Michael. *Power in the Kremlin.* New York: The Viking Press, 1969.

Tolischus, Otto. *Tokyo Record.* New York: Reynold and Hitchcock, 1943.

Trefousse, Hans Louis, ed. *What Happened at Pearl Harbor?* New Haven: College and University Press, 1958.

Trevor-Roper, H. R., ed. *Hitler's War Directives, 1939–1945.* London: Pan Books, 1966.

Trial of the Major War Criminals Before the International Military Tribunal. Vol. 26. Nuremberg: 1947.

Ulam, Adam. *Expansion and Coexistance.* 2d ed. New York: Praeger Publishers, 1974.

United States Army Forces, Far East and Eighth United Army. Office of the Military History Officer. Japanese Research Division. *Japanese Monograph.* (Undated).

Waite, Robert G. L. *The Psychopathic God: Adolph Hitler.* New York: Basic Books, 1977.

Wallin, Homer N. *Pearl Harbor: Why, How Fleet Salvage and Final Appraisal.* Washington, DC: U.S. Government Printing Office, 1968.

Waltz, Kenneth N. *Theory of International Politics.* Reading, MA: Addison–Wesley, 1979.

———. "Theory of International Relations." In *Handbook of Political Science.* Vol. 8. Edited by Fred Greenstein and Nelson Polsby. Reading, MA: Addison–Wesley, 1975.

Ward, Robert E. "The Inside Story of the Pearl Harbor Plan." Annapolis: U.S. Naval Institute Proceeding, 1952.

Warlimont, Walter. *Inside Hitler's Headquarters, 1939–1945.* London: Weidenfeld and Nicolson, 1964.

Washington Post, August 30, 1962.

Wasserman, Benno. "The Failure of Intelligence Prediction." *Political Studies* Vol. 8, No. 2, 1960, pp. 156–169.

Watson, Mark C. "Prewar Plans and Preparations." In *United States Army in World War II.* Washington, DC: U.S. Government Printing Office, 1950.

Whaley, Barton. *Codeword Barbarossa.* Cambridge: The MIT Press, 1973a.

———. "Stratagem: Deception and Surprise in War." Cambridge: The MIT Press, 1973b.

Wilensky, Harold L. *Organizational Intelligence: Knowledge and Policy in Government and Industry.* New York: Basic Books, 1976.

Wohlstetter, Roberta. *Pearl Harbor: Warning and Decision.* Stanford, CA: Stanford University Press, 1962.

———, "Cuba and Pearl Harbor." *Foreign Affairs,* July 1965, pp. 691–707.

Wu, Sun. *The Act of War.* Oxford: Clarendon Press, 1962.

Index

Abel, Ellis, 128–129, 149–150
Africa, 43
Agrarian Reform, 56–57
Alignment, 11; Arabs-USSR, 37, 77–78; Cuba-USSR, 115, 117, 145; Egypt-Syria, 39, 77–78, 82; Germany-Yugoslavia, 111; Israel-US, 39, 52, 79–81, 153, 159; US-West, 29, 93, 95; USSR-Germany, 41, 106–107, 109–110; USSR-West, 41–42, 131; USSR-Yugoslavia, 111
Allison, Graham, 6, 22, 46–50, 53, 62–64, 118–119, 142, 149–150
Analytical Induction, 18
Arbenz, Jacobo, 56–58
Argentina, 25
Armas, Castillo, 56, 58
Asad, Hafez, 39, 77
Austria, 40, 96–97, 100, 112
Axelrod, Robert, 25, 59

Baker, A.J., 87
Balkans region, 109–112, 114, 128, 133
Batista, Fulgenico, 57, 124
Belgium, 112
Bell, Coral, 79, 87
Ben-Zvi, Abraham, 5
Berlin, 47–48, 109–110, 122, 134
Betts, Richard, 21
Bissell, Richard, 57
Blitzkrieg, 43
Brecher, Michael, 55, 64, 95, 167
Bulgaria, 109, 111
Butow, Robert, 60, 67, 85

Central Intelligence Agency, 24, 57–58, 97, 137–139, 141–144
Chiang, Kai-shek, 29

China, 28–30, 140
Churchill, Winston, 43–44, 62, 114, 126, 132–134, 148
Cleason, S. Everett, 61
Cohen, Bernard C. and Harris, S.A., 23
Collier, Basil, 86
Converse, Philip, 60
Crowley, James, 60
Cry-wolf syndrome, 4, 69; Arab-Israel, 78, 83; Japan-US, 70; US-USSR, 137 (see also Deception by)
Czechoslovakia, 40

Dallin, Alexander, 62, 148
Dayan, Moshe, 51, 55, 76, 78–80, 97, 99, 103
DeWeerd, H.A., 3, 21
Deception, 7–9, 18–19, 151; by Arabs, 38, 77–83, 97, 100; by Germany, 42–43, 105, 107, 109, 113–114, 131; by Japan, 115–118, 137; by USSR, 115–118, 137; means of: capabilities, 58, 71, 77–78, 81–83, 99–100, 122, 125; intention, 68–70, 72–73, 78–79, 82–83, 97, 105; doctrine, 67, 74–75, 115, 137; target, 42–43, 66, 105–108, 113–114
Denmark, 41, 43
Dinerstein, Herbert, 128
Dobrynin, Anatoly, 117–118, 122, 140
Dulles, Allan, 57
Dulles, John Foster, 57
Dupuy, Trevor N., 61, 87

Eban, Abba, 54
Eckstein, Harry, 55, 64
Eisenhower, Dwight, 57
Elazar, David, 53, 79–80, 97

England, *see* Great Britain
Etheredge, Lloyd, 3

Falklands War, 25
France, 29, 31, 40–41, 74, 112
Fugate, Bryan, 62
Fukodome, Shigeru, 33, 60–61, 86
Fulbright, J. William, 50, 63

Gafencu, Grigore, 127
Geography (distance), 17, 124, 156;
    Arab-Israel, 84, 157; Germany-
    USSR, 43, 123, 135; Japan-US, 33,
    67, 157; USSR-Cuba/US, 115, 137
George, Alexander and/or Smoke,
    Richard, 4, 15, 21, 23–24, 36, 61,
    128, 149
Germany, 44, 65, 105, 111, 125–126,
    131–133, 147–148, 152, 154; and
    England, 41–44, 105–108, 113–
    114, 123, 132–134; and USSR, 19,
    41–43, 45, 123–125, 131–132,
    154–155, 167
Gilpin, Robert, 23
Goring, Hermann, 44
Grand v. tactical strategies, 8
Great Britain, 25, 57, 154; and Ger-
    many, 40–44, 107, 123–125, 132–
    134; and Japan, 28–30, 66, 70, 73,
    91, 93–94; and US, 91; and USSR,
    40–41, 105–106, 131
Greece, 111
Grew, Joseph, 69
Gromyko, Andrei, 36, 118
Guatemala, 54, 56–58, 129
Guevara, Ernesto "Che," 117

Halperin, Morton, 6, 21–22
Handel, Michael, 86–87, 95, 102–
    103, 167
Hart, Liddell, 7
Hegemony: Arabs, 54; Germany, 40–
    42, 109–112; Japan, 28–29; US,
    56–59; USSR, 41, 109–110
Heikal, Mohammed, 61, 87
Herzog, Chaim, 87
Hilsman, Roger, 63–64, 116, 128,
    137, 142, 144, 149–150
Hinsley, F.H., 62, 127, 148
Hitler, Adolf, 40, 44, 62, 111, 125,
    131, 147, 152, 164; and England,

40–44, 107–108, 113; and USSR,
    25, 41, 45, 62, 105–113, 125, 127
Horelick, A. and Rush, M., 64, 129
Hosoya, Chihiro, 60
Hull, Cordell, 29, 68, 91
Hybel, Alex, 64, 129

Ike, Nobutaka, 60, 68, 85–86
Immerman, Richard, 64, 129
Indochina, 29
Inter-American Conference, 57
Interactions, 10–11
Iriye, Akira, 60
Irving, David, 60, 124
Ishii, K. Kujiro, 60
Ismail, Ahmed, 38
Israel, 19, 38, 55–56; and 1967 war,
    36, 51, 54–56, 153; and 1973 war,
    3, 17, 25, 51–53, 55–56, 98, 153,
    157; and Arabs, 17, 25, 51–56,
    76–79, 99–101, 152–153, 157;
    and US, 25, 37, 52–53, 80–81, 153

Jackson, I.J., 128
Janis, Irving L., 102
Japan/Southeast Asia, 4, 17, 28, 35,
    52, 59, 85–86; and England, 28–
    30, 70, 73, 94–95; and US (Pearl
    Harbor), 1, 17, 27, 52–53, 83–84,
    155–157, 166; and West, 28–30,
    66
Jaring, Gunnar, 36–37
Jervis, Robert, 21–22, 24, 101–102,
    127, 136, 149
Jordan/King Hussein, 38, 54, 97

Kalb, Marvin and Bernard, 87
Kazakov, M.I., 134, 149
Kellogg-Briand Treaty, 28
Kennedy: Administration, 46, 49–50,
    121, 123, 129, 137, 139, 141, 144,
    146, 164; John F., 47, 49–50, 52–
    53, 63, 117–118, 122, 129, 137,
    139–140, 142–145, 147, 164;
    Robert, 117, 122
Khrushchev, Nikita, 46, 63–64, 115–
    116, 118, 125, 138, 152–153, 164
Kinhide, Mushakoji, 60
Kissinger, Henry, 79–81, 100
Knorr, Klaus, 15, 21, 54–55, 59, 64
Konoye, Fumimaro, 30, 66, 68, 70

Kuztnetsov, N.G., 149

Langer, William, 61
Leach, Barry, 61–62, 127, 148
League of Nations, 28
Lebow, Richard Ned, 21–23, 36, 60–61, 149

MacArthur, Douglas, 91
Manchester, William, 86
March, James, 23, 60
Matthews, Herbert L., 129
McSherry, James, 61–62, 127, 148
Mediterranean region, 44
Mefford, Dwain, 23–24
Meir, Golda, 3, 51–53, 80, 97–98, 159
Middle East War (1967), 36–37, 54–56, 75, 153
Miscalculation, 3–4, 16–17, 26–27, 59–60, 151–152; by Germany of USSR, 45, 62, 152, 155; by Israel of Arabs, 76–79, 84, 97–99; by Japan of West, 35–36; by US of Arabs, 80–81; by US of Japan, 27, 74–75, 83, 89–93, 155; by US of USSR, 115, 138; by USSR of Germany, 105–106, 113, 124, 131, 154–155; by USSR of US, 116, 121–122, 145–146
Misperception, 3–6, 12, 26–27, 165; by Germany of USSR, 45–46; by Israel of Arabs, 76–77, 79, 82, 84, 96–98; by Japan of West, 35–36; by US of USSR, 50, 115, 137–138, 145; by US of Japan, 4, 66, 75, 90–93, 95, 155, 166; by USSR of Germany, 105–106, 111–113, 124, 131–132, 135–136, 147, 154, 161–162; by USSR of US, 47, 138, 143
Mobilization, 8, 14; by Arabs, 78, 81–82, 84, 96–99; by Germany, 40–41, 107–108, 111, 114, 123, 132–136; by Israel, 55, 76, 96–98, 100; by Japan, 66–67, 69–73, 90–91; by USSR, 106, 111, 113, 116–119, 121–122, 131–132, 137
Morgenthau, Hans, 22
Morison, Samuel E., 30–31, 60, 68, 86, 101–102

Nagano, Osami, 32, 68
Nasser, Gamal Abdul, 36–37, 76
Nazi-Soviet Pact, 41, 106–108, 114, 135
Nekrich, A.M., 148–149
Netherlands/Dutch, 29–30, 66, 70
Netherlands East Indies, 29, 70, 91
Nixon, Richard, 36
Nomura, Kurusu, 29–30, 34, 68
Norway, 41, 112

Oikawa, Koshiro, 33
Onishi, Takijiru, 33
Open Door Policy (US), 28
Organization of American States, 58

Palumbo, Dennis, 23
Perlmutter, Amos, 21
Petrov, Vladimir, 148–149
Poland, 40–41, 108, 133
Power: *Balance of,* 85, 126, 151, 161; Germany-England, 40–41, 107, 113–114; Germany-USSR, 41–44, 105–106, 109–111, 114; Israel-Arabs, 36–39, 53, 55, 75–76, 84, 153; Japan-US, 52–53, 91–92; US-USSR, 47–51, 54, 63, 117, 121–122, 141–146, 164; *Capabilities,* 11–14, 26–27, 38, 126, 143, 158, 165; Arabs v. Israel, 37, 75–78, 82, 99, 152; Germany v. USSR, 123–125, 132–133, 164; Israel v. Arabs, 37, 39, 55, 76, 78; Japan v. West, 32–33, 89–91, 95, 155; US v. USSR, 48–50, 52–54, 120, 164; USSR v. Germany, 154; USSR v. US, 49, 63–64, 116–117, 122; West v. Japan, 29–30, 33–35, 89–92; *Differences,* 26–27, 156–157; Germany-USSR, 41, 45–46, 106–107, 110, 113–114, 124–125, 137; Germany-West, 40–41, 125; Israel-Arabs, 36–38, 54–55, 75–78, 98; Japan-West, 27, 29–30, 33, 35, 86, 89–91, 155; US-USSR, 47–51, 122, 126, 141–142; *Economic,* 11–13; Germany-USSR, 41, 105–106, 110, 114, 124; Israel-Arabs, 38–38, 55; Japan-West, 28–32, 35, 95; US-Cuba, 57; US-Arabs, 80; *Military,* 11, 13–14, 17, 19, 27, 148, 151–

152, 156–158, 164; Arabs v. Israel, 37, 51, 53–55, 75, 77–79, 82, 84, 84, 96–99; Germany v. USSR, 43–45, 106–108, 113–114, 123–125, 132–134; Germany v. West, 41, 43, 107, 111, 113–114, 125, 132, 134; Israel v. Arabs, 36–37, 39, 53–55, 152–153; Japan v. West, 31–32, 34, 51, 67–73, 75, 89–91; United Kingdom v. Argentina, 25; US v. USSR, 25, 48–51, 117–118, 139–140; USSR v. Germany, 111, 113, 132; USSR v. US, 47–49, 115–117, 122, 124, 137–138; West v. Germany, 43, 111, 131
Prange, Gordon W., 61, 86, 94, 101–102
Process-tracing procedure, 18, 20

Ribbentrop, J. von, 41
Rich, Norman, 61–62
Riker, William H., 23
Rogers, William, 37
Roosevelt, Franklin D., 29–30, 68, 72, 90, 160
Rumania, 110–111, 128, 133
Russett, Bruce, 60

Sadat, Anwar, 37–40, 51, 75, 77, 80, 152
Salisbury, Harrison E., 126–127, 148–149
Schlesinger, Arthur, 119, 128–129, 149
Schulenburg, Friedric W., 109, 112
Seaton, Albert, 61–62, 148
Shimada, Koichi, 86
Shlaim, Avi, 3, 21, 79, 87, 95
Simon, H.A., 22
Snell, John ed., 61
Snyder, Glenn and Diesing, Paul, 10–11, 22–23, 35, 61
Snyder, R.C., Bruck, H.W., and Sapin, B., 22
Sorensen, Theodore, 128–129, 150
Stalin, Josef, 110–111, 135–136, 153–154; actions re: Hitler, 109, 111–112, 131–132; manipulated by Hitler, 25, 105–107, 109–114, 131–132, 135–136, 147, 153–154, 160–161, 164

Stech, Frank, 21–22
Stein, Janice Gross and/or Tanter, Raymond, 64, 151, 159, 167
Steinbruner, John, 4, 22
Structure: societal/domestic, 38–39, 55, 141, 153; governmental, 3, 5–6, 39–40, 48, 55, 71–72, 81; international, 10–12, 40–41
Suez Canal, 36–37, 78, 98
Sugiyama, Gen, 68
Surprise: *dimension of* capabilities, 13–14, 19, 38, 75, 122, 142, 151, 158; doctrine, 14, 19, 67, 122, 158; intention, 1, 4, 13–15, 17, 19, 66–67, 83, 122, 147, 154–159; rationale, 13, 16–17, 19, 53, 75, 122, 153, 155, 158; target, 8–9, 14, 19, 66, 85, 123, 165; time, 14–15, 19, 85, 123; *strategies,* 8, 12–15; intention, 66–67, 85, 113, 122, 155–159; target, 42–44, 74, 107–108, 113–114, 155–159; time, 157–159

Tatu, Michael, 128
Thailand, 29
Theory: surpriser's school, 3, 7–8; victim's school, 3–6; Allison, 6, 46–50, 62–63, 118–119; Brecher, 55, 95; Butow, 67–68; DeWeerd, 5; Eckstein, 55; George and Smoke, 137; Handel, 4, 15, 95, 99; Hilsman, 137; Hybel, 142, 145–147; Jervis, 136; Knorr, 54; Lebow, 35; Morison, 30–31, 68; Prange, 94; Shlaim, 3, 95; Snyder and Diesing, 35; Stein, 151, 159; Steinbruner, 4–5; Waite, 44; Whaley, 7, 68; Wilensky, 5–6; Wohlstetter, 4, 31, 68, 70, 93–94, 136
Togo, Shigenori, 66, 69
Tojo, Hideki, 66, 68, 72
Tolischus, Otto, 66, 85–86
Toyoda, Teijiro, 68
Treaty of Versailles (1919), 40
Trefousse, Hans L. ed., 101

U-2, 120–123, 137, 139–142, 144–147
U-Thant, 36
USSR: mentality, 18, 115–119, 121–123; and Japan, 28; and Middle

East, 36–37, 75, 77–78, 84, 100;
and West, 40–41
Ulam, Adam, 129
United Nations, 36, 46, 62
United States, 25, 56–59; and Israel,
53, 76, 79–81, 85, 100, 153, 159;
and Japan, 27, 59, 83–84, 157–
160; and Middle East, 36–37, 80,
97; and USSR, 124–126, 129, 160,
164

Vulnerability, 12–13, 65, 84–85, 101,
148, 156–159, 161; Arabs, 37–39;
Germany, 43, 123–124; Israel, 77–
78, 82, 96–100, 155–158; Japan,
30–35, 95; US, 67, 70, 75, 83, 91–
93, 95, 115–116, 124–125, 138,
143–146, 148, 156–157; USSR,
105, 107–108, 113, 131, 148, 154

Waite, Robert G.L., 44–45, 62
Wallen, Homer N., 102
Waltz, Kenneth, 23
Ward, Robert E., 60, 85
Warlimont, Walter, 61–62
Washington Conference Treaties, 28,
60
Wasserman, Benno, 3, 21, 23
Watson, Mark C., 101
Western nations (generally), 28–30,
40–41, 106
Wilensky, Harold L., 5–6, 22
Wohlstetter, Roberta, 1, 4, 30–31, 60,
68, 70, 85–86, 89, 93–95, 101–
102, 129, 136–137, 149

Yamamoto, Isoroku, 33–35, 61, 67,
69–70, 72
Yugoslavia, 111–112, 133

About the Author

Alex Roberto Hybel is an assistant professor at the School of International Relations of the University of Southern California and a research associate with the Social Science Research Institute of the same university.